W9-CFO-249

AFRICAN HISTORICAL DICTIONARIES
Edited by Jon Woronoff

1. *Cameroon,* by Victor T. LeVine and Roger P. Nye. 1974. Out of print. See No. 48.
2. *The Congo,* 2nd ed., by Virginia Thompson and Richard Adloff. 1984
3. *Swaziland,* by John J. Grotpeter. 1975
4. *The Gambia,* 2nd ed., by Harry A. Gailey. 1987
5. *Botswana,* by Richard P. Stevens. 1975. Out of print. See No. 44.
6. *Somalia,* by Margaret F. Castagno. 1975
7. *Benin [Dahomey],* 2nd ed., by Samuel Decalo. 1987. Out of print. See No. 61.
8. *Burundi,* by Warren Weinstein. 1976
9. *Togo,* 2nd ed., by Samuel Decalo. 1987
10. *Lesotho,* by Gordon Haliburton. 1977
11. *Mali,* 2nd ed., by Pascal James Imperato. 1986
12. *Sierra Leone,* by Cyril Patrick Foray. 1977
13. *Chad,* 2nd ed., by Samuel Decalo. 1987
14. *Upper Volta,* by Daniel Miles McFarland. 1978
15. *Tanzania,* by Laura S. Kurtz. 1978
16. *Guinea,* 3rd ed., by Thomas O'Toole with Ibrahima Bah-Lalya. 1995
17. *Sudan,* by John Voll. 1978. Out of print. See No. 53.
18. *Rhodesia / Zimbabwe,* by R. Kent Rasmussen. 1979. Out of print. See No. 46.
19. *Zambia,* by John J. Grotpeter. 1979
20. *Niger,* 2nd ed., by Samuel Decalo. 1989
21. *Equatorial Guinea,* 2nd ed., by Max Liniger-Goumaz. 1988
22. *Guinea-Bissau,* 2nd ed., by Richard Lobban and Joshua Forrest. 1988
23. *Senegal,* by Lucie G. Colvin. 1981. Out of print. See No. 65.
24. *Morocco,* by William Spencer. 1980
25. *Malawi,* by Cynthia A. Crosby. 1980. Out of print. See No. 54.
26. *Angola,* by Phyllis Martin. 1980. Out of print. See No. 52.
27. *The Central African Republic,* by Pierre Kalck. 1980. Out of print. See No. 51.
28. *Algeria,* by Alf Andrew Heggoy. 1981. Out of print. See No. 66.
29. *Kenya,* by Bethwell A. Ogot. 1981
30. *Gabon,* by David E. Gardinier. 1981. Out of print. See No. 58.
31. *Mauritania,* by Alfred G. Gerteiny. 1981
32. *Ethiopia,* by Chris Prouty and Eugene Rosenfeld. 1981. Out of print. See No. 56.
33. *Libya,* 2nd ed., by Ronald Bruce St John. 1991
34. *Mauritius,* by Lindsay Rivière. 1982. Out of print. See No. 49.
35. *Western Sahara,* by Tony Hodges. 1982. Out of print. See No. 55.

36. *Egypt,* by Joan Wucher King. 1984. Out of print. See No. 67.
37. *South Africa,* by Christopher Saunders. 1983
38. *Liberia,* by D. Elwood Dunn and Svend E. Holsoe. 1985
39. *Ghana,* by Daniel Miles McFarland. 1985. Out of print. See No. 63.
40. *Nigeria,* by Anthony Oyewole. 1987
41. *Ivory Coast,* by Robert J. Mundt. 1987
42. *Cape Verde,* 2nd ed., by Richard Lobban and Marilyn Halter. 1988. Out of print. See No. 62.
43. *Zaire,* by F. Scott Bobb. 1988
44. *Botswana,* by Fred Morton, Andrew Murray, and Jeff Ramsay. 1989
45. *Tunisia,* by Kenneth J. Perkins. 1989
46. *Zimbabwe,* 2nd ed., by R. Kent Rasmussen and Steven L. Rubert. 1990
47. *Mozambique,* by Mario Azevedo. 1991
48. *Cameroon,* 2nd ed., by Mark W. DeLancey and H. Mbella Mokeba. 1990
49. *Mauritius,* 2nd ed., by Sydney Selvon. 1991
50. *Madagascar,* by Maureen Covell. 1995
51. *The Central African Republic,* 2nd ed., by Pierre Kalck; translated by Thomas O'Toole. 1992
52. *Angola,* 2nd ed., by Susan H. Broadhead. 1992
53. *Sudan,* 2nd ed., by Carolyn Fluehr-Lobban, Richard A. Lobban, Jr., and John Obert Voll. 1992
54. *Malawi,* 2nd ed., by Cynthia A. Crosby. 1993
55. *Western Sahara,* 2nd ed., by Anthony Pazzanita and Tony Hodges. 1994
56. *Ethiopia and Eritrea,* 2nd ed., by Chris Prouty and Eugene Rosenfeld. 1994
57. *Namibia,* by John J. Grotpeter. 1994
58. *Gabon,* 2nd ed., by David Gardinier. 1994
59. *Comoro Islands,* by Martin Ottenheimer and Harriet Ottenheimer. 1994
60. *Rwanda,* by Learthen Dorsey. 1994
61. *Benin,* 3rd ed., by Samuel Decalo. 1995
62. *Republic of Cape Verde,* 3rd ed., by Richard Lobban and Marlene Lopes. 1995
63. *Ghana,* 2nd ed., by David Owusu-Ansah and Daniel Miles McFarland. 1995
64. *Uganda,* by M. Louise Pirouet. 1995
65. *Senegal,* 2nd ed., by Andrew F. Clark and Lucie Colvin Phillips. 1994
66. *Algeria,* 2nd ed., by Phillip Chiviges Naylor and Alf Andrew Heggoy. 1994
67. *Egypt,* by Arthur Goldschmidt, Jr. 1994

HISTORICAL DICTIONARY OF GUINEA
Third Edition

by
THOMAS O'TOOLE
with
Ibrahima Bah-Lalya

African Historical Dictionaries, No. 16

The Scarecrow Press, Inc.
Lanham, Md., & London

SCARECROW PRESS, INC.

Published in the United States of America
by Scarecrow Press, Inc.
4720 Boston Way, Lanham, Maryland 20706

4 Pleydell Gardens, Folkestone
Kent CT20 2DN, England

British Cataloging in Publication Information Available

Library of Congress Cataloging-in-Publication Data

O'Toole, Thomas, 1941–
Historical dictionary of Guinea / by Thomas O'Toole with Ibrahima
Bah-Lalya. — 3rd ed.
p.   cm. — (African historical dictionaries ; no. 16)
Includes bibliographical references.
1. Guinea—History—Dictionaries.   2. Guinea—Bibliography.
I. Bah-Lalya, Ibrahima.   II. Title.   III. Series.
DT543.5.O88   1995   966.52'003—dc20   95–34783 CIP

ISBN 0–8108–3065–5 (cloth : alk. paper)

Printed in the United States of America

 The paper used in this publication meets the minimum requirements of
American National Standard for Information Sciences—Permanence
of Paper for Printed Library Materials, ANSI Z39.48–1984.

CONTENTS

For
Ann, Rachel and Phillip
Aissatou, Mariama and Alpha

ACKNOWLEDGMENTS

I thank several people for making this co-authored revised version possible. The most important is my wife, Ann, who as my companion, mentor, and editorial advisor saw me through the task while we both held full-time jobs. My daughter, Rachel, and my son, Phillip, both now caring, involved adults, and excellent scholars in their own right, give me reason to hope. Special thanks are also due Nancy Schmidt at the Indiana University library who offered invaluable assistance on bibliography and Elizabeth Schmidt, whose personal insight about Guinea was of great assistance. Four other friends who know Guinea well through Peace Corps service deserve mention, Jerome Pasela, Rebecca Schwartz, Denise Dauphannais, and Susan Poland. Carol Shaw assisted with some word processing.

Guinean friends, too numerous to name, offered insight into the present-day actualities of Guinea. Of these Guinean-born Professor Lansiné Kaba stands out for his special assistance. Not only was he my first guide to the understanding of Guinean history and African history in general, but he has continued to support me as a mentor and friend through the years. Without his help this revision would not have been possible. I would also note that Dr. Siba N'Zatioula Grovogui was also very helpful.

Finally, without the early support of my father, Philip O'Toole, and my mother, Dorothy Ann Trautt O'Toole, I would never have ventured beyond my southern Minnesota origins.

Thomas O'Toole

I would like to recognize, in a special way, three of my teachers: Karamoko Dioulde Bah; Maître Boubacar Karo Diallo, who is currently working for PAM (Programme Alimentaire Mondiale) at the Guinean Ministry of Education; and Dr. Clyde Maurice at

Florida State University. I would also like to recognize my entire family but most especially my wife, Aissatou "Djan Mama," and my two children, Mariama and Alpha. My teachers allowed me to dream and my family helped me to make these dreams come true.

Ibrahima Bah-Lalya

EDITOR'S FOREWORD

In 1958, upon gaining its independence as the only African state to reject the de Gaulle referendum and opt to become an independent republic outside the French Community, Guinea was a country with extraordinary economic, political and cultural potential. Under the dynamic leader, Sékou Touré, Guinea would have been a primary influence on the continent. Indeed, for a decade or so, Guinea, along with Ghana and Tanzania, led the struggle for decolonization, non-alignment and African socialism. However, even for those who were oblivious to the truth, the situation gradually took a turn for the worse under Touré's leadership. Although he was highly regarded internationally, the once popular president could only rule through force, crushing real and imagined enemies, constantly fearing plots and instilling fear in the hearts of the people of Guinea. The economy gradually collapsed and the political climate decayed. The cultural milieu was completely enmeshed with keeping Touré and his party in power.

Not until after Touré's death in 1984, when the Second Republic was established, would the world witness the reemergence of even the slightest movement toward democratic ideas within a framework of a military government. Political activity was cautiously restored. The economy showed few immediate signs of improvement though the future still held promise of a turnaround. Greater freedom of expression did began to take hold in the cultural realm. With the Second Republic Guinea's political, economic and cultural potential might finally begin to be fulfilled.

The ebb and flow of events in post-independence Guinea are traced in the third edition of the *Historical Dictionary of Guinea*. While events and people are depicted very soberly and objectively, it is impossible to read entries from the Touré era without realizing its full tragedy. Along with biographical sketches of renowned Guineans, both past and present, the dictionary covers important aspects of the country's economy and culture. The work also includes a useful chronology to help follow events. In addition, it provides an invaluable list of acronyms, without which it is hard to make sense of the literature. The bibliography was expanded and updated to help researchers find out more about a country for which information is still not easily obtained.

This latest edition was written by Thomas O'Toole with the help of Ibrahima Bah-Lalya. Dr. O'Toole, who authored the first two editions, is presently Professor of Interdisciplinary Studies at St. Cloud State University where he teaches in the African Studies program. He remains very interested in Guinea and has written extensively about Guinea and Africa. He is the translator of the *Historical Dictionary of the Central African Republic* in this series.

Dr. Bah-Lalya is currently Education Project Manager of the Critical Languages Institute at Florida A & M University. He has studied and worked with Guinea's local schools and institutions of higher education. Before moving to the United States from Guinea he last served as Interim General Director of Education at the National Ministry of Education. He, too, has written widely on Guinea and Francophone Africa.

Jon Woronoff
Series Editor

NOTE ON SPELLING

We are far from possessing a standard orthography for most of the indigenous languages of Guinea and only since independence has there been any real attempt to standardize spellings. The fact that French, Portuguese, and English variants for many terms exist along with different forms in the various African languages of Guinea only compounds the difficulty.

A single ethnic group, the Fulbé, can be labeled Peul, Pulo, Puulo, Fula, or Fulani depending on the source. Since Pulo (Puulo) is the singular and Fulbé (Fuulbé) is the plural used by Hapular (speakers of the Pular or Pulaar language) and there is actually an implosive sound in Pular which is not accurately represented by the "b" in Fulbé, in any case, they will be identified herein as Fulbé.

Likewise the Mandinka people are often referred to as Maninka, Malinké, or Mandingo. Though the usual Guinean usage is Malinké they are identified here, rather arbitrarily, as Maninka.

Generally agreed spellings of names and terms will usually be used even when they are not linguistically correct. When widely divergent spelling varieties exist the various forms will generally be given, with the most common term given first.

ABBREVIATIONS AND ACRONYMS

AFRIMAR	Société Africaine des Pêches Maritimes
AGF	Association des Guinéens en France
AGP	Agence Guinéenne de Presse
AID	Agency for International Development
ALCAN	Aluminum of Canada, Ltd.
ALIDI	Société d'Alimentation Diverse
ALIMAG	Société d'Alimentation Générale
AOF	Afrique Occidentale Française
BAG	Bloc Africain de Guinée
BAP	Brigade Agricole de Production
BATIPORT	Société Nationale d'Importation de Matériel pour le Bâtiment
BCEAO	Banque Centrale des Etats de l'Afrique de l'Ouest
BGCE	Banque Guinéenne de Commerce Extérieur
BIAG	Banque Internationale pour l'Afrique en Guinée

BIAO	Banque Internationale pour l'Afrique Occidentale
BICIGUI	Banque Internationale pour le Commerce et l'Industrie de Guinée
BIG	Banque Islamique de Guinée
BNDA	Banque Nationale pour le Développement Agricole
BPN	Bureau Politique National
CA	Conseil d'Administration
CAP	Coopérative Agricole de Production
CATC	Confédération Africaine des Travailleurs Croyants
CBG	Compagnie des Bauxites de Guinée
CC	Comité Central
CEFA	Comité d'Etudes Franco-Africain
CER	Centre d'Education Rurale; and Centre d'Education Révolutionnaire, beginning in 1966
CFA	Communauté Financière Africaine
CFAO	Compagnie Française de l'Afrique Occidentale
CFTC	Confédération Française des Travailleurs Chrétiens

CGCE	Comptoir Guinéen du Commerce Extérieur
CGCI	Comptoir Guinéen du Commerce Intérieur
CGT	Confédération Générale du Travail
CMR	Centre de Modernisation Rurale
CMRN	Comité Militaire de Redressement National
CNE	Caisse Nationale d'Epargne
CNF	Comité National des Femmes
CNPA	Centre National de Production Agricole
CNR	Conseil National de la Révolution
CNTG	Confédération Nationale des Travailleurs de Guinée
COPAC	Coopérative de Production Agricole et de Consommation
CTRN	Comité Transitoire de Redressement National
CUP	Comité d'Unité de Production
CUM	Comité d'Unité Militaire
DSG	Démocratie Socialiste de Guinée
EC	European Community
ECOWAS	Economic Community of West African States

ENPD	Ecole Normale Primaire de Dabadou
ENTRAT	Entreprise Nationale d'Accostage et de Transit
ESA	Ecole Supérieure d'Administration
FAC	Ferme Agro-Communale
FAO	Food and Agriculture Organization
FAPA	Ferme Agropastorale d'Arrondissement
FEANF	Fédération des Etudiants de l'Afrique Noire en France
FIDES	Fonds d'Investissement pour le Développement Economique
FLNG	Front pour la Libération Nationale de Guinée
FO	Force Ouvrière
GUINEXPORT	Société Guinéenne d'Exportation
HALCO	a consortium formed by Harvey Aluminum Company
IBA	Association Inter-Gouvernementale des Pays Producteurs de Bauxite
IFAN	Institut Français d'Afrique Noire

IMF	International Monetary Fund
INRDG	Institut National de Recherches et de Documentation de Guinée
IOM	Indépendants d'Outre-Mer
IPC	Institut Polytechnique de Conakry
IPGAN	Institut Polytechnique Gamal Abdel Nasser de Conakry
IPJNK	Institut Polytechnique Julius Nyéréré de Kankan
JORG	Journal Officiel de la République de Guinée
JRDA	Jeunesse du Rassemblement Démocratique Africain
LAMCO	Liberian-American-Swedish Minerals Company
LIBRAPORT	Société Nationale d'Importation de Livres et de Matériel Scolaire
MDR	Ministère de Développement Rural
MIFERGUI	Société des Mines de Fer de Guinée
MSA	Mouvement Socialist Africain

OAU	Organization of African Unity
OBETAIL	Office de Commercialisation du Bétail
OBK	Office des Bauxites de Kindia
OCA	Office de Commercialisation Agricole
OCAM	Organisation Africaine et Commune (formerly Organisation de Coopération Africaine et Malgache)
OECD	Organization for Economic Cooperation and Development
OERS	Organisation des Etats Riverains du Fleuve Sénégal
ONCFG	Office National des Chemins de Fer de Guinée
OUA	Organisation de l'Unité Africaine
PAI	Parti Africain de l'Indépendence
PAIGC	Partido Africão da Independência da Guiné e do Cabo-Verde
PASE	Programme d'Ajustement de l'Education
PDG	Parti Démocratique de Guinée
PGP	Parti Guinéen du Progrès
PND	Parti National pour le Développement et la Démocratie
PPG	Parti Progressiste de Guinée
PRA	Parti du Regroupement Africain

PRC	People's Republic of China
PRG	Présidence de la République de Guinée
PRL	Pouvoir Révolutionnaire Local
PRN	Parti du Regroupement National
PRP	Parti du Renouveau et du Progrès
PUP	Parti de l'Unité et du Progrès
PZ	Paterson-Zochonis
RDA	Rassemblement Démocratique Africain
RGE	Regroupement de Guinéens à l'Etranger
RPF	Rassemblement du Peuple Français
RPG	Rassemblement du Peuple de Guinée
SADA	Société Anonyme pour le Développement de l'Industrie de l'Aluminium de Tougue-Dabola
SBD	Société de Bauxite de Dabola
SCOA	Société Commerciale de l'Ouest Africain
SFIO	Section Française de l'Internationale Ouvrière
SGB	Société Guinéenne des Banques
SIAG	Société Industrielle et Automobile de Guinée
SIFRA	Société Industrielle des Fruits Africains

SIP	Société Indigène de Prévoyance
SMDR	Société Mutuelles de Développement Rural
SNA	Société Nationale d'Assurances
SOGUIKOP	Société Guinée-Koweitienne de Pêche
SOGUINE	Société Guinéenne d'Exploitation du Diamant
SOGUIP	Societe Guinéenne de Pétrole
SOGUIREP	Société Guinéenne de Rechapage de Pneus
SOMIGA	Société Minière Guinée-Alu-Suisse
SONATEX	Société Nationale de Textiles
SONIGUE	Société Nippo-Guinéenne de Pêche
UDSR	Union Démocratique et Socialiste pour la Résistance
UGTAN	Union Générale des Travailleurs d'Afrique Noire
UNP	Union Nationale pour la Prospérité
UNPG	Union Nationale pour la Prospérité de la Guinée
UNR	Union pour la Nouvelle République
UPG	Union pour la Prospérité de la Guinée; also Union pour le Progrès de la Guinée
USCG	Union des Syndicats Confédérés de Guinée

CHRONOLOGY OF MAJOR EVENTS

833	The Empire of Ghana is mentioned for the first time in European maps by the cartographer al-Khwarizmi (al-Fazari).
918–1076	Apogee of the Empire of Ghana. The country is inhabited by Soninké (Sarakholé, Sarakolé) lineages (Cissé, Diabi, Diané, Doukouré, Souaré and Tounkara, among others), Fulbé, and diverse other ethnic groups from the Manding cluster (Bambara, Mande, Susu). As part of a major population drift beginning in the tenth century elements of all these groups moved south and west, with some settling in present-day Guinea.
920–1050	Guinea is part of Empire of Ghana.
1076	The southern Almoravids were long-credited with conquering Ghana's capital, Kumbi-Saleh, in this year. Though actual conquest is unlikely there was certainly some armed conflict between Almoravids and Soninké.
1076–1200	The decline of the Empire of Ghana gives rise to smaller kingdoms such as Diara, Susu, and Mali which contend for supremacy in the region.
1200–1235	The Susu kingdom controls the region

and its leader, Sumanguru Kanté, builds a reputation as an oppressor.

1235–1255   Sundiata (Sunjata) Keita, a prince from the ruling family of Mali, defeats Sumanguru Kanté and drives the Susu back to the Futa Jalon highlands. The coalition he assembles to fight Sumanguru seals a pact at Kurugan which becomes the backbone of the Empire of Mali.

1312–1332   Kankan Musa (the "Rex Melli" or "King of the Gold Mines" on some European medieval maps) rules Mali.

1324   Kankan Musa's pilgrimage to Mecca.

ca. 1450   Increasing numbers of Portuguese raiding and trading ships make contact on the coast of present-day Guinea.

1470   Benedetto Dei, a Florentine, visits Timbuctoo.

early 1500s   Fulbé begin to arrive on the Futa Jalon plateau.

1513   Some 505 captives are sent as slaves to Portugal from the West African region (or perhaps the Gulf of Guinea in which case they could have come from anywhere from the Gambia to Angola). This marks the beginning of a large-scale trade in Africans as slaves.

1517   Beginning of the trade in Africans as slaves to the Americas.

post-1542   French privateers active on the Guinea coast.

March 12, 1591	The army of Songhay is defeated at the Battle of Tondibi by Moroccan troops and Spanish mercenaries. This marks the end of the era of great empires in the West African Sudan.
early 1600s	Beginning of Kankan and the Kingdom of Baté by Muslim Soninké (Sarakolé or Sarakholé) migrants from the Dynafunu, a province of ancient Ghana in present-day Mali.
ca. 1622	3,000 slaves sent annually from Guinea to Portugal.
1645	The Empire of Mali, attempting to regain power, is defeated by a coalition of Bamana (Bambara) forces.
1659	France establishes its first West African settlement in Saint-Louis (Senegal).
1675	Beginning of the second Fulbé migration to Guinea from Macina, the Futa Toro, and the Hodh (today's Sahel).
July 1687	English factory established at Rio Núñez.
1714	French Senegal Co. sets up factories on the Guinea coast.
1725	First major conflict and settlement between Muslim Fulbé under Karamoko Alfa's leadership and the Jalonka (Djalonka) and non-Muslims led by Mansa Dansa.
1751	Karamoko Alfa dies. The Fulbé encounter major setbacks in their holy war against a coalition composed of Jalonka and other

	non-Islamized groups. Ibrahima Sori steps in to lead the Fulbé army, win the war, and create the Sori dynasty.
1763	The Fulbé control the Futa Jalon highlands. This results in a massive movement of Jalonka and Susu ethnic groups from the Futa Jalon to the coast of Guinea.
1768	Moravian missionaries arrive on Guinea coast.
1795–1806	Mungo Park travels to Ségou in present-day Mali, but dies at Boussa during his second attempt to reach the Niger delta.
1808	British establish a naval patrol against slave traders in West African waters.
1827–1828	René Caillié leaves the Rio Núñez in northern Guinea (Boké) to begin his journey to Timbuctoo.
1838–1840	Al Hajj Umar Tall, a Fulbé cleric from Futa Toro in Senegal who introduced the Tijaniyya (Sufi order) to West Africa, sojourns in Kankan.
1840	A gentlemen's agreement is enacted between "Alfaya" from Karamoko Alfa's family and "Soriya" from Ibrahima Sori's house. By the terms of this agreement the Futa Jalon state is to be ruled by a two-party system with a complex election routine by a college representing the main Fulbé families and settlements.
1842	French treaties with Landoma and Nalou leaders in Guinea.

1850–1864	Al Hajj Umar Tall creates a theocratic state comprising the region between Dinguiraye, Nioro, Timbuctoo, and Mopti. His successors are unable to maintain unity and resist the French colonial troops.
1854	The jihad of Al Hajj Umar begins.
Aug.–Sept. 1860	French force Al Hajj Umar to retire to the Niger River.
1866	France acquires trading centers on Guinea coast.
1868	French posts established at Boké and Benty.
1880	French obtain railway concession in Guinea from some Fulbé leaders.
1880–1881	Siege of Kankan by Samory Touré, an emerging military leader and state-builder, who came from *dyula* (Maninka trader) origins along the forest borders of present-day Guinea.
1880–1898	Samory Touré builds a strong kingdom in the Guinean savanna, battles the French colonial troops for seven years (1891–1898), but is finally captured by the French on September 19, 1898, and is exiled to Gabon. He dies in 1900.
1881–1898	French expeditions against Samory Touré.
June 28, 1882	Anglo-French agreement on Sierra Leone and Guinea boundaries.

May 12, 1885	Franco-Portuguese Convention on Portuguese Guinea and French Guinea boundaries.
1894–1907	The forest ethnic groups, especially Guerzé, Manon, Toma, and Kissi, resist both Samory's troops and French colonial troops. It takes an alliance of French and British colonial troops to subdue their resistance.
June 15, 1895	AOF established.
1896	The last independent Fulbé leader of the Futa Jalon, Almamy Bokar Biro Barry is defeated by the French at the Battle of Porédaka. The Futa falls under French colonial rule.
March 10, 1896	The French colony of Guinea is officially established despite local resistance in the Futa Jalon, the Niger region and in the forest zones. This resistance continues until 1911.
April 8, 1904	A further Anglo-French convention on French Guinea boundaries.
Nov. 5, 1904	Franco-Portuguese treaty on Guinea boundaries.
1905	A number of anti-colonial struggles in French Guinea are in progress.
Sept. 18, 1907	Franco-Liberian agreement on Liberian-French Guinea borders.
Dec. 4, 1920	AOF reorganized.

March 30, 1925	Africans are elected to the colonial Conseil d'Administration in Guinea.
Dec. 7, 1942	AOF joins the Allies.
Jan. 30–Feb. 8, 1944	Brazzaville Conference.
Nov. 4, 1945	Yanciné Diallo and Mamba Sano from Guinea are elected to the First Constituent Assembly in Paris which was to draft a new constitution for the Fourth French Republic.
April 11, 1946	Corvée abolished in AOF.
May 7, 1946	French citizenship with a limited franchise given all AOF subjects.
Oct. 18, 1946	African leaders from French West Africa and French Equatorial Africa, including Sékou Touré, establish the Rassemblement Démocratique African (RDA-African Democratic Assembly) in Bamako.
May 1947	The Guinean branch of the RDA, the Parti Démocratique de Guinée (PDG-Democratic Party of Guinea) is formed without Yaciné Diallo.
1952	Sékou Touré becomes secretary-general of the Guinea branch of the RDA.
1954	The death of Yaciné Diallo, one of Guinea's deputies to the French National Assembly, allows Sékou Touré to make a strong showing in the election held to fill Diallo's seat.

1955	In Bandung, Indonesia, representatives from 29 "Third World" countries set goals for independence and cooperation among "developing" countries.
June 23, 1956	The Gaston Deferre plan is passed. It provides for some form of administrative and political decentralization for Africans in the colonial territories. Universal suffrage is extended for the first time. Sékou Touré is elected mayor of Conakry and becomes vice-president of the Government Council responsible for Guinea's internal affairs.
1956	The PDG-RDA sweeps the elections as Sékou Touré and Saifoulaye Diallo are elected to the National Assembly in Paris.
1956–1957	Ethnic and political riots in Guinea. Fulbé who are members of the BAG and PRA are mostly targeted.
1957	Under the *loi cadre* Sékou Touré's government abolishes the system of government-appointed "chiefs" and establishes elective councils in the villages, communes, and districts—the latter were redesignated *circonscriptions.*
Aug. 25, 1958	General Charles de Gaulle, head of the French government, visits Conakry seeking Sékou Touré's support for the referendum on the Constitution of the Fifth Republic.
Sept. 28, 1958	Guineans reject de Gaulle constitution by 1,136,324 to 56,981 votes.

Oct. 2, 1958   Guinea becomes an independent republic, with Sékou Touré as president.

Jan. 15, 1961   Nationalization program starts with takeover of power and water supplies.

Nov. 1961   "Teacher's Plot" put down; Daniel Solod, Soviet ambassador, expelled.

Dec. 1962   The Sixth Congress of the PDG in Conakry separates the leadership of the party from that of the state. Saifoulaye Diallo is elected general secretary of the PDG and Sékou Touré, though in the minority, remains head of government and state.

Jan. 1963   The National Assembly grants extraordinary powers to Sékou Touré against alleged plotters.

May 1963   The Organization of African Unity is created in Addis Ababa under the first generation of African leaders such as the president of Ghana, Kwame Nkrumah, the president of Guinea, Sékou Touré, the president of Côte d'Ivoire, Félix Houphouët-Boigny, the Emperor Haile Selassie of Ethiopia, the prime minister of Nigeria, Abubakar Tafewa Balewa, and the president of Tanzania, Julius Nyéréré.

Aug. 1963   A PDG national conference held in Kankan is transformed into the Seventh Congress and reinstates Sékou Touré as general secretary.

Nov. 1964   The government passes the *loi cadre,* a kind of enabling act aimed at controlling the growth of the private business sector and containing the political strength of the emerging "bourgeoisie."

Oct. 1965
A "plot" allegedly led by Mohamed Touré, known as "Petit Touré." The first serious attempt to form a legal opposition is put down. The leaders of this opposition, mostly traders, are arrested and executed in jail.

Nov. 1965
Ahmed Ben Bella, the president of Algeria and Touré's political ally, is overthrown by a military group led by Col. Houari Boumedienne.

Nov. 22, 1965
Diplomatic relations with France broken following October plot allegedly backed by French.

Feb. 1966
Ghanaian president, Kwame Nkrumah, a close political ally of Touré, is overthrown by a military junta. Nkrumah takes refuge in Guinea where Touré proclaims him co-president of the country. This causes the deterioration of relations between Guinea and such neighboring countries as Côte d'Ivoire and Liberia.

1967
The Eighth Congress of the PDG asserts the leadership of the PDG over the country's public life and the authority of its general secretary, Sékou Touré, over the party and the government.

March 1967
President Milton Margay of Sierra Leone is overthrown by Lt. Col. Andrew Juxon-Smith. Sékou Touré sends troops into Sierra Leone to restore order.

Aug. 2, 1968   Launching of the Socialist Cultural Rev-
                    olution.

Nov. 1968   Another of Sékou Touré's close political
                    allies, President Modibo Keita of Mali, is
                    overthrown by a military junta. This
                    coup d'état triggered a series of bold
                    political moves by Touré aimed at subdu-
                    ing the army leadership and increasing
                    PDG control over Guinea's public life.
                    As a result, several high ranking military
                    officers and civilian leaders are arrested
                    and executed.

Feb. 1969   The "Labé Plot." More than 1,000
                    Guineans are arrested. Several high rank-
                    ing army officers and many members of
                    the government are executed, including
                    the deputy commander of the Guinean
                    armed forces, Colonel Kaman Diaby, a
                    former minister of defense, Fodéba
                    Keita, and the main leader of the BAG,
                    Diawadou Barry.

June 24, 1969   Assassination attempt on Sékou Touré
                    during visit of President Kenneth
                    Kaunda of Zambia.

Nov. 22, 1970   Portuguese troops and Guinean exiles try
                    to take Conakry; they fail, 92 are con-
                    demned to death and 66 to hard labor for
                    life.

Jan. 1971   More than 70 persons are hanged in
                    Conakry and other towns throughout the
                    country for alleged participation in the
                    Portuguese invasion of Guinea. Among
                    those hanged are Barry III, the former
                    head of the PRA, Osumane Baldet, for-

mer minister of planning and finance, and Kara Soufiana, the director of police.

1971–1978   The Soviet Union establishes naval patrols to prevent attacks from Portuguese troops and protect Touré's regime against actions from externally based Guinean opponents assembled under Le Front, a political umbrella. In return the Soviets are authorized to use the Conakry airport and seaport facilities for shipment of military equipment and troops to Angola, Mozambique and the other Portuguese-controlled areas of Africa.

Jan. 24, 1971   Diplomatic relations are broken with Senegal, and, on January 29, 1971, with West Germany, on grounds that they had taken part in an abortive Conakry invasion.

Feb. 1971   Series of visits from heads of states starts with President Ngouabi of Congo-Brazzaville.

April 1972   President Sékou Touré is unanimously reelected president at the PDG's Ninth Congress.

Jan. 20, 1973   Amilcar Cabral, leader of the Guinea-Bissau independence struggle, is assassinated in Conakry.

May 9, 1975   Diplomatic relations with West Germany resume after a five-year lapse.

July 14, 1975   Diplomatic relations with France resume.

July 1975

Touré mediates the war between Burkina Faso (Upper Volta) and Mali.

Jan. 1976

Guinea agrees to participate in the Second World Black and African Festival of Arts and Culture in Lagos.

July 1976

The "Fula Plot"; Diallo Telli, former OAU secretary general, is arrested and later left to die of hunger without benefit of a trial.

Jan. 1977

An agreement is signed under which France will pay the pensions of 20,000 Guinean ex-servicemen while Guinea awards compensation to nationalized French companies.

Aug. 25, 1977

Demonstrations by market women in Conakry's Madina market against the brutality of police in charge of controlling economic affairs triggers riots throughout the country. These riots are brutally suppressed but do mark the beginning of a shift by Touré away from the totally controlled economy.

Sept. 1977

Touré interprets the Koran on Radio Conakry (The Voice of the Revolution) as supporting the PDG.

March 1978

The Monrovia Conference seals the reunion between Touré of Guinea, Senghor of Senegal, and Houphouët-Boigny of Côte d'Ivoire. This also marks a major step in the reconciliation between Guinea and France.

May 1978

A five-year arrangement for Soviet military aircraft to use Conakry as a base for Atlantic surveillance flights is canceled.

Dec. 1978

French president Valéry Giscard d'Estaing cements reconciliation with Guinea begun in 1976 with an official visit to Guinea.

May 1982

President Sékou Touré is reelected for his fourth term of office by a supposedly 99.98 percent vote.

1984–1985

Tension grows within the CMRN between President Lansana Conté and Prime Minister Diarra Traoré. The political differences between them seems to be aggravated by ethnic rivalries. Indications suggest that the army is aligned mostly with the president and the administration with the prime minister.

Jan. 1984

A group of 20 alleged mercenaries is arrested in Senegal, accused of planning to overthrow the Guinea government.

March 26, 1984

Sékou Touré dies in a Cleveland, Ohio (USA) hospital while undergoing heart surgery after a major heart attack. The impressive funeral organized by the PDG is attended by prominent representatives from Africa and the rest of the world. These include Vice-President Bush of the U.S. and the French prime minister. Touré was replaced by an interim president and almost the same government, composed of party members, continues to run the country.

April 3, 1984

Senior army officers and a group of civilians, mostly faculty from the

Teacher's Training School of Maneah, launch a successful coup against the interim government. The coup's success is assisted by the familial, ethnic, and regional dissensions within the government. The Comité Militaire de Redressement National (CMRN) is created to serve as a national leadership body to bring about the reform of the economic, political, and social life of the country.

Sept. 1984

More than 200 people are arrested at Kamsar following the death, in police custody, of Kerfalla Cissé, a criminal suspect. All but 16 are freed within 30 days.

Dec. 18, 1984

The position of prime minister is eliminated and the government is redesigned around four state ministries representing more or less the four regions and major ethnic groups of Guinea. Colonel Jean Traoré, Commandant Sory Doumbouya, Commandant Almamy Fofana, and Commandant Mamadou Balde emerge as key figures in the government and the CMRN.

Jan. 28, 1985

Guinea Foreign Minister Faciné Touré meets with Presidents Dauda Diawara of Gambia, João Bernardo Vieira of Guinea-Bissau, and Abdou Diouf of Senegal for the sixth summit of the Gambia River Development Organization.

Feb. 14, 1985

The International Court of Justice (World Court) rules in favor of Guinea in its border dispute with Guinea-Bissau over an offshore area said to be rich in oil deposits.

March 7, 1985 President Lansana Conté of Guinea and President Vieira of Guinea-Bissau meet at Kamsar, Guinea to discuss cooperation.

July 4, 1985 At ten o'clock in the evening a recorded message from former Prime Minister Diarra Traoré stating that he had seized power is broadcast over the radio. Troops loyal to Conté retake the radio station by morning and arrest Traoré and many of his followers. Traoré, some members of the Touré family, and several Maninka officers are executed without public trial.

Oct. 1985 The syli, the then national currency, is devalued by 96 percent.

Dec. 1985 The banking system is reformed. The value of the Guinean franc is reduced to 300 GF for one US dollar rather than the previous 25 syli for a dollar. State banks are closed and replaced by mostly French financial institutions such as the BICIGUI, BIAG, and SGB. State subventions are substantially reduced, commodity prices are freed from state regulations. A series of measures is undertaken to control the rate of inflation.

Feb. 1986 The IMF authorizes a $40 million credit and the World Bank provides a $42 million structural adjustment loan.

April 18, 1986 Debts are rescheduled with 12 Western nations (Paris Club).

May 1, 1986 Civil service wages are increased 80 percent.

Nov. 12–13, 1986   President Mitterand of France visits Guinea.

Jan. 1987   A series of sectoral adjustment reforms, advised by the World Bank and the International Monetary Fund lead to a 55 percent reduction of the civil service ranks, substantial reductions of programs subsidized by the government, major sectoral reforms in key national sectors, a general shift toward more public accountability, and the start of a market economy. One major and tangible effect of these reforms is the layoff of 45,000 civil servants who, together with university activists, build a strong pressure group known as Le Groupe des Déflattés.

Jan. 1988   Two students are dead and 50 people are arrested after two days of riots at the Madina market over the high cost of basic commodities such as rice (which jumped 300 percent in a few days). These riots force the government to increase the salary of civil servants by the same 80 percent that had already been granted to the military.

June, 1989   Fifty government enterprises including 17 from the industrial sector are closed as a result of the implementation of the structural reform plan advised by the IMF and the World Bank.

Oct. 1989   President Lansana Conté launches a movement for national democratic dialogue. This leads to the formulation of a *loi fondamentale,* a constitution providing a framework for democratic elections in Guinea.

	The Comité Transitoire de Libération Nationale (CTRN) is created to supervise the transition between the military regime and a nationally elected government.
1990	Another violent strike led by student activists and civil servants laid off as a result of structural reforms forces the government to make a 100 percent salary increase.
1990	First local and regional elections are organized throughout the country. In some areas, these elections are characterized by violent contentions between ethnic factions. Conakry, Kindia, and Nzérékoré are most affected by the conflicts.
Oct. 27, 1990	University students begin a strike against substandard conditions.
Nov. 22, 1990	Paramilitary police kill two demonstrating high school students.
Dec. 1, 1990	The military occupies the University of Conakry campus to break up the continuing strike.
Dec. 23, 1990	The government reports that 98.7 percent of the voters approved the *loi fondamentale* in a national referendum out of the more than three million voters who were said to have cast ballots.
March 1991	Mayoral elections in Conakry are marred by ethnic violence.
March–May 1991	A two-and-a-half-month student strike is followed by a ten-day teachers' strike,

and a two-day general strike in early
May.

Oct. 1991 — Government troops fire on demonstrators
in Kankan.

July, 1992 — The government bans all political demonstrations.

Aug. 6, 1992 — The Government of Guinea grants more
than 40 hectares (100 acres) of Mount
Nimba to an international mining consortium even though the area was established as a World Heritage Site.

Oct. 1992 — An attempt to assassinate President
Conté is unsuccessful.

Nov. 1992 — President João Bernardo Vieira of
Guinea-Bissau visits Conakry to discuss
the Liberian crises.

Jan.–March 1993 — A severe cerebro-spinal meningitis outbreak rages in Forest Region and parts of
Upper Guinea.

Feb. 1993 — President Conté meets with opposition
leaders but refuses to participate in a
government of national unity.

Feb. and March 1993 — Ethnic troubles flare in Kankan and Conakry.

Dec. 20, 1993 — Lansana Conté elected president.

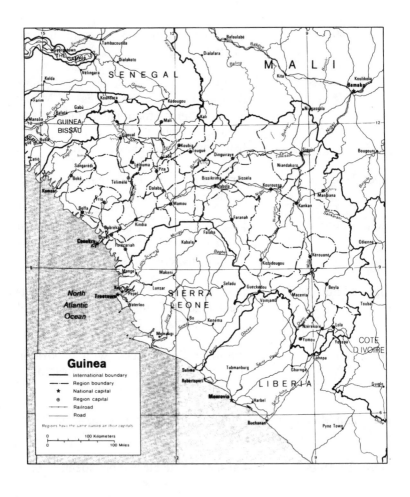

Guinea

- ——— International boundary
- —·—·— Region boundary
- ★ National capital
- ⊛ Region capital
- ┼┼┼ Railroad
- ——— Road

Regions have the same names as their capitals

0 ⊢————⊣ 100 Kilometers
0 ⊢————⊣ 100 Miles

Table 1:

Estimated Agricultural Production, selected years* (thousands of metric tons)

Food Crops	1964	1968	1972	1976	1980	1984	1990
Rice (paddy)	360	250	200	300	350	330	500
Cassava (manioc)	420	370	220	480**	550	600	450
Maize (corn)	70	68	48	320**	57	63	100
Sweet potatoes	85	80	30	120**	74	NA	105
Millet and other cereals	146	150	90	75	74	NA	94
Export crops							
Bananas	40	35	31	70	99	100	110
Pineapples	16	15	33	15	17	17	36
Palm kernels	23	25	30	10***	35	42	50
Coffee	13	15	7	5	15	15	6.9
Peanuts (groundnuts)	18	19	25	30	83	80	52

*Statistical information about Guinea under Touré can be accepted only with reservation and close analysis since there was a Guinean law against divulging such information. Furthermore, proponents and opponents of the regime often were politically motivated in their presentation of what little information did trickle out of the country.

**These FAO "estimates" are most certainly in error.

***Export only.

NA, not available

Sources: Harold D. Nelson, *Area Handbook for Guinea*, 2nd ed., Washington, DC: U.S. Government Printing Office, 1975; and FAO estimates.

Table 2:
Estimated Mining Production, selected years (thousands of metric tons)

	1965	1970	1975	1980	1985	1990
Iron ore	378	1,040	NA	NA	NA	NA
Bauxite	1,870	2,490	7,674	13,427	13,750*	17,530
Diamonds (thousand carats)	72	74	80	38	750*	146.6

*unofficial estimate
NA, not available

Sources: United States Statistical Yearbook and *Africa South of the Sahara*, London: Europa Publications, various years.

INTRODUCTION

The origin of the name Guinea itself is obscure. Some suggest that Guinea might be derived from the ancient Niger Basin trading center, Jenné. More likely it derives, through Portuguese usage, from the Berber *Akal-n-Iguinawen* or "Land of the Blacks." Yet another possibility is that it comes from the word *geenay,* meaning "women" among the coastal Susu, and somehow this name came to be applied to a widespread area of the African coast.

The modern Republic of Guinea faces southwest to the Atlantic on the western extension of Africa between 8° and 12° north latitude. Guinea touches on six other African nations; clockwise north to south they are Guinea-Bissau, Senegal, Mali, Côte d'Ivoire, Liberia, and Sierra Leone. Guinea is traditionally divided into four natural regions: (1) Lower Guinea (the coastal areas); (2) Middle Guinea, which consists chiefly of the highlands of the Futa Jalon, inland from the sea; (3) Upper Guinea, which descends gradually northwest towards the Sahelian savanna; and (4) the Forest Region, which stands astride the watershed between the Niger River drainage plains and the southward-flowing rivers which exit to the Atlantic through Liberia and Sierra Leone.

Climatically all of Guinea shares two alternating seasons: a dry season (November to April) and a wet season (May to October). Rainfall varies from region to region with as much as 432 cm (170 inches) a year at Conakry on the coast to less than 152 cm (60 inches) a year in Upper Guinea. The rainfall in Middle Guinea ranges from 160–231 cm (63 to 91 inches) a year while some areas in the Forest Region have more and 254 cm (100 inches) of rain a year. Temperature ranges also vary according to the different regions. On the coast and in the Forest Region the temperature averages 81° F. While the Futa highland of Middle Guinea may experience January daytime temperatures from 86° F to 95° F, nighttime temperatures may dip below 50° F. Midday highs of more than 100° F are not uncommon in Upper Guinea during the dry season.

The natural drainage systems include the fan-shaped system of the Niger River and its own main upper basin tributaries, the Tinkisso and the Milo, which drain over one-third of the country's total area including most of Upper Guinea and much of the Forest Region. In Upper Guinea, with an average altitude of 307 meters (1,000 feet) and great ranges in temperature and humidity, agriculture is mostly practiced in the river valleys. Both the Senegal and the Gambia Rivers have their sources in the Futa Jalon highlands of Middle Guinea. At 12,953 square kilometers (5,000 square miles) over 921 meters (3,000 feet) above sea level this area is relatively well watered and usually receives some rain throughout the year, though most falls in the four months of the wet season. Rivers such as the Rio Núñez, Konkouré, Fatala and Melakouré, which flow southwest to the Atlantic from the Futa, have hydroelectric and/or navigational value. A number of minor rivers drain the Forest Region boundary area and, because of the relatively short dry season and violent thunderstorms of the early rainy season, furnish water all year and often overflow their banks.

Most of Guinea is composed of savanna grasslands and orchard shrub with soils largely composed of silicates of aluminum hydrate except along rivers and the tidal areas. Major food crops include millet, maize, rice, manioc (cassava), and oil palms while some coffee and bananas are cultivated for export.

Guinea's population within the country's boundaries is estimated at 7.3 million in 1990. This high figure assumes that some exiles—the Guinean Diaspora—have returned to Guinea. In the mid-1980s there were Guineans living in France, Côte d'Ivoire (750,000), Senegal (700,000), Sierra Leone (250,000), Liberia (150,000), and Mali (100,000).

Since 1984 three significant population drifts have occurred within the Diaspora: 1) some returned to the homeland after Sékou Touré's death in 1984; 2) a major move back from Liberia and Sierra Leone as result of civil wars in the late 1980s, and 3) a substantial emigration from Guinea because of the deterioration of the economy and the uncertainties of the employment market. These movements have changed the composition and distribution of the population considerably. The first immigration movement was noticeable in the Futa Jalon and Upper Guinea, regions long opposed to Touré. The second significantly affected the Forest Region and Coastal Guinea. The third move mostly consisted of Guinean intellectuals, laid-off civil servants (the *déflattés*), and university students who faced a bleak employment future after graduation.

Along with such population shifts has come an unprecedented and uncontrolled growth of cities like Conakry, Labé, Kankan, Kindia, and Nzérékoré. This growth has been accompanied by major economic, health, and social problems. Conakry, for example, doubled in size in a decade as did the crime rate and social problems in such shanty neighborhoods as Koronti, Madina, Ratoma, and Bonfi. With this rapid urban growth the pressures on public facilities, health services, transportation, education, and utilities have escalated. Conakry faces major problems such as electric power breakdowns, lack of a good public sewer system, and growing air pollution. In spite of these problems Conakry has shown some growth in the private sector and more openness to international business.

Guinea's population is composed of a variety of ethnic groups. The present-day boundaries of Guinea were determined by colonial powers with little regard to the ethnic or linguistic groups of African people. These boundaries, therefore, often split ethnic and linguistic groups. Within the country, though, the four major geographic regions largely correspond to four major ethnolinguistic groups. In Lower Guinea, Susu, a Manding language closely related to the Dialonké language of Middle Guinea, has largely replaced that of the Landoma, Baga, Nalou, and other West Atlantic languages once widely spoken in the coastal areas. In the Futa Jalon of Middle Guinea, Pular, the Fulbé language is dominant, although minor indigenous ethnic groups like the Badyaranké, Bassari, and Konagi, continue to maintain some traditional ways. Maninkakan, the language of the Maninka, is spoken in Upper Guinea, and is widely used in Middle Guinea. It has long been penetrating the Forest Region where three very different linguistic groups are still dominant. These three linguistic areas, from east to west, are the Kpelle (Guerzé), Loma (Toma), and Kissi. A number of other minor ethnic groups exist in Guinea but the process of creating a national identity in Guinea has made considerable headway since independence.

As President Touré had suggested, ethnicity should not be denied but it should also be obvious that no ethnic group will survive if Guinea perishes because of inter-ethnic rivalries. The growth of the whole national community has largely taken priority over ethnic particularism in Guinea.

Based on official Guinea census figures the population density of Guinea in 1983 was 18 persons per square kilometer. But given the nature of slash-and-burn subsistence farming still widespread in large areas of Guinea and the persistent need to import food, it is unlikely that these figures are very accurate. The prefectures of Labé and Pita in the Futa Jalon, both having agreeable climates and fairly good soil conditions, probably have over 40 persons per square kilometer. In the forest region the rich agricultural areas around Guéckédou and Nzérékoré may have populations approaching 31 persons per square kilometer, especially given the influx of Liberian refugees in recent years. Except in fertile areas along the Niger and Milo Rivers, the large stretches of savanna and savanna woodland in Upper Guinea are very lightly inhabited. This region, encompassing two-fifths of Guinea's total territory, probably has as few as seven persons per square kilometer. The Conakry, Boké, Dubréka, and Fria regions in Lower Guinea have almost tripled their populations since independence as bauxite mining, bauxite processing, and other industries have grown. Conakry and its suburban environs on the Kaloum peninsula have over 2,500 people per square kilometer, while Fria and Dubréka have more than 40. Uneven urbanization of this sort is creating social, political, and economic problems for Guinea.

The pre-colonial history of Guinea still remains rather incomplete. Though archaeological research in Guinea has not made much progress, evidence seems to indicate that the area has been continuously inhabited by hunting-and-gathering populations for at least the past 30,000 years. It also seems probable that farming has been practiced in the area of Guinea for at least the past 3,000 years. There is considerable evidence that iron smelting dates back more than 2,000 years in this part of West Africa. But until further archaeological evidence is forthcoming, much of the early history of Guinea remains conjectural.

The pre-colonial history of Guinea becomes much clearer from about A.D. 900 as sources in Arabic and oral traditions become available. Travelers' accounts in Arabic and professional history keepers' oral narratives offer information on the genealogies of royal families and traditions of ethnic groups who lived in Guinea in the past millennium. For peoples like the Konagi, Baga, and Nalou, who now live on the Atlantic coast, ethnological evidence supports the view that they lived in the area of modern Guinea even before the Christian era. Others, like the Susu and Maninka, probably came into the area about A.D. 900, while the Fulbé, who arrived in large numbers in the seventeenth century, are almost newcomers.

Much of Upper Guinea's pre-colonial history is closely tied to the three great centralized savanna empires of West Africa—Ghana, Mali, and Songhai—which dominated the lands to the north and east of modern Guinea from about A.D. 900 to the mid-sixteenth century. Villages and small kingdoms of the Maninka people located on the headwaters of the Niger River began to achieve historical prominence in the thirteenth century. The gold fields of Buré near modern Siguiri greatly contributed to the wealth of all the trade-based empires of the western savanna but were certainly very important to the Mali Empire. Oral traditions maintain that the powerful empire of Ghana, which dates from at least the eighth century, forced the towns and villages of Upper Guinea to pay equal weights in gold for the salt that had to pass through Ghana from desert mines in the north. Oral historians or *griots* maintain that about A.D. 1235 a popular and effective leader, Sundiata Keita, united the various Maninka villages and groups and defeated Sumanguru Kanté, a war leader who had gained control over a number of kingdoms which had grown up after the destruction of the Ghana Empire about 1076. According to oral traditions and archaeological research, Sundiata was born in Niani, a Maninka village and the former capital of the Mali Empire. Niani is inside Guinea's present boundaries.

With the decline of the Mali Empire in the late fourteenth century new forces began to control the area of modern Guinea. In the late fifteenth century, Koli Tenguela (or Temala), a Fulbé leader, invaded and conquered part of the Futa Jalon with a small number of followers. Originally from the central Senegal River valley, he passed through the Guinean towns of Timbo and Labé during his incursion. Because Koli Tenguela's incursion was so ephemeral and involved mostly local populations as troops, the number of Fulbé involved was never large. The only long-term effect of these conquests was to establish the Kunda settlement in the northern part of the Futa Jalon and to push the Dialonka and Maninka groups to the coast where in later times they often established themselves as rulers over the local peoples. Not until 300 years later was a Fulbé-dominated Islamic theocratic kingdom established in the Futa Jalon by Karamoko Alpha and Ibrahima Sory Sambegu.

These coastal areas were drawn into European market systems from the mid-fifteenth century on. Local rulers on the coast began to grow in power by recruiting members to their groups with the promise of imported trade goods. Though not one of the major slave-trading areas of West Africa, Guinea was affected by the wars and disruption occasioned by this trade. By the end of the slave trade in the early nineteenth century, European trade goods had replaced many types of locally produced goods. Consequently the French and British commercial interests, which had achieved dominance on the coast, were poised to intervene even more deeply in internal African affairs.

It should not be supposed, though, that British and ultimately French trading interests played a very important role in the Guinean interior before the mid-nineteenth century. At the end of the seventeenth century, increasing numbers of Fulbé created a theocratic Muslim state in the Futa Jalon. This state itself was torn by internal dissent until the French incorporated the Futa Jalon into their colonial system in 1896 with the defeat of Bokar Biro at the Battle of Porédaka. The Fulbé leadership of this state firmly established the Islamic theory of a God-ruled state in the minds of many Guineans.

In the early 1840s a Muslim religious leader from the Futa Toro in upper Senegal returned to West Africa from Mecca and Sokoto. This man, al Hajj Umar Tall, spent a few years in Kankan and settled in the Futa Jalon. He began teaching a simple, devout form of Islam—the Tijaniyya. Pressured to leave the Futa Jalon as a potential threat to the existing Muslim state, he moved to Dinguiraye near the Buré gold fields in Upper Guinea. From there he gathered forces and launched an attack on his own original homeland and the Bambara states to the east. After his death internal revolts and French pressures destroyed his forces.

Not all African leaders were as easily defeated by the French. Almamy Samory Touré, a Guinean Maninka leader, had proposed an alliance against the French with Umar's son, Ahmad, in 1883 or 1884. Though Ahmad defeated this alliance, the story of Samory remains an important part of Guinean history. The first president of Guinea, Ahmed Sékou Touré, claimed descent from Samory and Guinean school children are taught that Samory was a forerunner of national independence because of his determined resistance to the French. As the leader of an independent Maninka state in southeast Guinea from 1880 until 1898, he did provide the French with more military resistance than they had bargained for. However, the French had the greater sources of supply. Samory was never able to obtain enough modern weapons to resist the French in the long run.

Samory's efforts at unification failed for a number of reasons. Though he saw the growing threat the French posed to African autonomy, his relations with other African leaders were hegemonistic. The Futa Jalon theocracy, for example, resisted associating with Samory for fear of being absorbed into his empire; Bademba of Ségu was reluctant to associate with the former aggressor against Sikasso during the Tieba era; Samory's attack on Kong made the Kong leaders very cautious in dealing with both the French colonial troops and Samory's forces; and groups in the southern forest region refused to join Samory since he often sold members of these groups into slavery.

Samory was captured by the French in 1899 and exiled. Belatedly and in isolation, small groups of Africans continued to resist the French until the end of World War I. But treaties with Great Britain and Liberia had by then already established the boundaries of colonial French Guinea.

French rule brought some important changes in the social and political structure of African societies. Large-scale African polities such as those which evolved under Samory Touré, al Hajj Umar Tall, and the theocratic states of the Futa Jalon were replaced by a French administrative structure. Private ownership of former communal land and the expansion of commercial and service occupations resulted in the development of civil servants, teachers, small shop and plantation owners, medical and military personnel, and transport operators. Gradually an urban elite evolved which adopted some of the salient aspects of French culture. However, this adoption was most often adapted to a national culture which continued to be fundamentally African and rural. Even for this elite the notions of family, ethnicity, and regional origins remained relatively unchanged and continued to play a significant role in political alliances and in public offices.

After World War II political activities among the chiefs and this French-educated elite grew. In the early 1950s some elements of this elite were politically affiliated with French socialists. In Guinea, Yaciné Diallo was one such person, but a number of more indigenous organizations were gaining prominence. In 1952 Sékou Touré became secretary general of the Parti Démocratique de Guinée (PDG) founded in May 1947 as the Guinea branch of the Rassemblement Démocratique Africain (RDA) which had been founded in Bamako in 1946. With the support of most Guinean teachers, the core of the "intelligentsia" and solid labor support Sékou Touré won country-area by-elections to the Territorial Assembly in August 1953, demonstrating his ability to attract the rural vote as well.

Overtly mobilizing the support of the rural populations, the youth, and the women PDG candidates Sékou Touré and Saifoulaye Diallo won two of the three seats in the French National Assembly. Touré and the PDG may well have also built covert, but strong, ties with the French colonial administration during the governorships of Cornut, Gentil, Messmer, and Mauberna. During the second half of the 1950s Sékou Touré continued to rise to the top of the Guinean leadership. In 1957 he became mayor of Conakry, and in the same year he was appointed vice-chairman of the Council of Government responsible for the colony's internal affairs. On the eve of independence both the French and local opposition forces realized that Touré was a major political leader. The result was a rather complex compromise between the main political factions in the colony. Touré and his partners had to deal with the colonial administration, on the one hand, and the local opposition groups, on the other.

The June 1956 passage of the Gaston Deferre *loi cadre* plan placed Touré in a difficult position. The law's provisions for the gradual devolution of legislative powers to the individual territorial assemblies would result in the Balkanization of both French West Africa and French Equatorial Africa with each territory dealing directly with the French Republic. Touré was forced to continue to operate within the French imposed system, increasing

Guinean initiatives while at the same time attempting to maintain some semblance of unity for French West and Equatorial Africa.

The June 1958 return to power of General Charles de Gaulle in France and the draft constitution of the Fifth Republic which lacked any provision for a federal structure for French West Africa (and also for French Equatorial Africa) heightened the tension. In a speech in Conakry in August 1958 General de Gaulle made it clear that there was no compromise possible. In mid-September the PDG under Touré called for a "no" vote in the draft constitution referendum. Other Guinean leaders joined with Touré and the PDG urging the rejection of this highly centralized and French-controlled constitution in the September 28, 1958 referendum.

The French reaction to the vote probably caught Sékou Touré by surprise. French government personnel, given no more than two months to assist in the transfer of authority, were often sent to posts elsewhere in French West Africa within days of the vote. On October 2, 1958, Guinean independence was formally proclaimed. Cut off from budgetary assistance and the favored-nation status of Guinean exports to France, faced with a shortage of trained administrators, teachers, military staff, and medical personnel, Guinea began independence with no resources other than a highly enthusiastic and hopeful population. The strong unifying force of a charismatic leader and a popularly based party in the early years of independence seemed to have begun to overcome interpersonal conflicts, the difficulties of rising expectations among the small Guinean elite, ethnic cleavages, and the great lack of economic resources and infrastructure for development.

Over the first ten years of independence, Guinea continued to occupy a special position among African states in its unqualified rejection of colonial control or economic domination by more developed nations. Taking a militant pan-Africanist stance in African affairs, one of "positive neutralism" in the cold war, and combining a unique articulation of African socialism and "cultural revolution" in internal affairs, Guinea, under the leadership of Sékou Touré, presented an image of racial experimentation in social and political development in Africa. Unfortunately the rate of economic development was rather slow and from 1960 on a number of attempts were made to overthrow the government of Sékou Touré by assassinations, coups d'état, and invasions. Touré made good use of the opportunities afforded by such attempts, both real and imagined, to purge his opponents in the party and the government. Koumandian was jailed for ten years in 1961, Diawadou was executed in 1969, Barry III was hanged in 1971, and Diallo Telli was tortured to death in 1976.

In April 1960 a plot to overthrow the government by the armed force was alleged by the PDG. The instigators of this plot were apparently Guinean citizens who resented the anti-capitalist socialist thrust of the PDG regime. In November 1961 Touré accused the Soviet embassy of supporting a teachers' strike, which was crushed with considerable severity. Thousands of students were jailed, and some died. All the schools were closed for a considerable period. Many prominent teachers fled to neighboring countries to reinforce the opposition to Touré. The government was reshuffled to strengthen Touré's control. The teachers' union was dismantled and its leaders received severe jail sentences. In late 1965 leaders of a group seeking to form an opposition party were arrested and charged with plotting to bring about the downfall of Touré's government. In February 1969 the army was purged along with other dissidents in the party and in June 1969 an apparent assassination attempt on Touré, blamed on an exile opposition group, was almost successful.

In November 1970 a seaborne invasion of Conakry, launched by Portuguese troops and Guinean exiles, proved abortive. Another purge of the Guinean political and administrative elite followed. In July 1971 the army officer corps was similarly purged and in April 1973 a number of cabinet ministers were accused by President Touré of plotting to overthrow his government. Though a substantial external anti-Touré force continued to grow, it was split into so many differing factions that its only noticeable effect was to make Touré and his regime apprehensive and inclined to deal ruthlessly with any internal opposition, even when such opposition was more in Touré's mind than real.

In 1975 the conflicts between Touré's regime and its opponents again took a violent form. In this year the regime concocted a so-called *Complot Cheytan* (Satan's Plot) to target merchants mostly from the Maninka ethnic group (especially those from Kankan, Guinea's second largest city). A year later, Touré focused on the Fulbé intellectual leadership and devised the *Complot des Peulhs* (the Fulbé Plot). Diallo Telli, the former

Secretary General of the Organization of African Unity, and several prominent Fulbé intellectuals along with Guineans of other ethnic groups, were killed without trial.

Weakening economic conditions added to Touré's troubles. Smuggling and illegal market activities grew. Touré's words gradually ceased to impress the majority of Guineans who were experiencing a declining standard of living. Popular support for Touré's highly centralized and personalized government declined. Finally economic mismanagement led to public riots in 1977 launched by market women of the Madina market in Conakry which forced Touré to make radical changes in his policies. To stay in office Touré had to solve pressing economic problems and he could not do this without external assistance. Warming the tone of his diplomatic overtures toward France, he renewed his ties with the West African Francophone community by restoring full diplomatic relations with Senegal and Côte d'Ivoire during the Monrovia Conference. At the same time he improved his relations with Sierra Leone and Liberia through the Mano River Union.

Simultaneously he was repairing relations with his West African neighbors. Touré launched an "Offensive Diplomatique" seeking to gain acceptance with the West, improve his public image with the rest of Africa, and gain financial support from the rich Arab countries. These diplomatic overtures laid the necessary groundwork for launching structural reforms that would, supposedly, bring about major changes in the country's economy. Touré called upon international organizations—the IMF, World Bank, and UNESCO among others—to help set a course toward a market economy. This shift of national priorities was slow to start since it was conducted under Touré's own leadership. His approach was to limit real changes in the economic sector and make cosmetic modifications in all other areas. Touré hoped to satisfy the Guinean people's demand for economic improvement without altering his tight control over the nation. Despite these precautions, the reforms of the late 1970s opened the doors to more drastic changes that ultimately led to the 1984 coup ending three decades of Touré's leadership.

Sékou Touré's death during an emergency heart surgery operation in Cleveland, Ohio, on March 26, 1984, came as a surprise to those outside the small group of predominantly Maninka associates, particularly his family, which occupied leading government posts. Initially little change was apparent. Prime Minister Lansana Béavogui was appointed interim president by the PDG leadership and an orderly transition seemed likely. Under the surface, though, disputes soon emerged over the succession among the inner clique many of whom were drawing illicit earnings from their positions.

On April 13, 1984, a day before the PDG congress was convened, the army seized power, arrested the members of the government and the *politburo*. A supreme military committee was set up with considerable popular support at the onset. The main force behind the military coup d'état was a group of army officers backed by a team of educated civilians from the teacher-training school of Maneah. Initially two main figures emerged. One of these was Deputy Chief of Staff, Colonel Lansana Conté, an officer of Susu origin who worked his way to the top of the military ranks through cooperation with President Sékou Touré and through service during the guerrilla war against the Portuguese in Guinea-Bissau. The second was Colonel Diarra Traoré, a Maninka officer and a PDG insider who had occupied several important positions including that of regional governor and member of the central committee of the PDG.

Very little unity existed from the start among those who seized power on April 3. At first the potential for conflict was diffused by the sharing of leadership; Colonel Diarra Traoré, the driving force behind the military takeover, accepted the post of prime minister, and supported Conté as the president of the Republic. A Comité Militaire de Redressement National was created to replace the legislative body and both Conté and Traoré played key roles in shaping the destiny of this committee. But the difficulty of establishing efficiency and order in the aftermath of Touré's Kafkaesque rule soon brought tensions to a head. An alleged coup attempt by ex-Prime Minister Diarra Traoré, whom President Conté had demoted after eight months, plagued by ethnic and personal rivalries, ended following several hours of fighting and anti-Maninka looting on July 5, 1985.

During the period immediately following the alleged coup attempt political prisoners from the First Republic government, most of them belonging to the Touré and Keita families, were executed without trials along with scores of Maninka officers. Persistent ethnic tensions and the social unrest caused by attempts at economic reforms, such as the devaluation of the Guinean currency imposed by the International Monetary Fund, posed major obstacles to President Conté's rule.

However, Conté was able to open a relatively democratic dialogue that led to acceptance of the *loi fondamentale,* a set of basic laws designed to guide the drafting of a constitution and the institution of a democratic system of public governance. These laws were passed in a context of volatile and fast-paced reshaping of Guinean public life. What was once a centralized monolithic public administration, ruled as a single party state by Sékou Touré and then the army after the 1984 coup, diversified rapidly. Public life in Guinea in the 1990s is a swirl of opposition parties, worker's unions, and newspapers opposed to the Conté regime. By October 1992 more than 40 political parties and associations existed. Although most of these parties were relatively minor their side-effects may prove more lasting. As the trend continued the country experienced an erosion of central authority, more public questioning of governmental decisions, and the development of significant opposition forces inclined to challenge the government.

These opposition forces were nurtured by the deterioration of living conditions in Guinea. Despite significant backup from important international institutions, economic adjustment reforms were undermined by rising inflation. Added to this were rapid population growth, uncertainties in the rural economy, an international decline of market values of Guinean mineral products, high levels of political conflict fueled by ethnic and regional diversity, and poor administrative and management structures that hampered any positive effects of reform.

The negative effects of the internal situation in Guinea were magnified by external factors beyond the control of the country's leadership. The Liberian civil war and political instability in Sierra Leone increased the migration of poor populations toward Guéckédou and Nzérékoré in the Forest Region while other towns, such as Boké, Conakry, Fria, Kankan, Kindia, and Labé continued to swell as rural populations sought the illusive hope of a better life. The urban infrastructures of these cities and towns could not support these influxes and shantytowns have developed in each of them.

Under such conditions, the implementation of programs based

on drastic political and economic changes was a considerable challenge to a military government torn between the need to transform the socioeconomic landscape and the fear of being swept away by the momentum. Only the future will reveal how well economic reforms put in place by Lansana Conté function.

On Sunday, December 20, 1993, General Lansana Conté received 51.7 percent of the vote in elections marked by some violence. None of the seven opposition candidates garnered a significant portion of the rest of the vote. The conduct of these countrywide elections for the national assembly and the president of the republic was not yet a clear test of the level of political maturity the country has achieved after almost four decades of self-government.

THE DICTIONARY

ACACIA (*Acacia senegal*). Spiny shrubs and thorn trees common in some areas of Upper Guinea (q.v.). These trees are a source of gum arabic, dye, tannin, building materials, and firewood throughout much of West Africa.

ADMINISTRATIVE ORGANIZATION. Although the party and the government were separate in the early years after independence and throughout the 1970s, until April 3, 1984 Guinea was a one-party state in which party and government were for all practical purposes, one. Major governmental functions were highly centralized in the hands of the executive and his appointed cabinet. In effect the president, as head of state and leader of the only legal party, the PDG or Parti Démocratique de Guinée (q.v.), dominated all branches of government. Reelected in January 1975 for his third seven-year term, President Sékou Touré appointed his own cabinet, all officials in public administration and all military officers. He drafted almost all laws and ruled, largely by executive decree or administrative fiat. Since 99.8 percent of the 2.4 million registered voters elected Sékou Touré unanimously in the 1975 election, this overcentralized executive office—responsible for the execution of all laws and signing all government acts—represented the sole source of all political power. With his prime minister and five party leaders the president ran a direct chain of command through every level of administration.

The cabinet under Touré varied from seven to 34 ministers and changes were constantly being made in the form and function of the ministries. In 1972 this basic system was reorganized with the creation of four distinct levels of ministry and an office of prime minister. The government was divided into seven domains presided over by "super-ministers" who dealt with all ministries and agencies concerned with some broad range of national interests. Originally one of these domains was headed by the president, a second by the prime minister and the other five by the other members of PDG's Bureau Politique National (q.v.), or BPN. Sékou Touré's brother, Ismaël Touré (q.v.), for example, was put in charge of the Economy and Finance Domain, which included the ministries of Industry and Power, Finance, Banking, Mining and Geology and Public Works, Urbanism, and Housing. His "brother-in-law," Mamadi Keita (q.v.), was in charge of education, culture, and sport.

In practice it was useless to chart carefully an administrative hierarchy or organizational structure because changes were made at will by the president. The PDG, the BPN, and the government of Guinea were ultimately no more than extensions of the will of the "Helmsman of the Guinean Revolution," Ahmed Sékou Touré.

The Comité Militaire de Redressement National (CMRN [q.v.]) assumed power on April 3, 1984. It abolished the constitution and the PDG and established the Second Republic. The 20-member CMRN is headed by an Executive Bureau of fewer than ten persons. The government is comprised of the president and 36 cabinet members including 4 ministers of state, 11 ministers, 15 secretaries of state, 2 governors, a chief of protocol, and a permanent secretary of the CMRN. Nine of the original cabinet members were civilians and one was a woman. The government is based on decrees and ordinances issued by the CMRN, the president, and various ministers. See ARRONDISSEMENT; LEGAL SYSTEM; LOCAL ADMINISTRATION; REGIONAL ADMINISTRATION.

AFRIQUE OCCIDENTALE FRANCAISE (AOF). French West Africa. One of France's two colonial African federations, the AOF encompassed the territories of Côte d'Ivoire (Ivory Coast), Niger, Burkina Faso (Upper Volta), Mauritania, Senegal, Mali (French Soudan), Benin (Dahomey), and Guinea. Established between 1895 and 1904 with a number of organizational changes over the years, this federation was the largest unit in the French colonial organization. In the post-World War II era the AOF was headed by a governor general in Dakar, Senegal, under the direct control of the Ministry of Colonies in Paris. The governor general was assisted by a Conseil de Gouvernement composed of five delegates from each territory with only consultative powers. Each colony had its own governor, responsible to Dakar, and a territorial assembly with severely limited deliberative authority. The AOF officially ceased to exist on January 21, 1959.

AGENCE GUINEENNE DE PRESSE (AGP). The Guinean Press Agency was a government information service supplying daily news releases to government officials and the foreign diplomatic corps. Its functions were largely allowed to lapse in the last years of the Touré regime as other government organs supplanted it. A revitalized press, still in government hands but far freer, has emerged since the April 1984 coup. See HOROYA; JOURNAL OFFICIEL DE LA REPUBLIQUE DE GUINEE.

AGENCE GUINEENNE DE SPECTACLES. Founded by the government of Guinea in May 1973 to replace the previous civil society, Syliart. This government institution under the Ministry of Youth, Art, and Sports provided support for Guinean artists, authors, and playwrights as well as pensions for retired artists whose works are in accordance with PDG (q.v.) views. See SYLIART.

AGRICULTURAL PRODUCTION. At independence in 1958, about 90 percent of the population lived in the rural sector. The country was almost self-sufficient in agriculture. Despite an increase in urbanization and manufacturing, over three-fourths of Guinea's population still farms. Yet, despite a generally favorable climate, relatively fertile soil, and increased mechanization, agricultural production drastically declined during the three decades of Touré's rule. By the late 1960s agriculture failed to supply the needs of national consumption. Coffee production for export, for example, fell from 11,000 metric tons in 1958 to 5,000 in 1976, though it recovered in the 1980s. Textile, fruit juice, and meatpacking plants built after independence have yet to operate at full capacity due to insufficient supplies and unsatisfied government tropical fruit export agreements with Eastern block countries.

According to Lansiné Kaba, among the many factors that crippled Guinea's agriculture and led to the famine of 1976 were lack of incentives, ill-planned and ill-managed cooperatives with costly equipment poorly adapted to Guinea, inadequate infrastructure such as transport and refrigeration facilities at Conakry (q.v.), and heavy taxation. Finally, general discontent among the farmers led to massive migration to neighboring countries. The relatively low prices paid producers in the PDG-controlled market coupled with the high prices and unavailability of consumer goods caused many producers to revert to subsistence agriculture and secret, local barter systems and/or resort to smuggling (q.v.) in order to survive (see Table 1).

AIR GUINEA. Funded in 1960 this semi-governmental agency has operated an irregular service of domestic flights from Conakry to laterite surface-landing strips at Boké, Kissidougou, Nzérékoré, Siguiri, Macenta, and Gaoual (qq.v.). Hard-surfaced airports now serve moderate-sized jet aircraft at Labé, Kankan, and Faranah (qq.v.). Occasional flights to neighboring capitals as well as government flights for officials, student groups, and Mecca-bound pilgrims are also made. Soviet-supplied aircraft and foreign as well as Guinean pilots and technicians continue a very diminished service at present. See AVIATION.

ALFA. The word derives from the first letter if the Arabic alphabet, Alef. In Muslim cultures, particularly among the Fulbé (q.v.) and Maninka (q.v.) of Kankan, it is used as a title of highest respect for the learned and religious/military leadership. It has gradually come to be used as a general proper name in this century.

ALFA KABINE KABA. See KABA, ALFA KABINE.

ALFAYA. After the death of the successful jihad (q.v.) leader,

Karamoko Alfa (Sambegu Ibrahima [q.v.]), in the mid-eighteenth century Futa Jalon (q.v.), rival factions developed. The party which favored the clerical supports of the family of Karamoko Alfa were called Alfaya and contended with the military group, the Soriya (q.v.), who supported the war leader Ibrahim Sori (q.v.). These two groups contended for the position of almamy (q.v.) in the Futa Jalon well into the twentieth century.

ALFA YAYA DIALLO (1830–1912). A Fulbé (q.v.) leader, the "king" of Labé (q.v.), the wealthiest province in the Futa Jalon (q.v.), who collaborated with the French conquest in order to achieve his own independence from the almamy (q.v.) of the Futa. When the French policy changed he was deported to present-day Benin in 1905. Upon his return at the end of his exile in 1911 he was accused by the French administration of attempting to retrieve his "slaves." He was then deported to Nouadhibou, Mauritania. The infamous military camp and jail for political prisoners was named after him. Sékou Touré's (q.v.) government cast Alfa Yaya as a heroic victim of French imperialism conveniently ignoring his earlier support of the French colonial occupation of the Futa Jalon.

AL HAJJ (literally, the pilgrim). Title of respect taken by any Muslim who has completed the recommended pilgrimage to Mecca (also spelled Alhadji, El Haji, El Hadj). See TALL, AL HAJJ UMAR.

AL HAJJ UMAR TALL. See TALL, AL HAJJ UMAR.

ALMAMY (or IMAM). Traditionally the spiritual leader in West African Muslim societies. An almamy was concerned with prayer, education, and general religious rule-making. The term gradually came to be applied to some secular as well as religious leaders in Guinea. A notable almamy was Samory Touré (q.v.).

ALUMINA. This aluminum oxide produced from bauxite is, along with the raw ore bauxite, Guinea's major export.

Produced by foreign investors, alumina and bauxite are the major foreign exchange sources for the government of Guinea with over \$428 million worth of alumina produced yearly in recent years. At present Guinea has not harnessed its hydroelectric potential to the production of aluminum and world market supplies of alumina and bauxite are such that the Guinean portion of the market is still negligible, but growing.

AMARIA. A small village on the Konkouré River upstream from the alumina plant and bauxite mines of Fria (q.v.). A 720,000-kilowatt hydroelectric plant was planned here as part of the Five Year Development Plan of 1973–1978. However, due to lack of finances, the plan was abandoned.

ANGLO-FRENCH CONVENTION OF 1882. By terms of the British Foreign Office this agreement granted most French claims along the coast between Conakry (q.v.) and Freetown. This convention was never officially ratified by the French Chamber of Deputies. It was, though, typical of European diplomatic activities of the nineteenth century which largely established today's national boundaries, but paid little or no heed to African realities.

ANIMAL HUSBANDRY. Guinea was a livestock exporter before independence but by the mid-1960s the flight of many Guinean herders to Côte d'Ivoire, Liberia, and Sierra Leone had made meat a very rare item in the diets of most Guineans. Scrawny chickens are found throughout the country along with an occasional duck and a rare turkey or Guinea fowl, but few of these animals are ever marketed. They are usually kept as a ready source of meat for the occasional village festival or honored guest. A few pigs are kept in the forest region. N'dama cattle, small, agile and strong with good resistance to disease, especially the tsetse fly (q.v.), which carries sleeping sickness, are allowed to wander and graze almost at will throughout much of Upper Guinea and the Futa Jalon (qq.v.). Small short-haired sheep and goats also exist in relatively large numbers throughout Guinea.

Dry season hunger keeps all of these animals from ever becoming very productive. Unselective breeding and the forced sale of animals by government requisition also militated against the creation of higher milk or meat yields under the Touré regime.

ARCHINARD, GENERAL LOUIS (1850–1932). French military officer who between 1888 and 1893 initiated a series of military campaigns, some without the approval of the French government, by which the Tukulor Empire and much of present-day Mali were brought under French control. He also launched several operations against Samory Touré (q.v.). After publication of his book *Le Soudan Français,* he was dismissed from his post as *commandant-supérieur* in 1893. When a civilian government was installed in French West Africa he was appointed in 1895 as director of defense in the Ministry of the Colonies and in 1897 was sent to Indochina.

ARDO. A Pular term for the leader of a transhuman (q.v. transhumance) community.

ARIBOT, AL HADJ SOULEYMANE. Nicknamed "Aribot Soda" this businessman and leader in the PDG (q.v.) was arrested by Sékou Touré in 1971. Born about 1921 this father of seven probably died in detention in Kindia (q.v.).

ARIBOT, FATOU. A teacher and prominent leader in women's organizations in Lower Guinea and Conakry (q.v.) in particular. Very active in the PDG (q.v.), she died in Conakry in 1993.

ARMED FORCES. Under the Touré constitution, the president of the republic was the commander-in-chief of the armed forces. From 1972 the minister of the people's army was under the domain of the prime minister with Namory Keita (q.v.) as chief of staff. Distrusted by Sékou Touré, the armed forces never played a very large role in Guinean affairs and were somewhat overshadowed by the militia (Milices Populaires [q.v.]), the Gendarmerie (q.v.), Sûreté Nationale, and Garde Républicaine (q.v.). The Army had fewer than 5,000 soldiers and its personnel were organized into four infantry battalions, one armored battalion, and one engineer battalion. Little information is available about the Air Force, with perhaps 300 members, and the Navy, with about 200 officers and personnel. Under Touré defense spending ranged from about 4–5 percent of the Guinea GNP to as much as 11.5 percent and the armed forces were often mobilized for developmental activities in agriculture and road building, so defense costs were perhaps not this high. The present government has not increased military spending substantially.

ARRONDISSEMENT. The administrative level between the regional and local levels. There were 220 such districts in 1974. Each *arrondissement* was presided over by an executive head called a commandant who was responsible to the governor of the region. Within the *arrondissement* party structures exactly paralleled those of the government. The *arrondissement* had been the basic administrative unit of the French colonial government in West Africa and the lowest over which a French officer presided directly. *Arrondissements* have been renamed *sous-préfectures* (q.v.) since 1984. See ADMINISTRATIVE ORGANIZATION.

ARTS, MUSIC. The traditional music of Guinea was, and to some extent still is, intimately linked with other cultural aspects of the country's various ethnic communities. Music was inspired by and enhanced religious, labor, war, magic, and leisure activities. In conjunction with dances performed by masked dancers in both the Forest Region and Lower Guinea (qq.v.) both vocal and instrumental music displayed rich polyphony and rhythmic variations. In Upper Guinea (q.v.) the high court music of the Mali Empire and the griot (q.v.) epic tradition are especially noted. In Middle Guinea (q.v.) the musical forms of the Fulbé (q.v.) included lyrical flute and stringed pieces with a rich heritage of poetry set to music.

From 1958 on, the PDG (q.v.) actively supported a

number of regional and national orchestras and choruses, some of which achieved international recognition for their innovative syncretization of modern and traditional instruments in a music of great originality and vitality. Popular dance band and individual solo performers, both voice and instrumental, have kept modern Guinean music very much at the forefront of popularity in Africa and the world.

ARTS, THEATER. Much Guinean theater during the Touré regime became a propaganda arm of the PDG (q.v.). It existed to glorify the party and President Sékou Touré (q.v.). The exceptions were the Ballet Africain (q.v.), and the Ballet National Djoliba. Founded in 1959 and 1964 respectively, these professional troupes used dance and song based on folk traditions to create a unique artistic and commercially quite successful performance genre. These troupes made Guinean music and dance better known throughout Africa, Australia, Europe, the United States, and even Japan.

ARTS, VISUAL. Most of Guinea's ethnic groups practiced pottery, and wall and mask painting. Wall painting was especially notable among the Kissi (q.v.), where the exterior white kaolin-plastered walls of houses were sometimes decorated with representations of village and household scenes in grayish monotones. Elsewhere in the country Muslims painted geometric raised relief patterns on their house walls. Sculpture in wood and stone was also once widespread in the country.

Ritual human figure statuettes in steatite (soapstone) and schist 10–20 centimeters (4–8 inches) high dated from the sixteenth century were once found throughout the Forest Region (q.v.). Wood sculpture, highly susceptible to decay in the Guinean climate, ranged from small wood figures among the Kissi to the notable drum support bases and large dance masks of the Baga (q.v.). Little wood carving beyond masks and small human and animal figures is commercially done today. Western style painting is infrequently practiced in Guinea at present.

ASKIYA. A dynasty of 11 Songhay (Songhai) emperors who

ruled from 1492 until the Moroccan attacks on the empire in the 1590s. The dynasty began with Mohammed Touré (also known as Askiya Mohammed and Askiya the Great), whose name some link to the Touré patronym, which is widespread in Upper Guinea (q.v.). Askiya Daoud (1549–1583) was the greatest of the Askiya emperors and much of Upper Guinea and some of the Futa Jalon (q.v.) were under his rule. Though the Moroccans and their descendants, between 1591 and 1750, gave the title to 18 individuals, the title had ceased then to have much meaning.

ASSEMBLEE DE L'UNION FRANCAISE. The representative body of the French Union which was created by the French Constitution of 1946. Indigenous people as well as French residents from the colonies were elected to this body which met at Versailles; its functions were purely advisory. Karim Bangoura (q.v.) was the best known of the Guinean representatives to this body.

ASSIMILATION POLICY. Some scholars argue that, at least in theory, this was the continuous cultural aim of the French in their African colonies. Derived from eighteenth-century French enlightenment thinking, the goal was that Africans would eventually be assimilated into French culture and become black French. Assimilation first became official policy during the French Revolution, was abandoned when Napoleon permitted slavery, reappeared during the revolutionary upheavals of 1848, and was maintained in uneasy coexistence with growing French racist attitudes in the nineteenth century. As awareness of the geographic size of the French colonies in Africa grew in the pre-World War I period, the policy was abandoned as impractical. In its place the policy of association (q.v.) became dominant. Prior to the *loi cadre* of 1956 only about 2,000 Africans in Afrique Occidentale Française (French West Africa, AOF [q.v.]) were able to meet the French language, dress, education, religion, and other requirements to obtain French citizenship and thus escape the *corvée* and the *indigénat* (qq.v.). The idea was revived, to some degree, after World War II and the *loi cadre* in 1956 allowed all Africans to become citizens.

ASSIMILE (OR ASSIMILATED). Name given to those few Africans who, within the French colonial system, met a whole range of educational, economic and social standards—in effect adopted the French way of life, and were thus, in theory, to be granted the full privileges of French citizenship. Until 1946, when reforms made French citizenship more readily available, only a handful of Guineans received this status.

ASSOCIATION DES ANCIENS COMBATTANTS. An association of World War I and World War II veterans plus veterans of the Indochina War. After World War II, this group became a political force in Guinea, especially in urban areas.

ASSOCIATION DES GUINEENS EN FRANCE (AGF). One of the two opposition groups in exile from Guinea during the last years of the Touré regime. Like its counterpart, the Front pour la Libération Nationale de Guinée (q.v.), it was composed largely of university graduates. These groups also counted former cabinet ministers and former Guinean ambassadors among their members.

ASSOCIATION INTER-GOUVERNEMENTALE DES PAYS PRODUCTEURS DE BAUXITE (IBA). Association of bauxite-producing countries formed in March 1974. Members are Guinea, Sierra Leone, Guyana, Jamaica, Yugoslavia, Surinam, and Australia.

ASSOCIATION POLICY. The colonial policy which by the 1920s had, in practice, replaced earlier theoretical attempts to assimilate Africans into the French culture. Under this policy Africans were considered to be incapable of becoming French in the near future so they were "allowed" to retain their manners, customs, and religion while political and economic control was in French hands. See ASSIMILATION POLICY.

AVIATION. Guinea's government-owned air service, Air Guinée (q.v.), functions as a public enterprise. It had cost the country more than $4 million by the early 1980s and offered little promise for increased profit. The Conakry-Gbessia airport (q.v.) is of international standard and receives scheduled flights of a number of airlines. This airport can take aircraft of the Boeing 737 size. The Labé, Kankan, and Faranah (qq.v.) regional airports can receive these aircraft both day and night while five or six other small unsurfaced, laterite strips are serviceable for daylight and dry season use by smaller aircraft.

- B -

BA, MAMADOU BOYE. The candidate of the Union pour la Nouvelle République (UNR) in the December 1993 elections. He campaigned on a platform of economic development and promised schools, dispensaries, and better roads. Calling for food self-sufficiency he spoke out particularly strongly against alleged corruption of the Lansana Conté (q.v.) government and ethnic divisiveness. He received about 13 percent of the votes in this election.

BADIARANKE (Badyaranké). An ethnic group closely related to the Konagi and Bassari (qq.v.) living on the Senegal-Guinea border. Beekeepers and farmers, they raised few cows but were once well known as cotton cloth weavers. Little assimilated into national life until relatively recently, they have maintained a larger degree of cultural and religious autonomy than most of Guinea's ethnic groups.

BAFING RIVER. The upper course of the Senegal River having its source less than 50 kilometers (30 miles) north of Mamou in the south-central Futa Jalon (qq.v.). From its source it flows north and northeast to the border of Mali and from there to the sea as the Senegal River.

BAGA. The largest of the minor ethnic groups in Lower Guinea (q.v.). Predating the later Susu (q.v.) populations in the coastal areas from Conakry (q.v.) to the Rio Núñez estuary, they were present on the coast from at least the sixteenth century. They became largely assimilated into the dominant

Susu populations of Lower Guinea by the 1950s. See LANDOMA.

BAH, AL HAJJ THIERNO IBRAHIMA. Born in about 1920, this administrative clerk served as a *chef de canton* in Dalaba (q.v.) under the French. He served successively as governor of Telimélé, Dubreka, and Kindia (qq.v.) under Touré. Married with four wives and 23 children, he was arrested in Kindia in 1971 and probably died in detention there.

BAH, MAMADOU (*Grand Bah*). A well-known lieutenant in the Guinean army arrested for alleged participation in a plot and executed in July 1971.

BAH, MAMADOU (*Mamadou Banque Mondiale*). An outspoken and leading figure in the opposition against Presidents Sékou Touré and General Lansana Conté (qq.v.). Mamadou Bah worked for the Touré government in the early 1960s before serving at the World Bank. In Abidjan he was involved in private financial and business affairs as well as politics. In 1969 he was condemned to death *in absentia* because of alleged participation in a plot against the Touré regime. After Touré's death in 1984 he returned from exile. His political party, the Union pour la Nouvelle République (UNR), is very active in the opposition against the military-backed government of General Lansana Conté.

BAH, MAMADOU (*Mamadou Libraire*). A teacher and librarian from the Labé Bah family. *Mamadou Libraire* became Director of BATIPORT and LIBRAPORT before being arrested in 1971 along with several family members for alleged participation in a plot against the Touré regime. He spent several years in Boiro political jail and although freed in 1977 he never fully recovered from the torture.

BAH, MAMADOU (*Mamadou Mangol*). A professor of linguistics and French. He held several positions in Guinean education including president of the Polytechnic Institute of Kankan before being appointed to several ministerial positions in the government including minister of information and tourism and minister of small and medium-scale businesses. Mamadou Bah found himself at odds with Touré's government after the "Fulbé" Plot (q.v.) in 1976. In the late 1970s he was appointed ambassador to Mozambique. After Touré's death he was removed from this post and later became director of the Afro-Arab Bureau of the Organization of African Unity (q.v.) in Addis Ababa, Ethiopia.

BAKOYE RIVER. An important tributary of the Senegal River taking its rise just inside the Guinea border north of Siguiri in the ancient gold-mining area of Buré (qq.v.).

BALAFON. The Maninka (q.v.) name for a wood xylophone widely played in the traditional orchestras throughout Guinea and elsewhere in West Africa.

BALDE. A common Fulbé (q.v.) family name especially for the many talented leaders who come from the Tougué (q.v.) region.

BALDE, DIAO. A native of Tougué (q.v.) who served in various positions in Sékou Touré's (q.v.) cabinet. Balde served Touré well, along with many others he mediated between Sékou Touré and his half-brother, Ismaël Touré (q.v.), and was able to retain Sékou Touré's trust until the very end.

BALDE, MAMADOU. An army commander and member of the military officers who organized the successful coup against the Touré regime in April 1984. In July 1985 he reportedly led the defense of Conakry (q.v.) against the military coup which attempted to overthrow Lansana Conté (q.v.). Since then, due to internal rivalries among the military leaders, he has played a less prominent role. He served as a member of the Comité Transitoire de Redressement National (q.v.) until 1992 then he was sent to Liberia to lead the Guinean troops with the West African forces fighting the Taylor rebels.

BALDE, OUMAR. This civil engineer served as director general of the Highways Department and secretary general of the Organisation des Etats Riverains du Fleuve Sénégal (OERS)

(q.v.) under Touré. Born about 1931 he probably died in detention in Kindia (q.v.) with neither trial nor sentencing.

BALDE, OUSMANE. An economist, president of the Banque Centrale de la République de Guinée (BCRG) (q.v.) and a long time minister of finance, Balde was arrested in December 1970 and charged with participation in the Portuguese invasion. He was sentenced without trial and hanged on January 25, 1971 along with Barry III (q.v.), Kara Soufiana, and Magassouba Moriba.

BALLA ET LES BALLADINS. One of the most popular Guinean musical groups. Balla is remarkable for his ability to incorporate Maninka folklore and traditional instruments (balaphon, kora, etc.) into modern ensembles.

BALLAY, EUGENE NOEL (1847–1902). First French governor of Guinea from the end of 1889 to 1900. After the Rivières du Sud (q.v.) were freed from the administrative control of Senegal on August 1, 1889, Ballay arrived in Conakry (q.v.) the next July to supervise construction of the territorial capital, develop communications for commerce, and establish an effective colonial administration and judiciary. A naval doctor by training he is the founder of the present city of Conakry. By the end of his governorship French control was quite firmly established in most of Lower Guinea and the Futa Jalon (qq.v.). He died of yellow fever on January 26, 1902, at Saint Louis (Senegal).

BALLET AFRICAIN. Founded by Fodéba Keita (q.v.) in the 1950s, this troupe displayed traditional West African art to the world. It was originally composed of singers, dancers, and instrumentalists from various parts of French West Africa. Constituted as a Guinea national ballet troop in 1959 it received government support and performed throughout Europe and America.

BAMA, MARCEL MATO. A former teacher, he served as PDG (q.v.) federal secretary in Guéckédou, governor of Dabola, minister of the interior, minister of trade, and minister-

delegate of Upper Guinea (qq.v.). Born about 1931, like many other alleged plotters, probably died in detention sometime later in Conakry (qq.v.) without trial or formal charges.

BANANAS (*Musa sapientum*). Representing an important export crop in Guinea, this large herbaceous perennial plant growing from three to nine meters (10–30 feet) high is best grown under irrigation in relatively sheltered well drained and fertile areas.

BANANKORO. An important diamond-mining town in the *préfecture* of Kerouané (q.v.) with a name etymologically meaning "under the banan tree" in Maninkakan. The rush for diamonds that began in the mid-1950s led to its phenomenal but ill-planned growth. With the creation of an official diamond-mining company, Sékou Touré's government forbade individual mining and destroyed a good part of Banankoro. Its twin-town, Gbenko, is the headquarters of AREDOR, a consortium established by the government with British partners. Gbenko has an airport. When Guinean private and individual mining resumed after 1984, serious problems concerning land rights and ownership arose between AREDOR and local populations. The diamond trade had contributed to the rise of a new and influential merchant class in Kissidougou, Kankan, and Conakry (qq.v.).

BANGOURA, KARIM. Born about 1926 into a prominent Susu family of Coyah (qq.v.). He was a primary school teacher and inspector. As an important member of the Bloc Africain de Guinée (BAG, [q.v.]) he was a representative to the Conseil de l'Union Française (q.v.) in France until 1958. A skilled administrator and diplomat, he served as director of the Guinean Press Agency, ambassador to Washington, and minister of industry and mines. Arrested in Conakry in 1971, he was never tried and was executed in 1972.

BANGURA, HADJA MAFFIRE. A tailor very active among the Susu (q.v.) women of Sanderval and Boulbinet in Conakry (q.v.), she spearheaded one of the first support groups for the

then unionist Sékou Touré (q.v.) in 1953. An influential member of the Parti Démocratique de Guinée (q.v.) she was a member of the Bureau Politique National (q.v.) and the government. She died in 1968.

BANKING. With the central bank under the direct executive control of President Touré, banking functions in Guinea largely consisted of maintaining credit and support functions for government agencies and state enterprises. Individual deposits and withdrawals in savings accounts were very rare and credit to the private sector consisted of less than five percent of total credit. Under the current administration mixed government and private banking institutions have been established. See BANQUE CENTRALE DE LA RE-PUBLIQUE DE GUINEE.

BANQUE CENTRALE DE LA REPUBLIQUE DE GUINEE (BCRG). Established on March 1, 1960, it operated, in principle, as a semi-autonomous institution, issuing currency, regulating the volume of credit, acting as banker for the government, and participating in the formulation of monetary and fiscal policies. In 1972 President Touré (q.v.) took over as governor of the bank and attached it directly to the presidency. Thereafter its previously limited freedom from executive control was totally lost.

On June 18, 1985, the Banque Internationale pour l'Afrique en Guinée (BIAG) was formally established and began operations in early August. The bank is 51 percent owned by the government and 49 percent by the Banque Internationale pour l'Afrique Occidentale (BIAO).

BANQUE CENTRALE DES ETATS DE L'AFRIQUE DE L'OUEST (BCEAO). French West Africa's central bank, established in Paris in 1958 with branches in all member states. Guinea's decision on March 1, 1960 to create an independent currency removed it from participation in this bank.

BANQUE DE L'AFRIQUE OCCIDENTALE (BAO). Until 1958, the Banque de l'Afrique Occidentale was the bank charged with issuing the currency in Guinea and the other French colonies in West Africa.

BANQUE GUINEENNE DU COMMERCE EXTERIEUR (BGCE). One of three specialized banks developed in 1961 after four or five French private commercial banks had their licenses revoked in August 1960. The Guinean Bank for Foreign Trade, like the other specialized banks, bases its credit expansion partly upon deposits made with them and partly upon borrowing from the central bank.

BANQUE INTERNATIONALE AFRICAINE DE GUINEE (BIAG). A branch of a French bank established in Guinea after the April 1984 military coup.

BANQUE INTERNATIONALE POUR LE COMMERCE ET L'INDUSTRIE DE GUINEE (BICIGUI). BICIGUI is affiliated with a French bank.

BANQUE ISLAMIQUE DE GUINEE (BIG). A branch of an American-Saudi bank established in Guinea in the 1970s during the economic boom of the Arab oil-producing countries. After Sékou Touré's (q.v.) death, this bank is encountering considerable competition from the French.

BANQUE NATIONALE POUR LE DEVELOPPEMENT AGRICOLE (BNDA). One of the three specialized banks developed in 1961 after four of five French private commercial banks had their licenses revoked in August 1960. The National Bank for Agricultural Development made possible the acquisition of tractors on easy terms by private entrepreneurs for a time, but credit to small-holders, which was extended by the cooperative (q.v.) system, was severely limited after 1964.

BAOBAB (*Adansonia digitata*). A large tree common to all of Africa. In some Anglophone countries it is called a monkey bread tree. In Guinea it has bell-like flowers which extended from the tree in late July and early August. Ground fruit and leaves are used to make sauces and animal fodder in the dry season. Because of the relative scarcity of trees on the savanna and the tree's striking appearance it came to be associated with magical phenomena among many Guinean peoples. The tree often serves as a shelter for village meetings.

BARO, EL-HADJI MAMADI. A graduate from the William Ponty School (q.v.) and a civil servant born near Kankan (q.v.). He was elected to the Guinean Territorial Assembly in 1952 on the Bloc Africain de Guinée (q.v.) list from Kankan (q.v.), and to the Grand Conseil of French West Africa. The victory of the Parti Démocratique de Guinée (q.v.) in 1956 cost him his seat. A survivor of the Sékou Touré (q.v.) era, with community leaders representing the Futa Jalon and the Forest Region (qq.v.), he built a coalition to ward off the attacks led by the Susu (q.v.) leaders in Conakry (q.v.) in 1991.

BARRY III. See BARRY, IBRAHIMA.

BARRY, ABDOULAYE. Born in 1927, this trained economist served Sékou Touré (q.v.) as *chef de cabinet* in the Ministry of Foreign Affairs. Arrested in Beyla (q.v.) in 1972, he was never tried or sentenced but apparently died in detention.

BARRY, ALPHA OUMAR. Born about 1921, this trained medical doctor was chief medical officer in Kindia (q.v.). He served Sékou Touré as PDG (q.v.) federal secretary in Kindia, minister-delegate of the Forest Region (q.v.), and minister of the *Domaine des Echanges*. Married, with several children, he apparently died in detention without a trial after his arrest in Conakry (q.v.) in 1976.

BARRY, BABA. This statistician served the government of Sékou Touré (q.v.) as technical advisor to the Ministry of Economic Development. Sentenced to hard labor for life after his arrest in 1971 in Conakry (q.v.) at approximately 35 years of age, he apparently died in prison.

BARRY, BOKAR (Boubacar) BIRO. The Soriya (q.v.) almamy

(q.v.) of the Futa Jalon (q.v.) who took over Timbo (q.v.) and refused to yield to the Alfaya (q.v.) faction which was scheduled to assume the alternating leadership in 1896. This offered the French an excuse to intervene, defeat his army at Porédaka and kill him and his son. His defeat by a coalition of French soldiers and Fulbé (q.v.) troops led by his own brother, Oumar Bademba Barry, ended independent Fulbé rule of the Futa Jalon and marked the beginning of French colonial rule. From 1896 to 1905 the French retained the Fulbé political organization but removed "chiefs" who opposed their rule.

BARRY, DIAWADOU. A son of the almamy of Dabola, this Fulbé political leader from the Futa Jalon (qq.v.) represented the traditional "chiefs" and most white residents of the Futa Jalon in the mid-1954 election for the delegate to the French National Assembly from Guinea. Barry was declared elected in an election rife with irregularities by the French colonial government in spite of the fact that Sékou Touré (q.v.) probably gained the majority of votes throughout most of Guinea. With the decline of traditional Fulbé authority in the late 1950s Barry's power waned. Arrested in April 1969 with Colonel Kaman Diaby, he was executed in prison, without benefit of trial for alleged participation in a military coup d'état.

BARRY, EL-HADJI IBRAHIMA SORY-DARA. A very influential "chief" in Mamou until 1957 and the paramount customary leader until his death in 1975. A Bloc Africain de Guinée (q.v.) party member of the Guinean Territorial Assembly, he was one of the two Guinean representatives to the Grand Conseil of French West Africa in Dakar until 1956.

BARRY, IBRAHIMA (BARRY III). Born of Fulbé peasants at Bantigrel in the Pita district he studied at William Ponty School (q.v.) and ultimately qualified as a lawyer in France. He ran for the post of deputy in the French National Assembly in 1954 and 1956, but was defeated on both occasions. As secretary general of the Mouvement Socialiste Africain (q.v.) and then as secretary general of a short-lived

Union Populaire de Guinée he opposed Sékou Touré (q.v.). He reconciled these differences in 1958 and served in the government through the mid-1960s. In 1971 he was hanged in Conakry (q.v.) allegedly for treason.

BARRY, IBRAHIMA (Sory). Succeeded Karamoko Alfa (Ibrahima Sambegu [q.v.]) as leader of the Fulbé Islamic state in the Futa Jalon (qq.v.) about 1751. This leader managed to establish, with the help of Muslim traders, a Fulbé-dominated state that brought the whole region under Islamic law by the late 1770s. When Ibrahima Barry died in 1784, the clerical supporters of Karamoko Alfa (whose given name was also Barry), the Alfaya (q.v.) and the alternate party, the Soriya (q.v.) which supported his descendants, contended for control of the Futa Jalon until the French occupation in 1897.

BARRY, KESSO NENE. Author of *Kesso, princesse peuhle* published in 1988. She is the daughter of the almamy (q.v.) El-Hadji Ibrahima Sory-Dara (q.v.) of Mamou. She had a successful career in high fashion in Paris where she lives with her French husband and her children.

BARRY, MAMADOU SAMBA SAFE. This former teacher served Sékou Touré as PDG federal secretary of Labé, governor of Labé, and governor of Kankan (qq.v.). Married with two wives and 14 children, he was arrested in Kankan in 1971 and apparently died in detention there without trial.

BARRY, MAMADOU SIRADIOU. This army major died in detention in Conakry (q.v.) sometime after his arrest in Conakry in 1971. Born about 1916 he served as deputy to the garrison commander in Kankan (q.v.), was commander of the Kindia Garrison, was a major in the Guinean Expeditionary Force (United Nations troops) to Zaire (the Congo), and was head of army ordinance.

BARRY, SORY. A forestry engineer who served Sékou Touré (q.v.) as director general of the forestry commission, minister of agriculture, minister-delegate for Upper Guinea, member of the National Confederation of Guinean Workers, and secretary general of the government. He was arrested in 1971 at approximately 45 years of age and probably died in detention in Kindia (q.v.) sometime after without trial.

BASSARI. This is one of the least Europeanized or Islamicized ethnic groups in Guinea. Historically among the oldest inhabitants of Guinea, the Bassari preserve their traditional matrilineal organization, religion, and way of life in the rugged areas of the Futa Jalon (q.v.) close to the Guinea-Bissau and Senegal border.

BASSE-GUINEE. See LOWER GUINEA.

BATEH. A region of Upper Guinea (q.v.) located between the right bank of the Niger River (q.v.) and the left bank of its tributary the Milo River (q.v.), and a significant precolonial crossroads that contributed to the rise of Kankan (q.v.) in the late sixteenth century. Bateh is also the name of the Muslim theocracy of which Kankan was the main center.

BAUXITE. Guinea has three major deposits of this aluminum-producing ore which are currently being exploited. The main contribution comes from the Boké (q.v.) mine which produces about 10 million tons a year. The Kindia (q.v.) mine, which has suffered persistent production and transport problems in recent years, produces about 3 million tons. The Friaguia bauxite alumina operation now produces around 615,000 tons of alumina and 1.35 million tons of bauxite a year. The deposits on the Ile de Los (q.v.) were exhausted in the mid-1970s but with more than 3.5 billion tons of known reserves Guinea will continue to be a major world exporter of bauxite for some years to come. See ALUMINA.

BEAVOGUI, LOUIS LANSANA. Born in Macenta (q.v.) in 1923, he was trained as a medic in Dakar. At the age of 31 he was elected major of Kissidougou (q.v.). In January 1956 he, Sékou Touré, and Saifoulaye Diallo (qq.v.) were elected to the French National Assembly from Guinea. Upon independence he was made minister for economic affairs and planning. In 1961 he became minister of foreign affairs, an office he held for almost eight years. He was active in the United Nations (q.v.) debate on the Congo in 1965. In October 1966, while en route to the OAU conference in Addis Ababa, he was held for months by Ghanaian officials at the Accra airport in retaliation for the refuge Guinea had offered to the exiled Kwame Nkrumah. In May 1969 he replace Ismaël Touré (q.v.) as minister of economic affairs.

On April 26, 1972, at the closing session of the Ninth Congress of the PDG (q.v.), President Touré announced that Béavogui was to fill the newly created post of prime minister. He was also placed in charge of the army, foreign affairs, planning, financial control, and information. President Touré trusted the dedicated and hard-working Béavogui very much, retaining him as prime minister into the 1980s. He served briefly as interim president in 1984.

BEAVOGUI, DR. MARIAMA. Physician in Conakry and daughter of Lansana Béavogui (q.v.). She is the leader of the Parti du Regroupement National (PRN), a party opposed to President Conté's military government.

BEAVOGUI, TOLNO. A former high school teacher, high school principal, university professor, regional education inspector, and member of several national commissions on education, he was a respected senior representative from the Forest Region (q.v.). In 1984 he was named ambassador to the United States and later to East Germany.

BEHANZIN, SENAINON. Born in Dahomey (now Benin), Behanzin played an important role in the educational policies of Guinea throughout the Sékou Touré (q.v.) years. Closely associated with the Touré regime, Behanzin was one of Sékou Touré's most trusted cabinet members. He was appointed minister of ideology and information at Sékou Touré's death and has since returned to his homeland in Benin.

BEMBEYA JAZZ. One of the most popular Guinean musical groups. With its leader and head vocalist, Demba Camara, Bembeya Jazz dominated the musical scene in Guinea and in

French-speaking West Africa in the 1960s and 1970s. It set
the example for other modern dance orchestras in all neighboring countries. Its 1968 "Concert" recording, composed in
honor of Almamy Samory Touré (q.v.), is a masterpiece of
modern Guinean music of the Sékou Touré (q.v.) era.
Demba's accidental death in Dakar in 1980 and the lack of
official support after April 1984 had a negative effect on the
orchestra. Like other Guinean orchestras, Bembeya Jazz is
struggling to survive.

BENTY. Once a relatively important trading town on the Mél-
kouré River south of Conakry (q.v.). This small port was still
active in banana (q.v.) exporting until the late 1960s, but by
the mid-1970s the small coastal transport lighters, which
served this and other small ports, had ceased operation and
Benty has declined in importance.

BERETE, FRAMOI. A long-time accountant at the Comptoir
Commercial Franco-Africain (CCFA) in Conakry (q.v.) and
the leader of the Union Mande, a voluntary organization that
joined with others from Lower Guinea, the Futa Jalon, and
the Forest Region (qq.v.) to create the Bloc Africain de
Guinée (BAG) (q.v.) party. Elected to the Territorial Assembly from Siguiri in 1946, he became its president as well as
the head of the BAG. He lost his seat to Fodéba Keita (q.v.)
in 1957. He died in Conakry in 1974.

BEYLA. A town and administrative region of the same name in
the northeast forest region on the Côte d'Ivoire border. Beyla
was the center of thriving tobacco-growing (q.v.) area until
independence. Though the Beyla region is also on the edge
of a major diamond-mining area, it remains a scarcely
populated subsistence agricultural area for the most part.

BIAG. See BANQUE INTERNATIONALE AFRICAINE DE
GUINEE.

BILHARZIA (*Schistosomiasis*). A common infectious disease in
Guinea caused by a parasite blood fluke which requires a
tiny fresh water snail as an intermediate vector. People are

infected by walking in, swimming in, or drinking water containing the larvae of the fluke. Since prevention and treatment are difficult, many Guineans suffer from this disease to varying degrees.

BINGER, CAPITAINE LOUIS GUSTAVE (1856–1936). French navy officer and explorer. He served in Senegal and Soudan (Mali) in the 1880s. In 1891 he traveled through the region from Bamako, Mali, to the coast of the Côte d'Ivoire through Wassulou (q.v.) and the eastern borders of Guinea. He wrote *Du Niger au Golfe de Guinée par le pays de Kong et le Mossi,* a very informative work on the dyula (q.v.) trade and the history of Kankan and Bateh (qq.v.) under Alfa Mahmoud Kaba (q.v.) in the 1850s.

BISSANDOUGOU. The capital of the short-lived Maninka Empire established by Samory Touré in the late nineteenth century near present-day Kérouané in Upper Guinea (qq.v.).

BLOC AFRICAIN DE GUINEE (BAG). Founded by a coalition of "conservative" leaders from Guinea's four regions. It was led primarily by Framoi Bereté (q.v.), Diawadou Barry (q.v.), Koumandian Keita, Karim Bangoura (q.v.), and El-Hadji Ibrahima Sory Barry (q.v.). The BAG controlled the Guinean Territorial Assembly and politics until 1957 when Sékou Touré's Parti Démocratique de Guinée (PDG) crushed it. After the referendum of September 28, 1958, and the attainment of independence, most of the main BAG leaders unilaterally joined the PDG, thereby ushering in the beginnings of a de facto one-party regime.

BOFFA. A town and region north of Conakry (q.v.) on the Atlantic coast which was an early site of European trade of colonial penetration. Largely a subsistence agricultural area in the twentieth century, its rice-producing possibilities and potential as a port for bauxite and alumina (qq.v.) exports have again given it importance.

BOIRO, MAMADOU. A Guinean military officer from the Foulakounda region of Koundata (q.v.) in the extreme northwest. He was apparently murdered by being thrown from an airplane while attempting to carry out Sékou Touré's (q.v.) orders for the arrest of other officers allegedly involved in a coup attempt. The Boiro military camp (named in his honor) in the center of Conakry (q.v.) became infamous in the mid-1970s and early 1980s as the scene of torture and execution of Touré's political opponents.

BOISSON, PIERRE. French administrator who served as secretary-general of the government of French West Africa (AOF [q.v.]) in 1936 and later as high commissioner for all of French West and Central Africa under the Vichy government. Under his administration, all political activities in Guinea were suppressed. He was removed from office in November 1942 after the allied invasion of North Africa.

BOKE. A town and region located on the Atlantic coast near the border with Guinea-Bissau. Established as a French garrison in 1866, today the Boké region is the center of the thriving bauxite-mining industry with a new railway and port facilities. The bauxite (q.v.) in the region has a 60–65 percent aluminum content with a very low silica content, making this perhaps 200-million-ton deposit one of the highest grade bauxite deposits in the world.

BOKE PROJECT. The most important, and to date, most successful of the industrial units established since independence. This bauxite-mining project was started in 1973 under the authority of a joint stock company owned 49 percent by the government of Guinea and 51 percent by a consortium of western aluminum companies. The project is expected ultimately to produce $50 million a year for the Guinean treasury and make Guinea one of the world's major bauxite (q.v.) producers. See COMPAGNIE DES BAUXITES DE GUINEE.

BOLON. A Maninka traditional musical instrument which consists of half a large calabash used as a sound box and a wooden pole that forms the neck. Unlike the kora (q.v.), the bolon has only two or three strings and produces deeper sounds. The bolon was used by marching armies to set the cadence while the kora is for relaxation.

BORDO. A suburb of Kankan (q.v.), the second largest city in Guinea, where the French established an arts and trade school during the colonial period. The school also had an agricultural experiment station. Functioning only marginally under a series of non-Guinean technical assistant groups the agronomy faculty of the national university was placed in charge of the agricultural station in 1971 and in 1981 the European Community expanded the experimental station.

BORGNIS-DESORDES, GENERAL GUSTAVE. French military officer and colonial administrator, in 1879 he was appointed commandant-supérieur du haut-fleuve and lieutenant governor of Upper Senegal. Under him the French conducted a series of military campaigns against the Tukulor Empire and Samory Touré (q.v.). He later served as an advisor to the colonial department. His protégé was Archinard (q.v.), whose military campaigns he supported.

BOUBOU. The traditional large robe customarily worn by Guineans and other West African males on public occasions. Women might also wear a voluminous transparent gauze *boubou* over a wrap-around piece of cloth (*pagne*), and a blouse of like color.

BOUET-VILLAUMEZ, LOUIS-EDOUARD. A French naval lieutenant charged by the French King Louis-Phillipe with surveillance of the slave trade (q.v.). On behalf of Bordeaux merchants, Bouet-Villaumez made treaties with local African rulers which permitted the establishment of the French trading posts known as Rivières du Sud (q.v.) from 1837 through 1842.

BRAZZAVILLE CONFERENCE. A meeting called by General Charles de Gaulle, leader of the Free French in Brazzaville (Congo, French Equatorial Africa) in January 1944. Presided over by Felix Eboué, the governor of Chad, its goal was to define the postwar evolution of the various African territories. This gathering of French colonial governors and administrators and non-Communist labor leaders reiterated their support of the colonial system though they promised to lessen the harshest aspects of colonial "native policy" after the war. The conference recommended the continuation of French assimilation (q.v.) policies and rejected the idea of autonomy for the colonies. It also emphasized the unity between the French and the overseas territories and opened the door for African representation in the political institutions of the Fourth French Republic (see CONSTITUTION OF THE FOURTH FRENCH REPUBLIC). Of most immediate significance was the abolition of the *indigénat* (q.v.) and elimination of the cosmetic distinctions between *citoyens* and *sujets indigènes* (q.v.).

BRIGADES AGRICOLES DE PRODUCTION (BAPs; also Brigades Modernes de Production). These work groups were a continuation of the *investissement humain* (q.v.) of the early years of independence in Guinea. Putting into practice the principle of *produire pour se suffire,* groups from all sectors of the Guinean population, including the army and students, were drafted into production brigades. Brigades were of two types: those in which all production plans were directed by the government and the government supplied all the equipment, and those in which local communities make the decisions. The 1973–1978 five-year plan called for 2,000 brigades in 1974, 3,000 in 1975, 4,500 in 1976, 5,500 in 1977, and 7,125 in 1978.

In the mid-1970s the BAPs were merged with the Brigades Motorisées de Production (BMP), which themselves became, in 1978, the Fermes Agropastorale d'Arrondissement (FAPA). The FAPAs were cooperative farms modeled on the agricultural communes of the People's Republic of China at the time. The FAPAs were conveniently used to control student activism and curb the unemployment figures, with graduates and university students from agricultural schools providing the largest part of the labor. The FAPAs met strong resistance from the general population (they were ridiculed as *faux pas*). At Sékou Touré's (q.v.) death they were among the first government institutions to be eliminated.

BURE (Bouré). This is the name of the ancient alluvial gold fields north of present-day Siguiri (q.v.). These gold fields were an important source of wealth for the empires of Ghana, Mali (q.v.) and Songhay. The production of gold in Buré during the 1920s and 1930s was very high. Since the 1970s higher gold prices have once again made these gold fields important and enlivened Siguiri.

BUREAU POLITIQUE NATIONAL (BPN). National Political Bureau. The seven-member central committee of the Parti Démocratique de Guinée (PDG [q.v.]). Made up of the president, the prime minister, and five other party leaders, this group controlled the government, appointed about one third of the National Assembly and, directly through the party, controlled all authorized political activity within the country.

- C -

CABRAL, AMILCAR (1926–1973). The founder in 1956 of the Partido Africão da Independência da Guiné do Cabo-Verde (PAIGC [q.v.]), which in 1963 launched the Guinea-Bissau war for independence from Portugal. Cabral was assassinated in Conakry (q.v.) in 1973 where the PAIGC had its headquarters.

CAILLIE, RENE-AUGUSTE (1799–1838). A Frenchman who traveled through part of Upper Guinea to Timbuctoo in 1824–1828. His accounts of this journey, published in 1830, whetted the European appetite for further exploration.

CAISSE NATIONALE D'EPARGNE (CNE). Under Sékou Touré (q.v.) the National Savings Bank was, along with a postal-checking system, a government-run agency with no real credit function.

CAMARA, AL HADJ BABA. A civil administrator and former directeur de cabinet at the Ministry of Trade as well as former director of the Department of Foreign Trade, former director of the National Banana Agency, and former governor of Kissidougou (q.v.). Married with two wives and ten children, he was arrested in 1971 and sentenced to hard labor for life. He probably died in detention in Kindia (q.v.) sometime later.

CAMARA, BENSALI. An early Parti Démocratique de Guinée (PDG [q.v.]) leader and unionist. He was a member of the *loi cadre* (q.v.) government and minister of labor and social affairs and a leading critic of Sékou Touré's (q.v.) autocracy at the Foulaya symposium in 1962. He was expelled from PDG leadership and jailed in 1965. He died in detention.

CAMARA, DIOUMA. Former staff officer of the combined Armed Forces (q.v.) and commanding officer of the Boké Military Camp, he was arrested in 1971 and probably died in detention shortly thereafter.

CAMARA, LAMINE ("Capi"). Born in Kankan (q.v.) in 1940 he was a graduate from the University of Conakry and active as a student leader in the Parti Démocratique de Guinée (PDG [q.v.]). Arrested and jailed at Camp Boiro, he was a member of the Comité Transitoire de Redressement National (CTRN [q.v.]). He was ambassador to France in 1993.

CAMARA LAYE. A Maninka from Kouroussa (qq.v.), Camara Laye is the best known Guinean author. His *L'Enfant Noir* (*The Black Child*) appeared in 1953 and was followed by *Le Regard du Roi* (*The Radiance of the King,* 1954) and *Dramouss* (1966). This latter novel, which appeared in France, depicts an African country under the control of a tyrannical dictator. Camara Laye lived in exile in Dakar, Senegal until his death in 1978.

CAMARA, MADAME LOFFO (ca. 1925–1971). A midwife and pioneering Parti Démocratique de Guinée (PDG [q.v.]) activist in Macenta (q.v.). She was a member of the Guinean Assembly and the PDG central committee and women's organization. She was arrested and hanged in Conakry (q.v.) in 1971.

CAMARA, MAXIME. Sékou Touré's son-in-law, a well-known soccer player from Kissidougou, husband of his daughter Aminata (qq.v.), and head of the cabinet of the Ministre de la Coopération Internationale before 1984. He is now living in exile.

CAMARA, MBALIA. A housewife and member of the Parti Démocratique de Guinée (PDG [q.v.]). Though pregnant, she was murdered by a Susu (q.v.) "chief" in about 1955. Her name was given to the main market in Conakry (q.v.) and other institutions during the Touré regime as a symbol of women's political awareness and militancy.

CAMARA, NANTENION. A professor of history at the University of Conakry born in Siguiri (q.v.), he was a member the Comité Transitoire de Redressement National (CTRN [q.v.]) in 1991 and minister of commerce in 1992.

CAMARA, SIKHE. A professor of law, writer and jurist, Dr. Camara held several ministry positions in successive Touré governments, including those of minister of higher education and minister of justice. After the 1984 coup, he was imprisoned and then later released by Lansana Conté (q.v.).

CAMARA, SORY KANTARA. Born in the Guéckédou (q.v.) in 1939 he became a professor of anthropology at the University of Bordeaux in France and authored the prize-winning book *Les gens de la parole,* Paris, 1978.

CAMP MAMADOU BOIRO. See BOIRO, MAMADOU.

CANTON. A regional administrative unit placed under an indigenous administrative agent or chief who was responsible to the *commandant de cercle* (q.v.) during the French colonial regime. See CHIEFTAINCY.

CASTE. Most Guinean ethnic groups, certainly the Maninka and Fulbé (qq.v.), had a tripartite status system which might be termed a caste system, remnants of which are still perceptible today. First there were the free persons, then came people belonging to endogenous occupational groups such as black-smiths, leather workers, or *griots* (q.v.). Finally came a class of servile bondspersons, sometimes called slaves. Though the three major divisions were a hierarchy of rank, many fine lines and divisions existed within each and wealth, power, and status did not always neatly line up in this ranked order.

CATHOLICS. The first French Catholic mission was established in Boffa (q.v.) in 1877 and 100 years later about 35,000 Guineans were Catholics. The White Fathers and the Holy Ghost Fathers (Spiritan) were the major Catholic missionary groups active in Guinea throughout the colonial period. European priests with their beards and *soutanes* were widely known throughout Guinea by the 1920s. Installed in small chapels and parish churches throughout the country they soon established elementary schools and dispensaries. A minor seminary was established in a Conakry (q.v.) suburb before the 1920s and some sources suggest that a major seminary may have also functioned there for a time. In 1962 Sékou Touré (q.v.) nationalized all church schools. In 1967 non-African missionaries were expelled from Guinea and in 1970 the African-born archbishop of Conakry Raymond Marie Tchidimbo (q.v.) was condemned to life imprisonment. He was released sometime later as a human rights gesture under pressure from Amnesty International and the Vatican. Today the Catholic Church is staffed by Guinean bishops and clergy.

CENTRE D'EDUCATION RURALE (CER). These secondary school institutions were designed by the party under Touré (q.v.) to retain rural families in the rural areas. Even when transformed into Centers for Revolutionary Education they were never truly successful and were mocked as "Centre des Enfants Ratés" (Centers for Failed Kids) by many Guineans. See EDUCATION.

CENTRE DE MODERNISATION RURALE (CMR). According to the first Three-Year Plan, these Centers of Rural Modernization were to be established in each administrative region. They were to serve as model enterprises for the training of local farmers, the demonstration of new materials, and the propagation of modern methods. Within three years of their creation in 1960 the CMRs were in ruins. Their property and especially the tractors were taken over for private use by officials. Their failure was due to inadequate finance and mismanagement.

CENTRE NATIONAL DE PRODUCTION AGRICOLE (CNPA). State farms which were to be organized under the first Three-Year Plan. Some of these were to be models of highly mechanized farming. But by mid-1963 none of the 20 CNPAs planned had been fully established and most were gradually abandoned in the next few years.

CERCLE. The basic unit of French colonial territorial administration directly controlled by the French. Each such area was headed by a district commandant, a civil official with extensive powers, who was directly responsible to the governor. See COMMANDANT DE CERCLE.

CFA FRANC. Originally the Colonies Françaises d'Afrique franc, the name was changed in 1962 to Communauté Financière Africaine. This is the freely transferable currency of most of the territories of the former French West Africa (AOF [q.v.]) and French Equatorial Africa except for Guinea (and Mali for a period), with the addition of Tunisia, Togo, and Cameroon. This currency is attached to the French franc. The central bank has been located in Dakar, Senegal since 1974. See CURRENCY.

CHERIF, CHEIKH MOHAMMED (Mamadi or Fanta-Mady). A prominent mystic and Muslim leader in Kankan (q.v.) who lived from about 1865 to 1955. He was referred to as "Karama-Sekoula" (the Great Teacher). His father, Karamo-Sidiki Cherif, was Samory Touré's (q.v.) spiritual teacher. Cheikh Mohammed's fame enhanced Kankan as an Islamic and commercial metropolis. He blessed the marriage of his namesake, Sékou Touré, (q.v.), in Kankan in 1950 and welcomed Kwame Nkrumah, a charismatic leader from the Gold Coast (Ghana), in 1954. His teachings had a strong impact on West African Islam.

CHERIF, SEKOU. One of the post-independence generation of party dignitaries who owed their position to Sékou Touré (q.v.). Married to Nouncoumba Touré (q.v.), Sékou Touré's sister, Chérif Sékou served as minister of the interior as well as in other positions with much the same degree of corruption and inefficiency as did other family members and allies in Touré's entourage.

CHIEFTAINCY. The process by which French colonial administration functioned at the lowest level. Appointed by the lieutenant governor on the recommendation of the *commandant de cercle* (q.v.), the "chief" was the African administrative agent responsible for tax collection, labor recruitment, and customary justice in his town or district (*canton*). In May 1957 Sékou Touré (q.v.) abolished the chieftaincy because so many "chiefs" supported the conservative Bloc Africain de Guinée (BAG [q.v.]).

CHINA. In 1960 the People's Republic of China began its aid program to Africa with an interest-free loan equivalent to US $25 million given to President Touré (q.v.) while he was on a state visit to Peking. Curtailed by the PRC government somewhat in the mid-1960s, aid continued to be an important source of development help. By 1970 China was Guinea's third largest source of imports. Guinea depended heavily on Chinese rice to meet continued food shortages during the late 1970s and early 1980s. The August 1968 Cultural Revolution, which sought to dissipate the pressure from university student activism by decentralizing the school system and dispersing the university campuses, was largely Chinese inspired. China also helped build the Kinkon hydroelectric facility which provides power to Dalaba, Labé, Mamou, and Pita in the Futa Jalon (qq.v.).

CISSE, AHMED-TIJANI. Born in Lower Guinea (q.v.) he studied in Paris. An essayist, playwright, and poet, he is the author of several books. He is an active leader of the Rassemblement du Peuple de Guinée (RPG) party along with Alpha Condé (q.v.).

CISSE, EMILE (EMILE MICHEL). A teacher and playwright born about 1926 whose publications in the 1950s dealt with the independence struggle. Once governor of Kindia and a major leader, he played an important role in the "kangaroo trials" that followed the Portuguese invasion in 1971 before falling victim to the very system he sought to reinforce.

CISSE, MADAME JEANNE MARTIN. Born in Kankan (q.v.) to the well-known Martin family, which is Muslim, the name notwithstanding. A teacher and Rassemblement Démocratique Africain (RDA [q.v.]) activist in Dakar, Senegal, during the 1950s she was a leading figure in the Parti Démocratique de Guinée (PDG [q.v.]) women's organization and a member of the central committee. Appointed ambassador to the United Nations in New York in 1973, she was the first woman to chair the Security Council. Arrested by the military government in April 1984, she has since been released and is living in Conakry (q.v.).

CLAN. In its primary meaning clan is an anthropological term for an extended kin group tracing descent from a common ancestor. It has come to be a political term useful in describing factions in Guinea's ruling elite, generally referring to political leaders or a coalition of leaders and their followers and dependents. Some social scientists call such association a patron-client network or an adaptation of pre-colonial superior-subordinate relationships or extended family ties. The clan remains in the post-colonial period a major socio-economic institution and is becoming reestablished as the basic political unit. Traditionally, every head of family in the Futa Jalon (q.v.) and elsewhere in Guinea had a patron either secular or clerical, whom he visited regularly for guidance, aid and to show respect. Many Guineans also depended on such patrons for access to land and a wife, in which case the patron was owed substantial services. Beneath the veneer of modern political and economic institutions the clan in Guinea remans the most viable means of getting jobs, promotions, and political favors.

CLIMATE. Coastal Guinea is part of the very western sector of West Africa which has a monsoonal climate. Thus Conakry (q.v.) has five to six months with almost no rain, then 4,300 mm (170 inches) fall in the remaining months of July and August. In the west center of the country, the Futa Jalon (q.v.), the climate is still monsoonal, but, although the total rainfall is lower (about 1,800 mm or 70 inches annually), it is more evenly distributed than on the coast as the rainy season is longer. The interior plains drained by the Niger and Milo Rivers (qq.v.) have less rain and the northeast especially has a typical Sahelian climate. Rainfall in the Forest Region (q.v.) of the southeast is significant (2,600 mm, 100 inches) falling in all but three or four months of the year with relatively high humidity and mist common throughout much of the year.

COCOLI. See LANDOMA.

COFFEE (*Coffea robusta*). Long an important export crop of the Forest Region (q.v.), coffee in Guinea faces a number of severe production problems. The coffees grown in Guinea are mostly robusta varieties which were long a surplus commodity on the world market. Cultivated in small holdings or inefficiently managed collective fields, Guinean coffee has suffered from recurrent onslaughts of disease. With government prices fixed far too low perhaps as much as 50 percent of the crop was smuggled out of the country through Liberia and Sierra Leone during the 1970s and early 1980s. Following the April 1984 military takeover, the Guinean authorities tried, with mixed results, to boost the production of coffee. However, it is hampered by overwhelming problems of road infrastructure, equipment, and strong international competition.

COMBES, ANTOINE. One of three colonels (with Louis Archinard and Georges Humbert) who fought the Maninka leader, Samory Touré (q.v.), intermittently from 1891 to 1898.

COMITE CENTRAL (Central Committee). From early 1975 this highest organ of the PDG (q.v.) was the policy-making and guidance body of the party, responsible for directing and controlling the country's political, economic, social, cultural, and administrative affairs through its executive agent the Bureau Politique National, which was chaired by President Touré (qq.v.). Along with the BPN, the Central Committee was composed of 12 other cabinet ministers, the party's permanent secretary, and four other appointed members.

COMITE D'ETUDES FRANCO-AFRICAINS (CEFA). An organization founded in Algiers and then transported to Paris in 1944 and to French West Africa (AOF [q.v.]) in 1945. It was an offshoot of the Comité Général d'Etudes (CGE) set up in 1942 by the resistance movement in France. The purpose of the CEFA was the study of Franco-African relations and the branch in Dakar started research on Africa to formulate assistance policy toward Africa. After the war, it became a center for Communist activity and, under increasing attack from the colonial administration, disbanded.

COMITE D'UNITE DE PRODUCTION (CUP). Committees of production which were supposed to be set up within administrative services and public enterprises so that workers could participate in the preparation and implementation of the production plan. Worker participation in budget formation and operation of the enterprise was to be ensured by these committees. By 1971 President Touré (q.v.) himself admitted that the CUPs had never really performed their function.

COMITE MILITAIRE DE PRODUCTION (CMP). This committee, comprised of military officers, was in charge of planning and carrying out production goals by the military. The committee also served as the political direction unit within the military under Touré (q.v.).

COMITE MILITAIRE DE REDRESSEMENT NATIONAL (CMRN). The group was formed to govern Guinea by Colonels Lansana Conté and Diarra Traoré (qq.v.) after assuming power on April 3, 1984. The 20-member CMRN was headed by an approximately 10-person executive bureau that advised a government comprised of the president and some 36 cabinet members including 4 ministers of state, 11 ministers, 15 secretaries of state, 2 governors, the chief of the army and gendarmerie (q.v.), the chief of protocol, and the permanent secretary of the CMRN.

COMITE NATIONAL DE LA JEUNESSE DE LA REVOLUTION DEMOCRATIQUE AFRICAINE. The special national youth committee of the JRDA (q.v.) with regional, sectional and local branches was disbanded in 1984.

COMITE NATIONAL DES FEMMES (CNF). Organized as an auxiliary to the PDG (q.v.) the CNF played an important part in the social and political affairs of Guinea. This organization was a pressure group within the party which watched over women's affairs. Cutting across ethnic, religious, and linguistic divisions, this single national women's organization helped unite the country and establish women (q.v.) on an equal footing with men in many important aspects of political activity.

COMITE TRANSITOIRE DE REDRESSEMENT NATIONAL (CTRN). The CTRN was created by the Comité Militaire de Redressement National (CMRN [q.v.]), the reputation and leadership of which was blemished by more than six years of internal dissension. The mission of the CTRN was, during the transition phase, to move toward democracy and a civilian government. From the beginning the CTRN was challenged by basic problems of legitimacy. First it was appointed by the military government to set the conditions for a non-military republic, so the military did not give it much authority. Secondly, since the CTRN, in theory, focused on many of the same issues that the opposition parties did it was hard for members of these parties to challenge directly the CTRN. Despite ambivalent attitudes on the part of both military and civilian groups the CTRN was able to draft a new constitution, *La Loi Fondamentale* (q.v.), to serve, along with some additional laws, as a basis for elections in December 1993. The mission of the CTRN terminated with those elections.

COMMANDANT DE CERCLE. A French official under the colonial regime in Guinea responsible for administrating a large district known as a *cercle* (q.v.) and divided into *cantons* (q.v.) headed by African "chiefs." Most present-day *préfectures* (q.v.) reflect these French administrative *cercles.* See CHIEFTAINCY.

COMMUNAUTE FINANCIERE AFRICAINE (CFA). Most French-speaking African states are members of this financial organization. Reserves are held in the French treasury and an exchange stabilization fund is maintained by the French. The community issues francs used as currency in member nations. Guinea withdrew from the CFA on March 1, 1960 and in 1986 began the process of readmission. The CFA is the name of the currency in use in most Francophone African countries. See also CURRENCY.

COMMUNAUTE FRANCAISE. The "free" association of auton-omous republics set up when the French Constitution of the Fifth Republic (q.v.) was ratified in 1954 by most of the French colonies in Africa. The only exception was Guinea, which opted for independence. In 1960 these associated republics attained jurisdiction over their own foreign policy, defense, currency, fiscal matters, and external communica-tions through an amendment to the French constitution.

COMPAGNIE DES BAUXITES DE GUINEE (CBG). A mixed enterprise in which the government of Guinea held 49 percent of the shares and took 65 percent of any net profits in taxes. The company operated the Boké bauxite mines with HALCO (qq.v.), a consortium of Alcan, Martin Marietta, Pechiney-Ugine-Kuhlmann, the Vereingte Aluminum Werke, and Montecatini-Elison. See BOKE PROJECT, HALCO.

COMPAGNIE FRANCAISE DE L'AFRIQUE OCCIDENTALE (CFAO). One of the major import-export corporations which dominated commercial life in Guinea during colonial times. These firms controlled the import-export and wholesale trade and some aspects of retail trade until the state-controlled enterprises severely curtailed operations after independence. See SOCIETE COMMERCIALE DE L'OUEST AFRICAIN.

COMPTOIR GUINEEN DU COMMERCE EXTERIEUR (CGCE). A state enterprise founded in January 1959 to handle Guinea's trade relations with the Eastern Bloc countries which had tied up much of Guinea's export production in a variety of aid-trade agreements. The CGCE was granted a full monopoly over rice, sugar, and cement imports along with a partial monopoly over banana, palm products, and coffee (qq.v.) exports. The *comptoir* was abolished in September 1961 because of its total inability to handle the job.

COMPTOIR GUINEEN DU COMMERCE INTERIEUR (CGCI). A state enterprise founded in May 1960 with a full monopoly over wholesale trade throughout the country. Regional *comptoirs* were established in the headquarters of each administrative region to serve as subsidiaries of the CGCI. Retail trade was left in private hands. The CGCI was abolished in September 1961 and a number of national commercial enterprises was established to replace this poorly managed internal trade monopoly.

CONAKRY. Like all of Guinea's major cities, Conakry, the country's capital and largest urban center, has grown at an unprecedented pace during the last two decades. The city's population has increased from 200,000 in the sixties to more than 700,000 in the early 1980s. Since 1978, it has doubled in size and population. With more than a million people in the 1990s, the Guinean capital is plagued with major economic, health, and social problems. Crime and civil disorder in its shanty neighborhoods—Koronti, Madina, Ratoma, and Bonfi—are becoming endemic. The immediate consequence has been to increase pollution, already high because of the mine-related seaport facilities. Also pressures on public facilities, services, and utilities are tremendous.

Electric power breakdowns and a lack of adequate sanitary sewers are some of the challenging problems facing Conakry today. In spite of these overwhelming predicaments, this West African coastal city has shown signs of extraordinary development in the private sector and a growing openness to the international business world.

CONAKRY-GBESSIA AIRPORT. An international airport on the Kaloum peninsula adjacent to Conakry (q.v.). It is served by scheduled flights of international air lines including Air Afrique. The landing facilities can take aircraft of the Boeing 737 size. An excellent new terminal was inaugurated on April 3, 1985. See also AVIATION.

CONDE, ALPHA. An activist student leader in the 1960s he was particularly known for his radical views and the book *Guinée: Albanie de l'Afrique ou Néo-colonie Americaine.* Condé returned briefly to Guinea in mid-1991, while political activity remained illegal, but chose voluntary exile following thinly veiled threats and a series of confrontations involving security forces and members of his party. His Rassemblement du Peuple de Guinée (RPG) systematically supported demonstrations against the government throughout 1990 and 1991. Returning to Guinea he received 19.55 percent of the vote for president in the December 20, 1993 elections.

CONDE, EMILE. A civil administrator who served as governor successively of Beyla, Macenta, Labé, and Conakry under Sékou Touré (qq.v.). Arrested in Conakry in 1971, he died in detention.

CONDE, MAMADOU. A captain and former commanding officer of the Nzérékoré Garrison and then of Camp Boiro. As a staff officer of the Combined Armed Forces under Sékou Touré he was arrested in Conakry (q.v.) in 1971 at approximately 40 years of age. Neither tried nor sentenced he is presumed to have died in detention in Conakry.

CONDE, YVONNE. A former teacher, an adult education spe-

cialist, and an official at the ministry of external trade under
Touré's government. A key member of the Comité Transitoire de Redressement National (CTRN [q.v.]), she has been
active in the areas of press and communications.

CONFEDERATION FRANCAISE DES TRAVAILLEURS
CHRETIENS (CFTC). Formed in France on November 1,
1919, with a program and ideology derived from the social
teaching of the Roman Catholic Church, the Guinean branch
was founded in 1946 under the leadership of David Soumah
with the aid of Antoine Lawrence, Firmin Coumbassa, and
Marius Sainkoun (qq.v.). The African branch of the CFTC
became the Confédération Africaine des Travailleurs Croy-
ants (CATC). After a congress in Ouagadougou, Burkina
Faso, in 1956, on November 24, 1956 the Guinean CATC
leader David Soumah joined with Abdoulaye Diallo (q.v.) of
the Guinean branch of the Confédération Générale du
Travail (CGT [q.v.]) in signing an interunion protocol with
Sékou Touré's (q.v.) Confédération Générale des Travailleurs Africains (CGTA) created in January 1956. This
ultimately led to the formation of the Union Générale des
Travailleurs d'Afrique Noire (UGTAN [q.v.]) after a conference in Cotonou, Benin, in January 1957.

CONFEDERATION GENERALE DU TRAVAIL (CGT). This
General Confederation of Labor was one of the earliest labor
unions in French West Africa (AOF [q.v.]); it was modeled
on French Communist labor confederations. As leaders of
this union's Guinean branch, Sékou Touré (q.v.) and his
closest associates first gained their mass following. By 1953
the CGT had 2,600 members, whom Touré led in a strike for
higher wages. Following Touré's election in Beyla to the
Territorial Assembly from Guinea in 1955 the union grew in
membership to 39,000. See LABOR UNIONS; UNION
GENERALE DES TRAVAILLEURS.

CONFEDERATION NATIONALE DES TRAVAILLEURS DE
GUINEE (CNTG). See LABOR UNIONS; UNION GEN-
ERALE DES TRAVAILLEURS.

CONIAGUI (See KONAGI).

CONSEIL DE LA REPUBLIQUE (Council of the Republic). Created by the French Constitution of 1946 as the upper house of the legislature and as an advisory group to the president. Several Guineans served in this house as representatives of their country between 1947 and 1958.

CONSEIL ECONOMIQUE NATIONAL. Council established by President Touré (q.v.) in June 1974 to oversee international agreements, exports and imports, domestic industries, development programs, prices, and salaries.

CONSEIL NATIONAL DE LA REVOLUTION (CNR). This was the representative body of the PDG (q.v.) which in Guinea was practically synonymous with government under Touré (q.v.). It was summoned in ordinary session twice a year and consisted of about 150 delegates from the 30 party federations throughout the nation. It was, in theory, a popular advisory body but in practice it had little more than a "rubber stamp" function as more and more power was assumed by the office of the president. See PARTI-ETAT.

CONSTITUTION. The constitution enacted immediately after independence in 1958 was, in theory, the governing document under which Guinea functioned until Sékou Touré's (q.v) death. In practice the constitution was altered, bent, and totally ignored as suited the objectives of President Touré and the PDG (q.v.). Only two amendments were formally added but numerous laws, regulations, and presidential decrees, many in direct and obvious conflict with the constitution, altered most of its provisions. See PARTI-ETAT.

CONSTITUTION OF THE FIFTH REPUBLIC (De Gaulle constitution). This 1958 act had two major provisions affecting French West Africa (AOF [q.v.]). First it dissolved the federation of French West Africa, dashing Touré's (q.v.) hope of a unified federation at independence. It provided that those states that so wished could regroup voluntarily, a dream which Touré never ceased to support and which the present government has suggested it might wish to pursue as well. Secondly, in the wake of British moves to grant colonial Africa independence, this French move offered a popular referendum to French West African voters. A "no" vote in the referendum meant independence would be granted immediately, ties with France would be completely severed, and no help (such as currency and banking, civil service, government records, and international and diplomatic relations) would be given in the transition. A "yes" vote meant each state would be granted internal self-government within a greater French Union (q.v.). Guinea's "no" vote undermined the concept of union and within two years all the other French possessions in West Africa won their independence under more amicable circumstances.

CONSTITUTION OF THE FOURTH FRENCH REPUBLIC (October 1946). The post-World War II government of France considerably liberalized relations with the colonies, hoping thus to perpetuate economic dominance and centralization by easing the more obnoxious aspects of colonial rule. The constitution established the French Union (q.v.) with an assembly in which voting membership was evenly divided between metropolitan and overseas France. African representation in the National Assembly and the Council of the Republic (q.v.) was also expanded. Locally in French West Africa (AOF [q.v.]) the status of *sujets indigènes* (q.v.) was eliminated. Voting rights were extended subjected to economic, educational, and administrative restrictions. Not until the *loi cadre* (q.v.) of 1956 was universal adult suffrage extended to the colonies. The 1946 Constitution did allow all of the French West Africa including Guinea to elect deputies.

CONSTITUTION OF THE SECOND REPUBLIC. A constitution drafted by the Comité Transitoire de Redressement National (CTRN q.v.) in the early 1990s under the *loi fondamentale* (q.v.) to serve as the basis for the fall 1993 legislative and presidential elections. This constitution called for the formation of a democratic, civilian government to replace the military government of Lansana Conté (q.v.).

CONTE, LANSANA. Born in 1934 at Loumbayba-Mousayah in the *préfecture* of Dubréka (q.v.) of Susu (q.v.) parents, Conté attended elementary school in the school for children of military troops in Bingerville, Côte d'Ivoire. His secondary schooling was in Saint-Louis, Senegal. Entering the French army in 1955 he asked to be freed of duty and returned to Guinea on December 21, 1958. He was integrated into the Guinean national army as a sergeant and rapidly rose in the ranks. He received his officer's training at Camp Alpha Yaya Diallo (q.v.) and then joined the Second Artillery battalion at Kindia (q.v.) as an instructor. In 1963 he was transferred to the special battalion in Conakry (q.v.). He occupied the new post of secretary general of the army chief of staff from May 1970. He was in charge of the defense of Conakry during the Portuguese invasion (q.v.) on November 22, 1970. Named captain, for the exceptional service he had rendered his country, he became adjunct chief of staff on May 19, 1975 and was promoted to colonel in 1982.

On April 3, 1984 Lansana Conté took power and proclaimed the second Guinean republic. He remained the head of state in Guinea until December 20, 1993 when he was elected to the presidency. In December 1984 he had demoted the Prime Minister Diarra Traoré (q.v.) to minister of education and after Traoré's alleged coup in July 1985 Conté was promoted to brigadier general and was named head of government by the Comité Militaire de Redressement National (CMRN [q.v.]). In the 1980s he appointed all government officials, served as the commander-in-chief of the armed forces (q.v.), and promulgated executive decrees which carried the power of law. During this period there was no legislature and Conté appointed military officers for each of the regions as well as provincial governors and civil servants. Conté obtained 51.70 percent of the 2,082,840 valid votes cast in the December 1993 election for the presidency in a race in which his Parti de l'Unité et du Progrès (PUP) often monopolized the radio and television.

COOPERATIVES. Originally established in 1960 in order to qualify for the credits, services, supplies, and rental tractors supplied by the government through rural modernization centers in administrative regions, village-producer cooperatives numbered some 492 in 1962 but never involved more than 4 percent of the country's cultivators. By 1964 most cooperatives were inactive. Revived in 1965 in conjunction with consumer cooperatives the agricultural cooperative movement in Guinea faltered because of poor management and lack of government support as well as lack of mass support.

COOPERATIVES AGRICOLES DE PRODUCTION (CAP). Under the Three-Year Plan these cooperatives of agricultural production were to be established to involve farmers in the collective use of new farming materials and, in some cases, to lead to the mechanized cultivation of collective farms. Only 291 of these cooperatives were formed by 1964, instead of the 500 envisaged in the plan. By 1965 few CAPs existed. See COOPERATIVES.

COOPERATIVES DE PRODUCTION AGRICOLE ET DE CONSOMMATION (COPAC). In 1965 this institution was created at the regional level to buy agricultural produce from farmers and sell it to the national export enterprise. In return it was to buy consumer goods from the national enterprises in charge and sell them to the farmers. In 1966 the function of supplying consumer goods was taken away. In 1970 the COPACs were abolished when it was found that they were not selling rural produce properly.

CORVEE. Forced labor imposed upon Africans for purposes of public construction and administration by French colonial officials until 1946 as part of the *indigénat* (q.v.). *Corvée* did not apply to the few Africans who achieved French citizenship but the vast majority of Africans were potentially victims of this onerous practice.

COUMBASSA, FIRMIN. A supporter of David Soumah (q.v.). in founding the Confédération Française des Travailleurs

Chrétiens (CFTC) to compete with the Marxist Confédération Générale du Travail (CGT) with which Sékou Touré
(qq.v.) was affiliated.

COUP D'ETAT. After some 15 real and alleged coups d'état
during the Sékou Touré (q.v.) regime, on April 3, 1984, eight
days after his death in a Cleveland, Ohio hospital, senior
army officers led by Colonel Lansana Conté (q.v) seized
power. Joined by Colonel Diarra Traoré (q.v.), Conté and
some 40 military officers established a Comité Militaire de
Redressement National (CMRN [q.v.]), which had the stated
goals of returning Guinea to economic and political stability.
Within eight months Conté demoted Traoré from prime
minister to minister of education. On July 4 and 5, 1985,
Traoré was alleged to have planned a coup against the Conté
government. Conté used this alleged coup as an excuse to
eliminate some opponents and to consolidate power.

COYAH. An important crossroad of commerce during colonial
times, this town is located at the juncture of the Conakry-
Kindia road and the road south to Forécariah (qq.v.) and the
Sierra Leone border.

CREDIT NATIONAL POUR LE COMMERCE, L'INDUSTRIE
ET L'HABITAT. The National Credit Institution for Trade,
Industry, and Housing was one of three specialized banks
developed in 1961 after four of five French private commercial banks had their licenses revoked in August 1960. This
bank bases its credit expansion partly upon deposits made
with it by government agencies and state enterprises and
partly upon borrowing from the central government.

CURRENCY. From March 1, 1960 to October 2, 1972, the
Guinean franc was the official currency of Guinea, replacing
the CFA franc (q.v.). The official exchange rate of the
Guinean franc from March 1, 1960 through December 31,
1971 was 246.8 Guinean francs per US $1. On October 2,
1972, the Guinean syli (GS [q.v.]) consisting of 100 cauris
became the official currency. It was officially exchanged at
a rate of US $1 for 22.7 Guinean sylis from October 2, 1972

through February 13, 1973; subsequently the rate was GS 20.46 for US $1. Guinean currency was non-convertible and clandestine sales often placed its value at a fourth or fifth of the official rate. In January 1986 the Guinean franc was reintroduced following the devaluation of the currency as part of the economic reforms package imposed on Guinea by the International Monetary Fund. At that time the official exchange rate was fixed at 340 Guineans francs for US $1. In 1992 the exchange rate was 1,100 Guinean francs for US $1.

- D -

DABOLA. A town and *préfecture* in the Futa Jalon between Mamou and Kankan (qq.v.) on the railway. Possessing untapped bauxite (q.v.) potential, Dabola remains a charming backwater town due to the poor roads and poor railroad service at this distance from the capital though a hydroelectric dam and a peanut oil factory were built there by the People's Republic of China (q.v.) in the late 1970s.

DALABA. A town and *préfecture* of the Futa Jalon between Labé and Mamou (qq.v.). Long an important regional market, Dalaba was also a favorite resort spot for Europeans in colonial times. Consequently the town has continued to produce considerable vegetables and fruits for Guinean markets. Once also a center of cattle production, it has declined in importance in recent years in spite of attempts at improving the local breeds.

DEFLATTES. A term commonly used for former civil servants who were laid off due to the structural reforms initiated under International Monetary Fund initiatives. *Déflattés* and post-1984 graduates from Guinean institutes of higher education constitute a major political force opposed to the Conté regime.

DE GAULLE, CHARLES (1890–1970). A French political and military leader who founded the Free French movement against the Germans in World War II. Receiving much support in Africa he called the Brazzaville Conference (q.v.) in 1944 to announce some political, economic, and social reforms for the French African colonies. In 1958 he took over the French government and established a new constitution (q.v.) which was to give the French colonies limited self-government in a French Community. This draft constitution sought to create a French community, with France's overseas possessions being granted some degree of autonomy. In a speech in Conakry (q.v.) in August 1958, de Gaulle stated that the rejection of this community in a referendum would cast Guinea out of the community; dire consequences were implied. Guinea went on to overwhelmingly reject the French community on September 28, 1958, and thus became an independent republic, much to de Gaulle's displeasure.

DEMOCRATIE SOCIALISTE DE GUINEE (DSG). A party associated with the socialist movement in France founded by Ibrahima Barry (q.v.) in 1954. In January 1957 the DSG had become a member of a Mouvement Socialiste Africain, but it never really achieved much power in Guinea.

DE SANDERVAL, OLIVIER. A French adventurer who dreamed of creating an African kingdom. He passed through Boké en route to Timbo (qq.v.) in 1880 and again in 1888. At Timbo he obtained important concessions from the almamy (q.v.). Ultimately these concessions led to a French protectorate over the Futa Jalon (q.v.). His private mercenary army assisted French troops and members of the Alfaya faction in defeating the Landoma (qq.v.) defenders of Boké.

DIABI, KAMAN. A colonel in the Guinean Army who was arrested during the 1969 "Labé Plot" (q.v.) and executed. See KEITA, FODEBA.

DIAKHANKE. A Mandé people whose contributions of learned Muslim scholars to the Fulbé (q.v.) community enabled them to form a privileged enclave at Touba in Middle Guinea near Gaoual (q.v.) until the early part of the nineteenth century. Claiming ancient ancestry in the historic

Empire of Ghana their descendants today still represent a force in Islamic and urban life.

DIAKITE, MOUSSA. An early member of the Rassemblement Démocratique Africain (RDA [q.v.]) and the Parti Démocratique de Guinée (PDG [q.v.]) and a key member of the Sékou Touré (q.v.) regime. After his class of engineering students was expelled in their final year from the Ecole de Travaux Publics in Bamako, he entered the federal civil service. He was among the first Africans to serve as commandant in Côte d'Ivoire. He was elected mayor of Kankan (q.v.) in 1956. In 1957 he was elected to the Guinean Territorial Assembly. A member of the Bureau Politique National (BPN [q.v.]) he served in almost every government under Sékou Touré (q.v.), holding such positions as minister of banks, security and internal affairs and finance and housing. He was arrested on April 3, 1984, and executed in Kindia in July 1985.

DIALLO, ABDOULAY (Portos). Born in 1935 and educated in law he served in Sékou Touré's (q.v.) government. Jailed for ten years following the Portuguese invasion (q.v.) in 1970 he went into exile after his release. Author of *La Verité du Ministre* (1985) about the Touré regime, Diallo led the Parti Guinéen du Progrès (PGP) in opposition to the Conté regime.

DIALLO, ABDOULAYE. Born of Fulbé (q.v.) parents in January 1917 at Konsondougou near Dabola (q.v.), Diallo was educated at the William Ponty School (q.v.) in Dakar. As a civil servant under the French he became active in the trade union (q.v.) movement. He first opposed and then joined Sékou Touré's Union Générale des Travailleurs d'Afrique Noire (qq.v.). Diallo returned to Guinea from the French Soudan (Mali) after the referendum of September 1958 and served in a number of governmental positions. As of March 1976 he was the minister of labor. He retired in the 1980s.

DIALLO, ALFA AMADOU. A veterinary surgeon who served Sékou Touré (q.v.) as secretary of state for foreign affairs and minister of information. He was arrested in Conakry in 1971 at approximately 60 years of age and probably died in detention in Kindia (qq.v.) shortly thereafter with benefit of trial.

DIALLO, ALFA OUMAR BAROU. Commandant Diallo started a teaching career in the 1950s before joining the military. After independence he was promoted in the Guinean army. In 1962, when Sékou Touré (q.v.) incorporated the higher education system into the army, Diallo was appointed military administrative officer. Falling out of favor with the Touré entourage he was discharged from the army and reappointed to civilian duties. After Touré's death in 1984 he held public offices as governor of Conakry (q.v.), minister of the interior, and government ministry representative for the province of Upper Guinea (q.v.). He left the office in early 1990 in opposition to General Lansana Conté's (q.v.) government.

DIALLO, ALFA YAYA. See ALFA YAYA DIALLO.

DIALLO, AL HAJJ OUMAR KOUNDA. Trained as a teacher he served Sékou Touré (q.v) as ambassador to Sierra Leone and governor of Gaoual and Kérouané (qq.v.). Arrested in 1971 he died in Camp Alfa Yaya.

DIALLO, AMIROU. A professor of geography who served as a school director, regional director of education in the Forest Region (q.v.), and a national inspector of education for almost 20 years.

DIALLO, BOUBACAR TELLI. Born in 1926 at Porédaké in the Mamou (q.v.) region, he earned a doctorate in law in Paris in 1946 and served the French colonial administration as a magistrate. He also served as an assistant public prosecutor in Senegal and Dahomey (Benin). In 1957 he became secretary-general of the Grand Council of West Africa, but when Guinea voted for independence in 1958, Diallo returned to Guinea.

He served as Guinea's permanent representative at the

United Nations (1958–1961). He was elected the first secretary-general of the Organization of African Unity (q.v.) on July 21, 1964, and served in that capacity until June 1972. Appointed minister of justice on August 22, 1972, he was able to convince Touré that he was still a loyal party member after his long absence from the country and remained one of the few Fulbé (q.v.) representatives in the government until August 1976. At that time he was accused by President Touré of complicity in a plot against the government. Married with three children, he died in prison in Conakry (q.v.) without a trial.

DIALLO, MAMADOU. A colonel and deputy chief of staff under Sékou Touré (q.v.), this married man with six children presumably died in detention after his arrest in Conakry in 1971. He was born about 1911.

DIALLO, MAMADOU OURY ("MISKOUN"). A senior tax inspector and national director of the Registry Office under Sékou Touré (q.v.), he also served as inspector of administrative and financial affairs. He was arrested in Conakry (q.v.) in 1971 at approximately 45 years of age. Never tried or sentenced, he is presumed to have died in detention in Kindia (q.v.).

DIALLO, SAIFOULAYE. Born in 1923 at Diari near Labé, Diallo received a normal school education at William Ponty School (q.v.) in Dakar. He served throughout French West Africa (AOF [q.v.]) as a civil servant and was frequently moved because of this trade union (q.v.) activity. He was active in RDA (q.v.) affairs throughout the AOF and in January 1956 he was elected to the French National Assembly. In March 1957 he was elected to the Guinean Territorial Assembly and served as its first president. At independence he was elected president of the National Assembly. In 1963 he was appointed minister of state for finance and planning and in May 1969 he replaced Béavogui (q.v.) as minister of foreign affairs. Ill health caused him to be less active, and his appointment as minister at the presidency in June 1972 was largely honorary, though he continued to hold ministerial rank through at least 1976.

DIALLO, SIRADIOU. An economics graduate of the Universities of Dakar, Senegal, and Paris he was a journalist for *Jeune Afrique* in Paris. He was a leader of a Guinean student organization and a major movement opposed to the Sékou Touré (q.v.) government until Touré's death in 1984. His name is associated with the Portuguese-led invasion (q.v.) of Conakry in 1970. He led the Parti du Renouveau et du Progrès (PRP) in opposition to President Conté.

DIALLO, T. M. CELLOU. Trained as an engineer, he served as inspector general under several agricultural ministries between 1964 and 1971 before being imprisoned for political reasons by President Touré (q.v.). He spent six years in Boiro political prison. Freed in late 1976 he has held various academic and professional positions. He was an active member of the Comité Militaire de Redressement Nationale and the Comité Transitoire de Libération National (qq.v.).

DIALLO, YACINE. A "socialist" member of the French assembly from Guinea which adopted the 1946 constitution making French Black Africa a part of the French Republic as members of the French Union (q.v.). He was head of the Democratie Socialiste de Guinée (q.v.) until his death in 1954.

DIALONKE (Djallonké, Dyaloké, Jallonké). A Mandé population of the south and central part of the Futa Jalon who inhabited the Futa before the Fulbé (qq.v.) state was established in the eighteenth century. Accepting Islam (q.v.) and staying on as allies of the Fulbé, or fleeing south and east, these people are one of many Mandé populations scattered throughout West Africa by events of the past 500 years.

DIAMONDS. Guinea produces both gem and industrial diamonds in some quantity. Alluvial deposits between Kissidougou, Beyla, and Kérouané (qq.v.) produced 643,000 carats in 1959. During the Touré years, reliable production figures were not readily available, though informed sources indicate that there was considerable smuggling (q.v.). Aredor Sales, the Swiss-based subsidiary of Aredor Holdings (the consortium that owns 50 percent of Aredor Guinea, Guinea's diamond-mining enterprise), sold 47,435 carats of diamonds in 1984, its first year of operation. The Guinean government owns 50 percent of both Aredor Guinea and Aredor Sales and reported the production of over 100,000 carats of diamonds with almost 95 percent gem quality in 1985.

DIANE, DR. CHARLES. Born in Kankan (q.v.) in 1932, he graduated from the University of Paris in medicine and practiced as a surgeon in France, Liberia, and Gabon. He was the president of the militant Fédération de Etudiants Africains en France (FEANF [q.v.]) in 1957. The author of several pamphlets on Sékou Touré's (q.v.) Guinea and a book, *La FEANF: les grandes heures du mouvement syndical etudiant noir* (1990) he was condemned to death *in absentia* in 1971.

DIANE, EL-HADJI IBRAHIMA. Born in Kankan (q.v.) and graduated from William Ponty School (q.v.) he was a civil administrator in Beyla and Kindia (qq.v.) and served in Côte d'Ivoire as head of the financial services of the Public Works and Construction Department. An early member of the Parti Démocratique de Guinée (PDG [q.v.]) he was head administrator of the city of Conakry (q.v) in 1957 after Sékou Touré (q.v.) was elected mayor. He served as head of the Guinean custom service but was arrested and jailed at Camp Boiro from 1971 until 1980. Returning from exile he has been an active community leader in Conakry since 1984.

DIANE, EL-HADJI KABINE. Koranic school teacher and leader born in Kankan (q.v.) he was *imam* (q.v.) in Bouaké, Côte d'Ivoire, from 1949–1958. He wrote an abbreviated translation of the Koran into French and was *imam* of the Koleah mosque in Conakry (q.v.) in 1968. He was also the representative of the World Islamic League in Guinea and organizer of yearly pilgrimages to Mecca. He died in March 1993.

DIANE, LANSANA. At independence Diané was appointed governor of Kankan and Nzérékoré (qq.v.). In 1960 he was major-general of the Guinean army and served as the head of the 749-man battalion sent to the Congo (Zaire) as part of the United Nations (q.v.) peace force. He was appointed governor of Labé in 1961 and helped to still persistent resistance to Touré's (qq.v.) regime in that area. He served in a variety of ministerial positions until November 20, 1970, when Portuguese and Guinean opponents to Touré's regime captured him during an attack on Conakry. He apparently escaped, but was for a time relegated to lesser party positions by the president. Diané was minister of defense when Sékou Touré died. He was imprisoned by the new government after the April 3, 1984 coup. He was executed in Kindia in July 1985.

DIANE, SEKOU. A notary public and businessman born in Kankan (q.v.). Known as Diane "*nettsec*" because of his dry cleaning complex in Conakry (q.v.), he was arrested in 1971 and died in detention in Kindia (q.v.).

DIASPORES. A term commonly used for the more than two million Guineans who fled the country for economic or political reasons during the Touré (q.v.) era. Some *diasporés* have sought to return to Guinea since Touré's death. But Guinea's economic conditions hamper a massive return of the large population that went into exile in the 1970s.

DIECKE FOREST. A reserve of primary forest in the Nzérékoré region (q.v.) which was to supply the sawmill at Nzérékoré built in 1964 by the Soviet Union. Even with careful selective cutting and reforestation, this forest could not have supplied the plant's capacity of 50,000 cubic meters (1.75 million cubic feet) a year and still have exported lumber to the Soviet Union through Liberia as planned. The few valuable species in the forest have been decimated in the intervening years and the sawmill, if operating at all, must be producing far below capacity.

DIEPPE MERCHANTS. The First French traders to trade openly on the Guinea coast despite Portuguese (q.v.) claims to a monopoly of trade in all of Western Africa. By 1570 they had made contact with some coastal peoples in what is today the Republic of Guinea.

DIETE NOIRE. The *diète noire* (black diet) was a particularly long, drawn-out and painful form of execution used under the Touré (q.v.) regime. It consisted of total deprivation of food and water until the prisoner starved to death. Following the major waves of arrests in 1970, 1971, and 1976, it was applied against prisoners who proved insufficiently "cooperative" during the torture sessions which accompanied interrogations, and who were unwilling to "confess" to being members of an international conspiracy against Sékou Touré. Most prisoners on the *diète noire* reportedly died within two weeks, after undergoing extreme pain and distress. According to witnesses, the screams and groans of dying prisoners were often heard throughout the prison block at Camp Boiro in those years.

DINAH, SALIFOU. See SALIFOU, DINAH.

DINGUIRAYE. A historical town and administrative region of Upper Guinea located at the headwaters of the Tinkisso River north of Dabola (qq.v.). The original retreat of the Fulbé leader Al Hajj Umar Tall (q.v.) in the mid-nineteenth century, Dinguiraye is a potentially rich agricultural and cattle-producing region.

DONZO, KEFING (ca. 1910–1980). Born in Beyla (q.v.) he became a civil administrator and was the first Bloc Africain de Guinée (BAG [q.v.]) member of the Guinean Territorial Assembly and then a prominent Parti Démocratique de Guinée (PDG [q.v.]) leader in Beyla. He served as a member of the National Assembly and the PDG central committee.

DORE, JEAN MARIE. The candidate of the Union pour le Progrès de la Guinée (UPG) in the December 1993 elections. Largely campaigning from Conakry (q.v.) and on television he did campaign especially strongly in the Forest Region (q.v) as well. He promised better roads, water supplies, and electrification and called for national unity. He received less than one percent of the votes in this election.

DOUMBOUYA, SORY. Colonel Doumbouya was the governor

of Siguiri and a member of the party central committee during the Touré (q.v.) era. After the fall of Diarra Traoré (q.v.) in the second republic he seems to have been able to manage a successful political career. Apparently representing Maninka interests in the army and in General Conté's (qq.v.) government, he was the minister of defense for several years. In 1993 he was the president of the CTRN and one of the few members of the original CMRN (qq.v.) selected to draft the constitution of the second republic.

DRAME, ALIOUNE. A tax inspector, Dramé served Sékou Touré (q.v.) as minister, of finance, minister of planning, ambassador to Côte d'Ivoire and inspector of administrative affairs. Arrested in Conakry (q.v.) in 1976 at approximately 55 years of age, he presumably died in detention with benefit of a trial.

DRY SEASON. Depending on the area of Guinea, this season of little or no rain lasts from late October through April. In Upper Guinea (q.v.) the dry northwesterly winds of the period are called the harmattan (q.v.).

DUBREKA. A town and *préfecture* of Lower Guinea located just inland from Conakry on the road north toward Boké (qq.v.). Once an Atlantic trading center for products of the interior and later a banana-producing (q.v.) center, Dubréka now produces rice and palm nuts as well. The town is the birthplace of President Conté (q.v.).

DYAMA. See AL HAJJ MANSOUR KABA.

DYELI (Jeli, Griot or Gewel). A Maninka traditional social group commonly referred to in French as *griot* and corresponding to the Wolof *gewel*. The *dyeli* constitute an endogenous professional group specialized in music and oral traditions. As such, they are part of the *nyamakala* (q.v.) category that has some characteristics of a caste (q.v.). The Diabaté (Dioubaté or Jabati), the Diawara (Jawara), the Kouyaté, and the Kamara *dyeli* are among the best known *dyeli* clans (q.v.).

DYULA (Jula or Dioula). A Maninkakan word meaning "trader."
The *dyula* have had a major role in the history of the Niger
River valley. Professor Yves Person spoke of a "dyula
revolution" to explain the rise of Samory Touré (q.v.) in the
nineteenth century. In the Côte d'Ivoire *dyula* applies to the
Muslim northerners who speak a variation of Maninkakan.

- E -

ECOLE GEORGES POIRET. A vocational school for Africans
opened by the French colonial administration in Conakry
(q.v.) in the early 1930s. It offered two- to four-year
post-primary courses. It trained only as many artisans and
foremen as the French administration felt it needed.

ECOLE SUPERIEURE D'ADMINISTRATION (ESA). An important part of the Institut Polytechnique de Conakry (IPC),
this school of administration was charged with training
political individuals for upper civil service levels. The
school was originally established in 1957 under the *loi-
cadre* government, became, in 1964, the College Prépara-
toire d'Administration to train middle level officials,
and was converted to a center for senior administrators
under the name Ecole National d'Administration in 1963. In
1964 it became the ESA and in 1965 it was integrated into
the IPC.

ECOLE WILLIAM PONTY. See WILLIAM PONTY SCHOOL.

ECONOMIE MIXTE. Economic goal under the Five-Year Plan
1973–1978 in which "the people" assume control over
formerly private capitalist enterprises. Leadership was to be
African, though some foreign private businesses would
continue to participate.

ECONOMY. See AGRICULTURAL PRODUCTION; ANIMAL
HUSBANDRY; BANKING; CURRENCY; ELECTRIC-
ITY; FINANCES; FISHING; FOREIGN AID; FOR-
ESTRY; INDUSTRY; LABOR; MINING; PETROLEUM;

PLANNING; TRADE—INTERNAL; TRADE—EXTER-NAL; TRANSPORTATION.

EDUCATION. From 1968 until 1984 schools were renamed Centres d'Education Révolutionnaire (CER [q.v.]), which were work-study centers expected to contribute materially to national economic development. Resembling similar centers in the People's Republic of China (q.v.) and in Cuba, the CERs, especially in rural areas, were supposed to help create the cadres of socialist cooperatives.

With the exception of Muslim Koranic schools, all education was nationalized in 1962 under Touré (q.v.). Education from primary school to the university has been made available to more and more students since independence, although the goal of universal compulsory education has not yet been accomplished. Most schools through secondary level, though, now have Guinean rather than foreign teaching staffs and some success in Africanization of the curriculum has been accomplished.

School organization under Touré consisted of six years of primary school (first cycle), three years of lower secondary school (second cycle), three years of higher secondary school (third cycle); vocational and technical schools were also on this level, as was a new thirteenth grade established in the 1973–1974 school year. Course length varied somewhat for the vocational and technical schools. Finally there are four or more years of the fourth cycle, higher education (q.v.).

As late as 1974 few urban schools operated on the CER principles. But 85 active CERs existed in 1972 at the level of the third cycle and 8,000 trained cadres, mostly from rural areas, would have been ready to staff cooperatives (q.v.) in the fall of 1973 if the planned agricultural cooperatives had been ready. Under the Conté (q.v.) government a return to French patterns with some French teachers and materials had been projected.

ELECTRICITY. Guinea has tremendous potential for hydroelectric development. Currently only a small part of this potential is harnessed. Pita, Labé, Dalaba, and Mamou (qq.v.) are served by the dam and power station built by the People's Republic of China (q.v.). in the mid-1960s at the Kinkon gorge near Pita (q.v.). A dam on the Tinkisso River at Dabola provides electricity to Dabola and Faranah (qq.v.). Conakry is also served by a power station at the Grandes Chutes near Kindia (qq.v.), which generates about 20,000 kilowatts. Plans for a hydroelectric station on the Koukoutamba, which enters the Tinkisso south of Dingui-raye, are to furnish power for processing the bauxite of Tougué and Dabola as well as lighting the towns of Dingui-raye, Siguiri, Labé, Kouroussa, and Faranah (qq.v.). The Boké bauxite (qq.v.) project promises increased use of hydroelectric power produced on the Konkoré. Thermal plants at Kankan, Siguiri, Gaoual, Boké, Sangaredi, and Kamsar (qq.v.) produce 114,000 or more kilowatts while small diesel generators operate part-time in many smaller towns.

ETHNIC CONFLICT. Since many of the earliest political groups in Guinea were ethnically or regionally based, there was intense ethnic rivalry until a Guinea branch of the RDA (q.v.) was founded in 1947. Susu, Dialonké, Konagi, Bassari, and Badiaranké could remember that the Fulbé (q.v.) rulers had oppressed their ancestors. Other ethnic groups also recalled historic animosities and perhaps some lingering anti-Fulbé feelings still plague the governments, but to a considerable extent the PDG and Sékou Touré (qq.v.) had successfully overcome ethnic differences and created a strong sense of Guinean nationalism. See ETHNIC GROUP.

ETHNIC GROUP. The term is best used to mean a group of human beings who, for the most part, have a common culture. Unfortunately, European anthropologists and administrators, in order to distinguish among the various peoples of Guinea, conjured up muddled biological, historical, and territorial groups which hardly corresponded to African perceptions. Linguistic, cultural, and historical groups do exist in Guinea but they are and have been constantly fluid. Guinean nationalism is gradually superseding ethnic difference for many young people though a few major historical and linguistic groups still maintain considerable allegiance. See ETHNIC CONFLICTS.

ETUDES GUINEENNES. In 1945 the Institut Français d'Afrique Noire (IFAN [q.v.]), which had been created in 1938 in Dakar, Senegal, established a Guinea territorial branch. As director of this branch, Georges Balandier founded and edited the branch's journal, *Etudes Guinéennes*. This journal published original research in physical science, ethnology, economics, and African culture and crafts from 1947 to 1956. In 1959 the newly formed Guinean Institut National de Recherches et de Documentation (INRD [q.v.]) began publishing *Recherches Africaines* (q.v.) as successor to *Etudes Guinéennes*.

EVOLUE. A term that was commonly used during the colonial period in French West Africa to designate an African who had received a French education or had sufficiently acquired French culture, in the eyes of the French, to be allowed to change his legal status from *sujet* to *citoyen* by means of being classified as an *assimilé* (q.v.). Most Africans continued to be regarded as subjects rather than citizens throughout the colonial period. See AFRIQUE OCCIDENTAL FRANCAISE; ASSIMILE; INDIGENAT; SUJETS INDIGENES.

- F -

FABER, MAITRE PAUL. Prominent jurist born in Conakry (q.v.) and active in the 1950s. Minister of justice from 1958–1961 and legal adviser to Sékou Touré (q.v.). He was head of the African Affairs Division of the International Monetary Fund in Washington, D.C., from 1963–1967, and while in exile served as professor of law and international affairs at the University of Abidjan, Côte d'Ivoire. Retired in Conakry he was a top adviser to President Lansana Conté (q.v).

FAIDHERBE, GENERAL LOUIS L. C. French governor of Senegal from 1854–1861 and from 1863–1865. He was one of the designers of the early French foreign policy in West Africa. He stopped the expansion of Al Hajj Umar (q.v.) into the coast and laid the groundwork for the eventual French expansion into West Africa.

FAMINE. Sahel droughts have made famine a historic fact of life for part of Upper Guinea (q.v.). However, the more widespread recent food shortages in Guinea are the result of population pressures, poor governmental planning, and declining fertility of the generally fragile laterite soils of much of this part of Africa.

FARAGUE, JEAN. A Parti Démocratique de Guinée (PDG [q.v.]) activist in the Forest Region (q.v.) in the 1950s, he was elected to the Territorial Assembly in 1957. He served as a member of the government and the PDG Central Committee and was a leading critic of Sékou Touré's (q.v.) leadership at the Foulaya symposium and the PDG Sixth Congress in 1962. He was expelled from the PDG leadership in 1964 and arrested in 1965.

FARANAH. A town and region of Upper Guinea located between Dabola and Kissidougou (qq.v.) on the border of Sierra Leone. The birthplace of President Touré (q.v.), this small town was made more important by Touré's intervention in the late 1970s and early 1980s.

FEDERATION DES ETUDIANTS DE L'AFRIQUE NOIR EN FRANCE (FEANF). An organization of active African students in France who opposed the *loi cadre* (q.v.). They offered support to Sékou Touré (q.v.) when he challenged the territorialist thrust of this law with the Rassemblement Démocratique Africain (RDA [q.v.]) from 1956 through 1958. The Guinean, Charles Diané (q.v.), led the FEANF in 1956 and 1957. These students, like Touré, wanted a West African federation of former French colonies rather than separate territories tied to France. The FEANF was opposed to the disintegration (Balkanization) of French West Africa and, therefore, withdrew its support from Houphouët-Boigny and other like-minded leaders. The French government disbanded the FEANF in 1958.

FERME AGRO-PASTORALE D'ARRONDISSEMENT (FAPA). Based on a People's Republic of China (q.v.) model, these communal farms were established throughout the country by the party during the Touré years. The FAPAs were never truly successful and were mocked as "faux-pas" by many Guineans.

FILARIASIS. A name given to a number of infectious diseases caused by a string-like worm that lives as a parasite in human soft tissues. River blindness (onchocerca infection) is the most serious. It is spread by the bite of a small black fly whose maggots are hatched in the fast-flowing streams of Upper Guinea (q.v.). Repeated infections over several years result in worm infections around the eyes causing blindness. Because the fly disperses so widely, only massive cooperation with neighboring countries will allow Guinea to eradicate this disease. See also ONCHOCERCIASIS.

FINANCES. Critical to Guinea, as it is to any developing country, is the capital for financing development. Deficit financing of development projects through foreign loans, grants, and trade arrangements has caused a tremendous inflationary pressure on Guinea's nonconvertible currency (q.v.). Guinea has mortgaged its mining and export agricultural production for many years into the future and now can only hope that mining enterprises like the Boké project (q.v.) can help the government of Guinea maintain solvency.

FISHING. Guinea has an abundance of fish both in the rivers and along with coast. These have long been used as an important food source. Inland fishing is done with baskets, traps, poisons, hook and lines, and dynamiting, though the last is supposedly outlawed. Some 4,500 "barks" holding up to six fishermen and over 3,000 dugout canoes allow some 10,000 traditional fishermen to earn a living in coastal waters. The larger barks are motor or sail equipped. Three mixed fishing enterprises with trawlers and refrigerator boats also operate out of Conakry (q.v.), producing over 9,000 metric tons of fish per year. These industries are owned jointly by the Guinean government and companies from the United States,

Japan, and Kuwait. See also SOCIETE AFRICAINE DES PECHES MARITIMES; SOCIETE DES PECHES DU KAMSAR; SOCIETE DES PECHES INDUSTRIELLES DU KALOUM; SOCIETE GUINEO-KUWEITIENNE DE PECHE; SOCIETE NIPPO-GUINEENNE DE PECHE.

FOFANA, COMMANDANT ALHOUSSEINI. A military officer born in Lower Guinea (q.v.). He was a member of the Comité Militaire de Redressement National (CMRN [q.v.]) and was appointed minister of agriculture in April 1985. He was considered a major figure in the events of July 1985 that led to the arrest and murder of Colonel Diarra Traoré (q.v.) and scores of Maninka officers and civil servants. He is now blind, retired from public service, and lives in Conakry (q.v.).

FOFANA, DR. IBRAHIM KALIL. Born in Dabola (q.v.) and graduated from the University of Conakry and the University of Moscow in economics. A former instructor at the University of Conakry, this bank executive and the head of the Union of Guinean Bankers served as the general secretary of the Parti National pour le Développement et la Démocratie (PND).

FONDS D'INVESTISSEMENT POUR LE DEVELOPPEMENT ECONOMIQUE ET SOCIAL (FIDES). A law passed by the French Parliament on April 30, 1946, authorized creation of the fund to finance systematically all of France's overseas dependencies according to an overall development plan. The fund was to receive annual subsidies from the metropolitan budget and contributions from the territories concerned. After the independence vote of September 1958 Guinea no longer received any of this aid.

FONIO (*Digitania exilis*). Often termed a millet, this African cereal grain is the least productive of the grains raised in Guinea, but given dietary preferences developed since birth it is considered a special treat by many Guineans. Often giving little more than a two-to-one return for seeds planted and rarely as much as six-to-one, this cereal has little commercial value in world markets. It is rich in essential amino acids and is a good energy source. Fonio is easy to digest as well, will grow in the poorest ground, and is often planted on marginal land as an insurance against failure of the major grain crops like maize and rice. See MILLET.

FORCED LABOR. See CORVEE.

FORECARIAH. A town and region of the same name on the Atlantic coast between Conakry (q.v.) and the Sierra Leone border. Forécariah was the capital city created by Muslim traders from Kankan-Bobeh in the eighteenth century who descendants are known as the Susu or Moreah. This region was formerly a major banana-growing area with a small international shipping facility at Benty (q.v.). Largely over shadowed by Conakry in recent years it still has future potential as an important rice and palm (qq.v.) production area. Its location on the Conakry to Freetown, Sierra Leone, axis should also prove economically advantageous.

FOREIGN AID. Published information on foreign aid to Guinea is uncoordinated and fragmentary, but it seems clear that Guinea has received more than $3 billion in foreign aid including private investment. Interest rates have ranged from loans from the Soviet Union and Eastern European countries at around 2.5 percent to direct credits from the import-export bank at 7 to 8.5 percent. Guinea's official and private foreign debt in 1971 was equivalent to 84 percent of the country's 1970 GNP—one of the highest rates of indebtedness in the world. Some sources contend that Guinea's great mineral productivity is mortgaged for the next 30 years for debt repayment. Having relied upon Western and Eastern European, American, Chinese, (then) Soviet, Israelis aid since independence, Guinea turned to a number of Arab states for help in the mid-1970s. As one of the world's 25 least developed countries, Guinea received some help from the United Nations Development Program. Unless funds are better managed and overall development plans better coordinated, it is unlikely that great strides in agricultural or industrial output will soon be achieved under the present government though World Bank, UNDP, USAID, and French aid have once again become available since Touré's death.

In 1989 there was a major shift as Guinea sought and received a $27 million grant from USAID to finance the implementation of a national program of structural adjustment in education (the PASE, Programme d'Ajustement Structurel de l'Education). This grant and World Bank aid are playing a flagship role for other investments in Guinean social and economic sectors. They have also led to better coordination of donor activities in Guinea. Despite these positive developments, foreign aid to Guinea is hampered by overwhelming economic problems, among which are uncontrolled inflation, a lack of basic infrastructure, and endemic mismanagement of scarce national resources.

FOREIGN RELATIONS. As a "non-aligned" nation, Guinea found it ideologically easier to cooperate with Eastern European countries and the People's Republic of China (q.v.) than with Western European countries, the United States, and Canada, yet pursue a stated policy of "positive neutrality." Guinea found it theoretically and pragmatically impossible to avoid accepting considerable economic aid from Western bloc countries. In practice, Guinea maintained a very closed and guarded stance toward most nations. From the abrupt break with France to the continuing periodic moments of patriotic fervor generated by real and imaginary "plots" (see PLOTS) and "aggressions," the psychological sense of being a nation besieged by external enemies, both African and non-African, was an important element of Guinea foreign policy. National solidarity was, to some extent, achieved in Guinea by a paranoid "hot and cold" relationship with the rest of the world. The present government continues to reestablish more cordial relations with Western nations and neighboring countries.

FOREST REGION. One of the four geographic regions into which Guinea is usually subdivided. The Forest Region makes up the southeastern extension of Guinea. Its major feature is the Guinea Highlands which range from 500 meters (1,600 feet) above sea level in the west to over 1,000 meters (3,250 feet) in the east with some peaks of 1,300 meters (4,225 feet) and more. Possessing some dense rain forest below 700 meters (2,200 feet), much of the Forest Region is now derived savanna and even the forest is largely secondary growth because of the long presence of farming peoples in the area who practice slash-and-burn agriculture and keep increasing numbers of grazing animals. The Forest Region is a true land of pluralism with different ethnic groups.

FORESTRY. Guinea has some teak and ebony trees as well as a few rubber and quinine plantations. However, with the exception of locally used sawmill output, the lumber industry in Guinea has never been too productive. Less than 4 percent of Guinea has substantial forest cover and valuable species have come very rare. A sawmill at Nzérékoré and particle board factories at Kissidougou (qq.v.) and Sérédou near Macenta (q.v.) have never operated to capacity and lumber reserves have been so depleted that it is unlikely they ever will.

FRENCH LANGUAGE. Under Touré French was the official language of Guinea along with eight national languages: Poular, Maninkakan, Susu, Kissi, Guerzé (Kpelle), Toma, Konagi, and Bassari (qq.v.). Unfortunately, in spite of UNESCO help, literacy in national languages was somewhat hampered by a lack of funds for books and teachers, and parent-student resistance to the reform. French thus continued to fill the need for administrative, technical, and business communications inside the country and for inter-African and international relations. It was understood by about 20 percent of the population and was used as a lingua franca among educated Guineans of different ethnic groups. It was the language of instruction beginning with the fifth year of school and was taught from the third year. It appears that French skills declined in the late 1970s and early 1980s. French, under the current government, has been restored to its primary place as official language of instruction and for government purposes.

FRENCH UNION. This structure was established under the French constitution (q.v.) of October 1946. It allowed a measure of representation for French colonial territories in the policymaking process of government. The mainland African colonies were classified as overseas territories over which France felt it "must continue to exercise its domination." Only "evolved" (evolué [q.v.]) Africans were granted full French citizenship. Some African deputies were granted seats in the French National Assembly though, and elected territorial assemblies were given very limited legislative powers in territory affairs.

FRIA. A town and region of the same name located just inland from the coast in Lower Guinea between the Dubréka and Boffa (qq.v.) regions. This town is a highly industrialized "island" with its own railway line, oriented towards the outside world well into the 1960s. Under pressure from the Sekou Touré (q.v.) government the African presence in management grew in this mining and aluminum-processing industrial zone, long of major importance of Guinean finances.

FRONT POUR LA LIBERATION NATIONALE DE GUINEE (FLNG). This group of Guineans in exile opposed to Sékou Touré's (q.v.) regime was very active in the mid 1960s. Like its counterpart, the Association des Guinéens en France (AGF [q.v.]), it was composed of university graduates, Guinean veterans of the French military, former Guinean cabinet ministers, and a few former Guinean ambassadors. The group declined in the 1970s as its support from France, Senegal, and the Côte d'Ivoire waned.

FULA. Maninka term for Fulbé (qq.v.). This term has also been adapted into French, English, and general Guinean usage for the Fulbé of the Futa Jalon (q.v.).

FULBE (also Peul, from the singular Pullo, or Fulani and Fula, from Hausa and Maninka sources). Claiming descent from nomadic pastoralists in present-day Mauritania the *hapularen* (Poular-speaking) peoples of Guinea mostly lived in

the Futa Jalon (q.v.). They are part of a large ethnic/
linguistic group spread through much of West Africa from
Senegal to beyond Lake Chad in a belt between the rain
forest and the Sahara. In Guinea, people with family names
such as Bah, Balde, Barry, Diallo, Sow, Tall, and Thiam are
generally of this ethnicity. In the Maninka (q.v.) areas of
Wassulu people with names like Sangaré and Diakité are
included but do not speak Poular. The name Boiro includes
descendants of Koli Tenguela's forces in the pre-Islamic
migrations. Members of this ethnic group created a centralized state in the Futa Jalon in the eighteenth century and
maintained a dominant position in the area almost until
independence in 1958.

"FULBE" OR "PEUL" PLOT. One of more than a dozen or so
alleged attempts to overthrow the Touré government. This
second major purge (see PORTUGUESE PLOT) took place in
1976, when President Sékou Touré announced that an attempt
on his life by Fulbé had been foiled. Touré is reported to have
declared: "We will annihilate them [the Fulbé] immediately,
not by race war, but by radical revolutionary war." Between
June and August 1976, many Fulbé were arrested. New
"confessions" of "counterrevolutionary" activities, extracted
under torture, were broadcasted and published in Guinea. The
National Council of the Revolution (CNR [q.v.]) was convened as a revolutionary tribunal and resolved in advance that
all prisoners convicted of involvement in the "Peul Conspiracy" would be sentenced to death. However, no trial proceedings took place and no publicity was given to any
sentences. Among those arrested at the time were such
prominent individuals as Diallo Telli (q.v.), former Guinean
ambassador to the United Nations and the USA, and Aliouné
Dramé (q.v.), former minister and ambassador. Many died in
jail under reportedly atrocious conditions.

FUTA JALON (Fouta Djallon). A highland area in Guinea with
elevations up to 1,500 meters (4,800 feet). It is the source of
the Gambia, Senegal, and Niger rivers (q.v.) as well as a
number of other smaller rivers which flow directly south and
west into the Atlantic. In the early eighteenth century, Fulbé

(q.v.) reformers created a theocracy there with the state controlled by elected almamies (q.v.). This Futa Jalon experience served as a model for Islamic reformers in other area of West Africa. The state of Futa Jalon remained independent until the almamy placed it under French protection.

- G -

GALLIENI, MARSHAL JOSEPH SIMON (1849–1916). French soldier and colonial administrator. He served as a member of the Commission for the Reorganization of French West Africa (AOF [q.v.]) where he favored a civilian government unlike his successor, Archinard (q.v.), who favored a military one.

GAMBIA RIVER. This river gives the Gambia its name. It rises northeast of Labé in the Futa Jalon (qq.v.) and flows northward toward the Senegal border and then on to the Gambia.

GAOUAL. A town and *préfecture* of the same name in the Futa Jalon highlands of Middle Guinea, between the Koundara and Boké (qq.v.) regions on the Guinea-Bissau border. One of the best roads in Guinea was completed by the Italians in the early 1980s from Boké to Gaoual as part of a vast development program planned for the Boké, Gaoual, and Mali (Guinea) areas. Thermal springs are found in the region and a major earthquake occurred there in 1984. Gaoual is a potentially rich agricultural and cattle-producing area.

GARDE REPUBLICAINE. This paramilitary organization reinforces the Gendarmerie and polices the rural areas in administrative regions. In Conakry (q.v.) the Garde provided the band and the motorcycle escort for official welcoming ceremonies as well as guarding the president's palace. One company guarded Camp Boiro near the Donka Hospital. See GENDARMERIE.

GENDARMERIE. A paramilitary force charged with law enforcement, public safety, and security throughout the country. At least one brigade of from six to 36 gendarmes commanded by a lieutenant or senior noncommissioned officer appointed by the president was assigned to each administrative unit. In the regions along the country's border extra frontier brigades were assigned to help the Customs Service. In Conakry (q.v.) there were port, airport, and city brigades as well as mobile detachment. Two criminal brigades in Conakry and the Futa Jalon (q.v.) conducted investigations, took depositions, collected fines, and made special reports in connection with specific infractions.

GHUSSEIN, ISMAEL. Born in Dabola (q.v.) in 1936 he was a civil administrator and secretary general of the Parti Démocratique de Guinée (PDG [q.v.]) of Conakry (q.v.). This former head of the Guinean petroleum office in 1991 became the head of the head of the new PDG-RDA in adamant opposition to the Lansana Conté (q.v.) government.

GOMBO (also gumba, *Hibiscus esculentus* or okra). A common food in Guinea, it is prized as an ingredient of soups and sauces.

GOMEZ, ALSEINY. Army Commandant Gomez was a member of the CMRN and an important figure in the Conté (qq.v.) government. During his tenure he held several key positions including minister of defense and general secretary of the government. From 1992 as minister of internal affairs he was perceived as the second most important figure in the Conté government.

GOURAUD, GENERAL HENRI. The French captain whose troops captured Samory Touré (q.v) at Guélémou on September 29, 1898. He was the author of *Au Soudan* (Paris, 1939) which is indispensable for the study of Samory's last period.

GOVERNMENT. Until April 1984 the Republic of Guinea was a single-party state in which executive, legislative, and administrative power was tightly controlled by the president, his prime minister, and five other ministers of domain who were also members of the Bureau Politique National (q.v.), the executive body of the Parti Démocratique de Guinée (PDG [q.v.]). Local and regional governments were under the control of the minister of the interior and security. The 34 administrative regions had a governor appointed by President Touré. Each region was divided into *arrondissements* (q.v.) presided over by a commandant. At the local level, the Pouvoir Révolutionnaire Local (PRL [q.v.]), a party group whose chairman served as major, directed all governmental activities, including production and consumption cooperatives (q.v.), and was responsible to the commandant of the *arrondissement* and the regional governor (see PARTI-ETAT).

The Comité Militaire de Redressement National (CMRN [q.v.]), which assumed power on April 3, 1984, abolished the constitution and the single political party and established the Second Republic. The previous government was based on decrees and ordinances issued by the CMRN, President Conté (q.v.) and various ministers. The country is divided administratively into eight provinces headed by governors, who are directly responsible to the CMRN. The provinces are divided into *préfectures* (q.v.), sub-prefectures, and districts known as quartiers in the cities.

GOVERNOR GENERAL. The position of governor general of French West Africa (AOF [q.v.]) was established by decree in 1904. Under this decree, the governor general, who resided in Dakar, had enormous powers over all of the territories. He alone reported to Paris, all of the lieutenant governors, who headed individual colonies, reported to him. He had almost complete control over taxation and the budget of the individual territories.

On June 16, 1916, a government general was created for French West Africa by decree. It unified Senegal, French Soudan (Mali), Côte d'Ivoire, and Guinea. The governor general who resided in Saint-Louis, Senegal, was also governor of Senegal. The first governor general was Chaudie. Two decrees, one in October 1902 and one in October 1904, gave the governor general additional powers.

The government was transferred to Dakar by the 1902 decree and the 1904 decree gave the governor general complete control over taxation and budgets in all of the French West African territories. This system lasted until the reforms of 1946 when considerable autonomy for each territory and representative institutions were established. Some of the important governors general included: Roume (1902–1908), Van Vollenhoven (1912–1918), Carde (1923–1930). Boisson (q.v.), who sided with the Vichy government, was replaced by Cournaire in 1943.

GRIOT. See DYELI.

GRIS-GRIS. A slightly derogatory term applied to the leather-bound verses of the Koran which many Guinean Muslims traditionally wore in much the same way westerners carry St. Christopher medals.

GUECKEDOU. This town and region in the Forest Region (q.v.) bordering on Sierra Leone and Liberia has long been important in the production of coffee, rice, and palm (qq.v.) nuts. Relatively densely populated, Guéckédou is still a rather isolated town in spite of its productivity. Never of great importance in colonial times, Guéckédou, with little mineral wealth and connected with Macenta and Kissidougou (qq.v.) by very poor roads, had been drawn very little into the national development programs. A tiny local soap factory closed in 1958 and reopened in the 1960s represents Guéckédou's sole non-agricultural industry.

GUERZE (more properly called Kpelle). An ethnic group which in Guinea is mainly concentrated in the Nzérékoré (q.v.) administrative district. They are linguistically most closely related to the Mende of Sierra Leone and thus represent an ancient intrusion of more northern people into the rain forest areas of the southwesternmost part of western Africa.

GUILAVOGUI, GALEMA. Born in Macenta this member of Forest Region ethnic group was among the first graduates of the Institut Polytechnique de Conakry (qq.v.). He was appointed minister of pre-university studies and literacy under Sékou Touré (q.v.).

GUINEE FORESTIERE. See FOREST REGION.

- H -

HAJJ. The pilgrimage to Mecca, one of the five pillars of Islam (q.v.) obligatory for all Muslims who can afford it. People from Guinea accomplished the journey by at least the thirteenth century. During the fourteenth, fifteenth, and sixteenth centuries pilgrims from Guinea traveled for several years, on foot or by camel caravan, receiving hospitality and stopping to study and trade along the way. Pilgrims from Guinea joined with others at a number of points to cross the Sahara to Cairo. During the colonial period, the government encouraged the hajj by organizing charter boats. Today's charter flights, which fly several hundred Guinean pilgrims annually to Mecca, have transformed the tradition though many pilgrims still stay to study. See AL HAJJ.

HALCO. A consortium formed in 1962 by Harvey Aluminum Company to work bauxite deposits in the Boké (q.v.) region. See BOKE PROJECT, COMPAGNIE DE BAUXITE DE GUINEE.

HAMANA. A region in Upper Guinea between Kankan and Kouroussa (qq.v.).

HARMATTAN. A hot dry wind generated by the Saharan air mass during the summer months. It blows from the interior to the coastal and forest regions of Guinea. The effect of the harmattan is most intense in Upper Guinea (q.v.) where it can cause the relative humidity to drop from 70 percent at night to 20 percent by late afternoon. Daytime temperatures also soar with the harmattan, often exceeding 37° C (100° F). Vegetation dries as well as people's skin, and dust fills the air on many days of the harmattan season.

HAUTE-GUINEE. See UPPER GUINEA.

HAUT-SENEGAL-NIGER. The name for the French Soudan (now Mali) from 1904 to 1920. Title of an important three-volume work by Governor Maurice Delafosse.

HEALTH. All institutions providing health facilities in Guinea are run by the government. By 1970, there were 29 at least moderately equipped regional hospitals, compared to the single one existing at independence. Over 200 new dispensaries have been opened and the number of doctors doubled. A school of medicine and a school of pharmacy are supposedly now functioning. It should be noted, though, that the ratio of doctors to inhabitants remained about one to 37,000. Bad management, incompetent administration, and drug and equipment pilferage continue to hamper adequate health care delivery. Equipment and supply shortages also remain a severe problem. Preventive medicine can hardly be said to exist. For most Guineans, hospitals are a last resort and pharmacies and dispensaries seldom can do more than apply dressings and dispense a few drugs rather than actually provide adequate community-wide health care and preventive medicine.

HIGHER EDUCATION. In 1961 Guinea nationalized all private educational institutions and required that post-secondary scholars prove their "fidelity to the party and the country." In 1962 the regime established a polytechnic in Conakry (q.v.). In 1968 the teacher-training institute the Ecole Normale Julius Nyéréré in Kankan (q.v.) was upgraded with the Conakry Polytechnic (later called Institut Polytechnique Gamal Abdel Nasser de Conakry [q.v.]) to form a national university with the following faculties: social science, administration, electrical and mechanical engineering, civil engineering, natural science, pharmacy and medicine, chemistry, agriculture, geology and mining.

In the late 1970s, the mining and geology faculty was moved to Tamakené outside the town of Boké (q.v.). An agricultural faculty was established in each administrative region creating increased staffing problems. Textbooks and teachers were always in short supply. It was common to see students sitting on the floor during class for lack of chairs in these expanded centers. After the military took power in 1984 the number of agricultural faculties was reduced to 12 for a transition period. At present there are four located in Foulaya (near Kindia), Faranah, Bordo (near Kankan) and Macenta (qq.v.).

Primary school teachers are trained in Koba, Pita, Dabadou, and Guéckédou and at more advanced schools in Faranah and Macenta. Besides the secondary teachers graduating from the university, the government sought in 1973 to construct two new secondary teacher-training institutes at Labé and Kindia. Yet low pay, low morale, and subsequent lack of interest in teaching continued to plague teacher-training programs throughout Guinea in the late 1970s and early 1980s. Higher education in the second half of the 1970s grew to more than 23,000 students on 43 campuses dispersed throughout rural Guinea. Confronted with management and financial difficulties most of these small campuses were closed or merged into l'Université Guinéenne with only three main campuses at Conakry, Faranah and Kankan (qq.v.) between 1979 and 1984. See EDUCATION.

HIVERNAGE. French term used to describe the rainy season. Usually beginning in May in the forest and Atlantic coastal zones and in northeastern Guinea by late June or early July, it ends from north to south between September and the end of October.

HOLY GHOST FATHERS (Pères du Saint Esprit). Founders of the first Catholic mission in Guinea at Boffa (q.v.) in 1877. This Roman Catholic order also established a number of schools in colonial times. After the 1967 Africanization of clergy, the order virtually ceased to function in Guinea during the Sékou Touré (q.v.) years. President Conté (q.v.) has permitted the return of French missionaries, and the church is again beginning to play an active role in Guinean life. See CATHOLICS.

HOROYA (Freedom). Beginning in April 1961 this four- to eight-page daily became Guinea's only newspaper. Officially an organ of the PDG, it consisted mostly of speeches and statements by President Touré (qq.v.). Visits by foreign dignitaries and information on economic and social developments were covered. Various government and party reports as well as full texts of important laws and decrees appeared regularly as well as Guinea sports news. Occasionally international and African news items were published along with specifically signed editorials and political poems. Circulation was somewhat more than 20,000. The creation of more than 40 different political parties in the early 1990s led to a blossoming of newspapers, most of which proved ephemeral. These included *Balafon, Le Citoyen, L'Echo, La Guinée Nouvelle, L'Indépendent, Lama Dore, Le Lynx, La Nation, La Nouvelle République*, and *Le Progrès*.

HOSPITALS. See HEALTH.

HOUSING. Though in many areas European-style construction with cement walls and floors and metal roofs has become the norm, many Guineans still live in one of two types of traditional houses. In the forest a few rectangular houses, their walls consisting of a lattice-work woven frame coated with puddled mud, are still constructed. Round houses of sun-dried brick supporting roofs of wood poles and thatch with a single wooden door (and perhaps a single wooden shuttered window) are the more common form of traditional housing.

HUMBERT, GEORGES. One of three colonels (with Louis Archinard and Antoine Combes) who fought the Maninka leader, Samory Touré (qq.v.), intermittently from 1881 until 1898.

HYDROELECTRIC POWER. Guinea has the greatest hydroelectric production potential of any nation in West Africa. The country has good rainfall and many fast-flowing streams which descend from the Futa Jalon (q.v.) through deep and narrow valleys. Total potential is estimated at 63.2 billion kilowatt-hours, of which one-third is on the upper reaches of the Niger, 16 percent on the upper reaches of the Senegal River (Bafing), and 19 percent on the Konkouré. Immediately harnessable sources on the Konkouré, Tominé, Baring, and upper Niger could yield 13.6 billion kilowatt-hours. Only a small fraction of this potential is currently being used, but plans for harnessing more are numerous, as adjuncts to ambitious plans for future production of aluminum, iron, and steel.

The World Bank and aid agencies from Canada, Belgium, France, and West Germany are assisting the Société Nationale d'Eléctricité (SNE, sometimes referred to in Guinea as the Société de la Nuit Eternelle, due to very frequent breakdowns) to develop a long-term plan for development of hydroelectric power.

- I -

ILES DE LOS. A number of small islands five or six miles southwest of Conakry in the Atlantic Ocean. They include Kassa with its now mined-out bauxite deposits, Tamara with its excellent beaches, and Raume which was once a slave trade and smuggling (qq.v.) depot. This latter island later became a British anti-slavery headquarters and perhaps inspired Robert Louis Stevenson's description of Treasure Island.

ILES TRISTAO (Unhappy Islands). A number of small islands in the estuary of the Kogon River (q.v.) on the border with Guinea-Bissau. These islands were named by the Portuguese in the sixteenth-century as were the Iles de Los (q.v.) and other points along the Guinean coast.

IMAM. Poular and Maninkakan (qq.v.) adaptation of the Arabic title al-imam, designating the one who leads the congregation in prayer. By extension it also means the head of a mosque, head of a particular clerical community, or head of a country ruled by clerics. See ALMAMY.

IMPORTEX. A government agency formed in August 1975 to take charge of the export-import trade. This was but one of a long series of attempts to bring all trading activities under governmental control during the Touré years. This agency was eliminated as part of the return to free enterprise begun by the military in 1985.

IMPORTS. In order of importance, Guinea has to import large amounts of food, textiles, vehicles, transportation equipment, petroleum products, and building materials.

INDEPENDENCE. After the *loi cadre* in 1956 Sékou Touré (qq.v.) served as deputy to the French National Assembly and head of the first territorial government. According to Professor Lansiné Kaba, opposing the French-sustained chiefs (q.v.) who dominated political and economic life in the rural areas, gained Touré increased popular support. Touré criticized the *loi cadre* for its lack of provisions for effective autonomy and its inherent trends toward Balkanization. When the crisis in Algeria and the subsequent return of General Charles de Gaulle (q.v.) to the French presidency in May 1958 brought down the Fourth French Republic, the stage was set for a Guinean rejection of the new de Gaulle constitution. The constitution established a strong presidential regime in France, with direct bilateral ties between the French government and the government of each territory at the expense of the sixty-year-old federal system that most Guinean political leaders had come to see as a prerequisite for viable political development. The PDG (q.v.) under Touré's leadership and the opposition parties reached common ground on this issue of unity and unanimously opposed de Gaulle's constitutional referendum. Guinea's overwhelming NO vote resulted in Guinea's independence on October 2, 1958, and its ostracism by France for two decades.

INDIGENAT. A collection of laws which were once basic to French colonial policy in Guinea. Assuming under the policy of association (q.v.) that most Africans could not measure up to the standards of French culture required of

African *assimilés* (q.v.) who had adopted the French life-style, the French treated most Africans as subjects (see SUJETS INDIGENES) rather than citizens. The French afforded strict treatment and fewer rights to the African "subjects" under a separate legal regime. Established by decree in 1924 the *indigénat* restricted African civil liberties (e.g., rights of association and movement) and permitted forced conscript labor or *corvée* (q.v.) to build roads and other public works. French and French-trained administrators were given a free rein to punish African subjects for violations as minor as hindering traffic or responding disrespectfully to administrators. Condemned by administrators themselves at the 1944 Brazzaville Conference (q.v.), the *indigénat* was finally abolished in 1946.

INDUSTRY. With the exception of the Fria (q.v.) mining complex owned by a European and American consortium, Guinea had little industry at independence. A few privately owned, small scale enterprises existed. These concerns process food (baked goods, canned fruit and juice, beer, soft drinks, syrups, and so on) or produce other light consumer goods like perfume essences, raincoats, sandals, metal construction materials, soap, and nails. Many of these functioned at a seriously curtailed level or ceased functioning altogether after independence.

In the first 15 years of independence a number of industrial operations were created. These projects included a textile complex, two palm oil-processing concerns, a canned fruit factory, cigarette and match factory, a canning plant, a slaughterhouse, a military clothing and leather goods complex, a tea-processing plant, bicycle and truck assembly plants, a tire-recapping operation, and factories for the production of tiles, particle board and aluminum products. A number of important mining firms were also created in the Touré years. All of these projects were public or semi-public enterprises.

Many of the public and semi-public industrial enterprises were badly planned and very badly managed. Most were launched with insufficient preparation. Canning plants functioned far below capacity because inadequate supplies of fruit, vegetables, and meat could be obtained. Many Guinean managers were ill-trained and incapable of running the enterprises to which they were entrusted. Furthermore industrial "islands" like Fria and Kamsar (q.v.) drew workers from farming and helped contribute to Guinea's total production deficits.

Yet many projects still hold great promise, especially those in the mining area. Gradually better trained and competent Guineans will perhaps lead to better functioning of mixed and privately owned industries in the future.

INSTITUT FRANCAIS D'AFRIQUE NOIRE (IFAN). Research institute with headquarters in Dakar, Senegal, with branches in most territories of French West Africa (AOF [q.v.]), founded in 1938. The Guinea branch was founded in 1945 by the French sociologist Georges Balandier, who also founded and edited the branch's journal, *Etudes Guinéennes* (q.v.), which appeared between 1947 and 1956. After independence the institute's name was changed to Institut National de Recherches et de Documentation (INRD) (q.v.).

INSTITUT NATIONAL DE RECHERCHES ET DE DOCUMENTATION (INRD). A Guinean national continuation of the Institut Français d'Afrique Noire (q.v.). Charged with administering the national archives, national library, and national museums as well as a nature reserve at Mount Nimba, in 1959 INRD began publishing the quarterly journal *Recherches Africaines* as the successor to *Etudes Guinéennes* (qq.v.), previously published by the Institut Français d'Afrique Noire.

INSTITUT PEDAGOGIQUE NATIONAL (IPN). This institute was the center of production and diffusion of teaching materials used throughout the country. During the agricultural campaign when students were sent as agricultural laborers to villages to help the Pouvoir Révolutionnaire Local (PRL [q.v.]), the IPN provided course handouts and brochures for these students. Under Sékou Touré, when Guinea was largely closed to the outside world, the IPN materials were often more important to teachers than materials from the National Library.

INSTITUT POLYTECHNIQUE DE KANKAN (IPK). Originally founded as a teacher-training institute for secondary school teachers, this school was upgraded in 1968 to include faculties of natural science (mathematics, physics, chemistry, and biochemistry), social science (history and geography), literature, and linguistics. The IPK was ultimately merged with the Institut Polytechnique Gamal Abdel Nasser (q.v.) and other institutions (see HIGHER EDUCATION) to form the present University of Guinea. After the military took over in 1984, the faculty of agriculture at Bordo near Kankan (qq.v.) was given autonomy.

INSTITUT POLYTECHNIQUE GAMAL ABDEL NASSER DE CONAKRY (IPGAN). In 1974 this institute of higher learning in Conakry (q.v.) had 13 schools and faculties, including medicine and pharmacy. Along with the Ecole Normale Julius Nyéréré in Kankan, it constituted the national university. Established in 1962 with Russian aid, it concentrated on administration, science, and technology for training personnel to forward the industrial and agricultural development of the nation. Also called Institut Polytechnique de Conakry (IPC).

INVESTISSEMENT HUMAIN. It is a self-help program launched by the PDG (q.v.) in 1958. The "masses" were mobilized to participate in development projects through party recruitment. By the end of the first Three-Year Plan (1960–1963), projects including hundreds of schools, dispensaries, markets, mosques, roads, and bridges worth about three billion Guinean francs had been completed through investissement humain. The coercion necessary to continue this mobilization as well as numerous technical and administrative difficulties caused the mass involvement program to be gradually abandoned in the 1960s. Many Guineans were disenchanted when, after having worked on local schools and dispensaries, no teachers or nurses were made available to staff them. Student and army mobilization largely replaced the *investissement humain* in the mid-1970s.

ISLAM. An Arabic word meaning "submission," it is the name of the religion preached by the Prophet Muhammed in the seventh century. A follower of Islam is a Muslim. Spread to West Africa by clerics and traders in the ninth century, it flourished in the great West African Empires of Mali and Songhai as well as in the eighteenth- and nineteenth-century theocracies of Al Hajj Umar and Samory Touré (qq.v.). It is the dominant religion in Guinea today.

- J -

JEUNESSE DE LA REVOLUTION DEMOCRATIQUE AFRI-CAINE (JRDA). This youth organization of the Parti Démocratique do Guinée (PDG [q.v.]) was declared the single national youth institution in Guinea by the party leadership on March 26, 1959. The JRDA concentrated on three areas of activity: culture and sports, national defense, and "revolutionary" morale. As guardians of "revolution-ary" morale, JRDA militants patrolled hotels and dance halls against prostitution and "capitalist" music, manners, and dress. Through the JRDA the PDG exercised control over all aspects of the performing arts and forced a sterile conformity to a narrow definition of Guinean drama and music in order to remove "tainted" French and European standards. By giving officially approved focus to the recreational activities of young people and involving them in political work, the JRDA served as a training ground for future party leaders. Occasionally this "shock force of the revolution" tended to outrun the adult PDG leadership and to present it with the task of keeping youthful impatience from changing into left-wing opposition. As Milices Populaires (q.v.), JRDA members threatened to become an uncontrollable vigilante group persecuting any they defined as "enemies of the nation" according to their own whims. The military abol-ished the JRDA in 1984.

JIHAD. A religious duty imposed on Muslims by the *sharia* or Muslim law for the maintenance of Islamic orthodoxy.

Popularly known as "holy war" it is waged against apostates, threatening unbelievers, and enemies of Islam. See MUSA, IBRAHIM; TOURE, SAMORY; UMAR AL HAJJ.

JOLIBA. See NIGER RIVER.

JOURNAL OFFICIEL DE LA REPUBLIQUE DE GUINEE (JORG). The name under which the official journal of French colonial administration in Guinea was continued after independence. Appearing, more or less on a biweekly basis, it published laws, decrees, ministerial orders, notices of civil service appointments and changes, and various other official pronouncements.

JULA. See DYULA.

-K -

KABA. A patronym spread among the Maninka-Mori (Muslim Maninka) settled in Kankan and its adjacent region of Bateh (qq.v.). All of these Muslim communities trace their origins back to the Soninké (Sarakolé) world of the Empire of Ghana (northwestern part of present-day Mali and southeastern Mauritania). The ancestors of the Kaba clans began to settle in Bateh near the end of the sixteenth century and later founded Kankan as an emporium and defensive post on the kola (q.v.), gold, and salt trade routes.

KABA, ALFA KABINE. A mystic and Muslim leader of Kankan (q.v.) in the eighteenth century. He led the resistance of the Kingdom of Bateh, of which Kankan was the metropolis, against an anti-Muslim invasion head by Kondeh-Birama. The alliance he concluded with the almamy (q.v.) of the emerging theocracy of Futa Jalon (q.v.) proved beneficial for both states. Throughout Upper Guinea (q.v.), Alfa Kabiné is revered as a hero and the patron saint of Kankan. His grave, known as "Mbemba Kodon" is an important place in Kankan.

KABA, ALFA MAHMUD. King of Kankan (q.v.), teacher, and military leader, he was the host and friend of Al Hadjj Umar Tall (q.v.). He died in 1865.

KABA, AL-HADJI DIAFODE. A civil servant and later a contractor and business person, he was born in Kankan (q.v.) about 1906. He was a member and vice-president of the Guinean Territorial Assembly (1946–1952). A founder of the Union du Mandé voluntary association, he was elected as second deputy mayor of Kankan in 1957. He died in detention in Camp Boiro in 1976.

KABA, AL HAJJ LAMINE. Born about 1914 of a prominent Muslim family, Al Hajj Kaba was arrested in 1960 by Sékou Touré (q.v.). Since he was *imam* (q.v.) of the Coronti mosque in Conakry (q.v.), Kaba's arrest caused considerable dissatisfaction in Guinea, but he was executed nevertheless.

KABA, AL HAJJ MANSOUR. The candidate of the DYAMA ("Masses") party in the December 1993 elections. Kaba, a construction engineer born in Kankan (q.v.), was the youngest candidate in the election. He campaigned on a platform of hard work and national reconstruction. He received less than one percent of the votes in this election.

KABA, KABAKAROU-SEKOU (1928–1962). A prominent lawyer in Paris and Conakry (q.v.) from 1955–1958, he was an adviser to Sékou Touré (q.v.), executive head of the ministry of justice and member of the constitutional committee responsible for the first Guinean constitution.

KABA, COMMANDANT KABINE. An officer in the Guinean army, he was a member of the Comité Militaire de Redressement National (CMRN [q.v.]) that overthrew the Parti Démocratique de Guinée (PDG [q.v.]) regime in 1984. Named governor of the central bank he fled to Mali and the Côte d'Ivoire in the aftermath of the anti-Maninka (q.v.) riots of July 1985. He is the author of pamphlets critical of President Lansana Conté's (q.v.) management and policies.

KABA, KARAMA-DAYE. A military person and younger brother of the King of Kankan, Karamo-Mori Kaba (qq.v.). After Samory Touré conquered Kankan (qq.v.) in 1880, he sought French assistance in Soudan; and subsequently played a role in Samory's defeat.

KABA, KARAMO-MORI (ca. 1835–1918). Religious figure and king of Kankan (q.v.). He was a foe of Samory Touré (q.v.).

KABA, KARAMO-TALIBI (ca. 1880–1962). With Cheikh (Mamadi) Mohammed Cherif (q.v.), a prominent religious leader in Kankan (q.v.). A prolific writer in Arabic and Maninkakan, he is remembered for his intellectualism and the prediction of Sékou Touré's (q.v.) "bloody rule."

KABA, LAMINE-SADJI (ca. 1898–1962). School teacher in Dakar, Senegal, and founder of the French Koranic school (Ecole Franco-Arabe) there. An author, he was known as "Sadji" or "The Ram" because of his temper. He was a candidate for *député* to the French National Assembly in Paris in 1946 but the riots that accompanied his campaigns in Kankan (q.v.) resulted in a military intervention from Soudan and his arrest. He served seven years in prison in Mauritania and in 1957 he was elected to the Guinean Territorial Assembly for Kankan and become that body's vice president. He died in 1962.

KABA, LANSINE. A scholar and writer born in Kankan (q.v.) and graduated from the Sorbonne in Paris and Northwestern University in Evanston, Illinois, he was professor of history and department head at both the University of Minnesota and the University of Illinois at Chicago. He is the author of many works on Guinea, Islam, and politics in Africa. He was co-founder of the Parti National pour le Développement et la Démocratie (PND), a party critical of President Lansana Conté's (q.v.) regime and politics.

KABA, LAYE (ca. 1918–1971). A prominent businessman in Kankan and Conakry (qq.v) he was arrested and hanged in Conakry in 1971.

KABA, MADY-AMIATA. Born in Kankan (q.v.) about 1935 he was a store manager and businessman in Nzérékoré (q.v.) in the 1950s. Secretary general of the Parti Démocratique de Guinée (PDG [q.v.]) in Kankan from 1961–1965, he served as governor in the Futa, and then minister of commerce 1970–1971. He was jailed in Camp Boiro in 1971 and returned to business after his release in 1981.

KABA, MAMADI. Born in Conakry (q.v.) about 1928, he was Sékou Touré's (q.v.) early companion in the trade union and the Parti Démocratique de Guinée (PDG, q.v). Once chairman of the Guinean labor movement and a former governor, minister of labor, and member of the PDG *politburo,* he was arrested on April 3, 1984, and released in 1988. He serves as honorary chairman of the new PDG.

KABA, MASSA-SEKOU. Born in Kankan (q.v.) about 1930 he was a civil servant in Dakar, Senegal, a member of Sékou Touré's (q.v.) staff and cabinet. Arrested on April 3, 1984, and released in 1988 he lives in exile in Abidjan, Côte d'Ivoire.

KABA, EL-HADJI NFALY (1899–1972). The best known and most influential businessman in Kankan (q.v.) in the 1940s and 1950s. President of the Bloc Africain de Guinée (BAG [q.v.]) until 1958, he retired from business in 1964 and was buried in 1972 in the Bemba-Kondon Cemetery, the holiest place in Kankan.

KABA, HADJA NYAMAKORO (1915–1970). Although she was the sister of El-Hadji Nfalay Kaba (q.v.), she was among the first organizers of the Parti Démocratique de Guinée (PDG [q.v.]) in the Kankan (q.v.) region. Elected to the Kankan municipal council in 1956 and a member of the PDG national women's committee, she died in Kankan in 1970.

KABA, EL-HADJI SIMKOUN (ca. 1900–1970). Born in Kankan (q.v.) he was a civil servant in the Forest Region, the Futa Jalon, and Conakry (qq.v.). Considered Sékou Touré's (q.v.)

unofficial "guardian," he was an early member of the Conakry (q.v.) branch of the Parti Démocratique de Guinée (PDG [q.v.]). He was a member of the PDG central committee and the government.

KADE. This area in Gaoual, where the village Ndama is located, is considered the limit of the Futa Jalon (qq.v.).

KAKE, IBRAHIMA BABA. Born in Kankan (q.v.), he graduated *agrégé* in history from the University of Paris. A former student activist, he founded an opposition movement to Sékou Touré (q.v.) along with Siradiou Diallo (q.v.). A *lycée* teacher in Paris, he is a prolific writer, and the author of *Sékou Touré: le héro et le tyran* (1987). He is also the producer of a radio program *Mémoire d'un continent* on Radio-France Internationale and the publisher of *Silatigui,* a bimonthly journal critical of President Lansana Conté's (q.v.) government.

KAMSAR. Until the 1970s this was a small town on the Atlantic Ocean just south of Iles Tristão (q.v.) on the Guinea-Bissau border. In 1973 the completion of an 137-kilometer (85-mile) railroad connecting the Sangarédi bauxite deposits with the coast at Kamsar (qq.v.) and the establishment of the headquarters for bauxite mining and exporting of the Compagnie des Bauxites de Guinée (CBG [q.v.]), a joint Guinean and HALCO (q.v.) corporation, transformed Kamsar into the second major port in Guinea overnight. Kamsar today is a classic example of the "implanted" city and is critical to Guinea's economy.

KANKAN. The second largest city in Guinea and a *préfecture* (q.v.) in Upper Guinea (q.v.) which borders on the Côte d'Ivoire and Mali. The city was founded by the Kaba (q.v.) and other Muslim clans at the end of the sixteenth century.

KANKAN, MUSA. See MANSA MUSA.

KANTE, SUMANGURU. King of Susu (q.v.), one of the warring kingdoms that competed for hegemony in the Niger River (q.v.) valley in the early 1200s long after the decline of the Empire of Ghana. He conquered the Mali Empire (q.v.) and other neighboring states due in part, according to the oral traditions, to his magical powers. About 1235, he was defeated by Sundiata (or Sunjata) Keita (q.v.), heir to the throne of Mali. He is considered to be the "ancestor" of the blacksmiths.

KARITE. See SHEA-BUTTER TREES.

KEITA, ANDREE. Sékou Touré's second wife and mother of Mohamed Touré (qq.v.).

KEITA DYNASTY. A dynasty of Manding rulers who directed the Mali Kingdom and its successor the Mali Empire (q.v.) from the eleventh century until 1600. The most important emperors were Sundiata (1130–1255) and Mansa Musa (1307–1332; qq.v.). The last emperor was Mama Moghan (ca. 1600).

KEITA, FADIALA. A lawyer who for a long time served in Kankan (q.v.) before independence. Adviser to the appeal Court, attorney general, and ambassador to both the (then) USSR and the USA. As managing director of the Kindia Bauxite Agency (OBK), he was arrested and died in detention in Conakry (q.v.).

KEITA, FODEBA. Born in Siguiri (q.v.) in February 1921, he was educated at the William Ponty School (q.v.). A choreographer, songwriter, and playwright in Paris in the late 1940s, he wrote *Aube Africaine* and founded the Ballet Africain (q.v.), the first international group specializing in the interpretation of West African folklore and dances (especially focused on Maninka forms). As a radical, anti-colonial poet, his works were banned throughout French Africa. Elected to the Guinean Territorial Assembly in 1957 he served as minister of administrative affairs, defense and security, and agriculture under Sékou Touré (q.v.). Arrested and sentenced to death for alleged complicity in the so-called "Labé Plot" (q.v.), he was executed.

KEITA, HADJA TATA. The younger half-sister of Sékou Touré's wife, Andrée, and wife of Moussa Diakité, whose son was married to Ismaël Touré's oldest daughter, Mama Kountou (qq.v.).

KEITA, MAMADI (1933–1985). Born in Kankan (q.v.), while a philosophy student in Paris he became the leader of the West African Student Organization and was expelled from France in 1961. He received his doctorate in philosophy from the University of Geneva, Switzerland, and subsequently was a professor, dean, and president of the University of Conakry. He served in Sékou Touré's (q.v.) government as minister of education and was a member of the Parti Démocratique de Guinée (PDG [q.v.]) politburo responsible for ideological affairs. A member of the large Keita lineage of Kankan and Kouroussa (qq.v.) which included Sékou Touré's wife, Madame Hadja Andrée Touré, with whom he was influential. He was arrested on April 3, 1984, and executed in Kindia (q.v.) in July 1985.

KEITA, NAMORY. Army chief of staff who replaced Noumandian Keita (q.v.) after the latter was executed for alleged treason in 1971.

KEITA, N'FAMARA. Born at Molota in the Kindia region in 1924, he completed some secondary studies in Dakar before becoming a court clerk in Macenta (qq.v.) in 1947. Chosen by Touré as an active trade unionist, he rose in politics as a member of PDG (qq.v.) and was elected mayor of Kindia in 1956. Upon independence he was appointed secretary of state in the office of the presidency. In March 1960 he was appointed minister of planning. Transferred to the Ministry of Trade in January 1961, he served in that post, with other brief assignments through 1972. He was minister of the Superministry of Rural Development in 1975 and a member of every one of Sékou Touré's cabinets. He died in prison after the military seized power and arrested him in 1984.

KEITA, GENERAL NOUMANDIAN. The chief of the combined armed forces' general staff, Keita was arrested in July 1971.

In prison he was forced to confess to spying for the West German government in relation to the November 1970 invasion of Guinea by Portuguese (q.v.) and a Guinean exile groups, the Régroupement des Guinéens en Europe.

KEITA, SEYDOU (1934–1985). A cousin of Mamadi Keita (q.v.) and Hadja Andrée Touré, the wife of Sékou Touré (q.v.), he studied economic planning in Paris. He held many positions in Guinea before being appointed ambassador to West Germany and Italy. He was arrested on April 3, 1984 and executed in Kindia (q.v.) in July 1985.

KEITA, SUNDIATA (Soundiata). The founder of the Mali Empire (q.v.) who ruled from 1230 to 1255 or 1260. Sundiata inherited a small kingdom centered on his capital, Niane, that had been ruled by the Keitas since the twelfth century. When Sundiata assumed power Mali was a small vassal state of Susu (Sosso, Sousou [q.v.]), a powerful kingdom to the northeast that had emerged as the Ghana Empire disintegrated. Named Mari Djata, he was later called Sundiata meaning the "lion prince." Oral traditions about Sundiata are still recited in those areas of West Africa which were once part of the Mali Empire. Between 1230 and 1234 Sundiata expanded his small kingdom into a large empire through armed conquest. As his military power grew he was able to attack Susu and in 1235 he defeated Sumanguru Kanté (q.v.), king of Susu, at Kirina, north of present-day Koulikoro, Mali. After this conquest he controlled all of Susu and its vassal states. In 1240 he moved north into what is now Mauritania, where he conquered the remains of the declining Ghana Empire.

KEROUANE. This town and *préfecture* on the headwaters of the Milo River is the major diamond-producing (qq.v.) area of Guinea. Between the savanna region of Kankan and the forest regions of Macenta and Beyla (qq.v.) on the border with Côte d'Ivoire, Kérouané remains a rather isolated town. Historically this region on the flanks of the Simandou Mountain range was the area from which Samory Touré (q.v.) launched his revolution at the end of the nineteenth century. The region appears destined to remain an economic backwater until hydroelectric (q.v.) resources, iron-mining potential, and better transportation facilities are developed.

KINDIA. A town and *préfecture* of the same name located between Coyah and Mamou (qq.v.) on the border with Sierra Leone. The town was important in colonial times as a trade and transportation center for plantation crops and to a lesser extent still is so today.

KISSI. A relatively large rice-growing ethnic group in the Guéck-édou and Kissidougou (qq.v.) regions. Other Kissi live just inside the borders of Sierra Leone and Liberia. Culturally and linguistically they are unrelated to the dominant Mandé-speaking populations to the north and hence have been somewhat neglected in the political and economic life of present-day Guinea.

KISSIDOUGOU. Town and *préfecture* of the same name in the Forest Region south of Kouroussa and Kankan (qq.v.). Between the forest and savanna, the town of Kissidougou has long been an important trade center. The region is a rich agricultural area producing rice, coffee, maize (qq.v.) and other food crops.

KOGON RIVER. Rising in the Futa Jalon just west of Telimélé (qq.v.) this river flows in a wide arch northwest and then southwest to a large Atlantic estuary on the Guinea-Bissau border. Though it passes close to the major bauxite deposits at Sangria in the Boké (qq.v.) region, the river has yet to be named as a major source of potential hydroelectric (q.v.) power.

KOKULO RIVER. One of three major tributaries of the Konkouré River, flowing from the Pita region toward Fria (qq.v.). A dam and power station at the Kinkon gorge on this river was completed by the People's Republic of China (q.v.) in 1966; it supplies electric power to the towns of Pita, Labé, Dalaba, and Mamou (qq.v.).

KOLA NUTS (*Cola nitida* or *Cola acuminata*). A golf ball-sized kernel traditionally traded by West African peoples. Containing considerable caffeine, this kernel was a mild stimulant; commercially it is today used in the production of cola drinks. The kola nut trade in Guinea represented one of the principal trade items in non-European trade especially between the Forest Region and Upper Guinea (qq.v.).

KOMOYA, COMMANDANT FODE. A military officer who was commander of Camp Alfa Yaya in Conakry (q.v.) and very active in the events of July 1985 that led to the arrest and execution of Colonel Diarra Traoré (q.v.) and scores of Maninka (q.v.) officers. He was commander of the Camp of Kankan (q.v.) from 1989–1991 and a member of the Comité Transitoire de Redressement National (CTRN [q.v.]). He was blind, retired from service, and living in Conakry in 1993.

KONAGI (also Coniagui). An ethnic group akin to the Kassari (q.v.) currently occupying a small part of the Younkounkoun area and a small area of eastern Senegal. Oral traditions suggest that they once were sparsely settled throughout eastern Senegal, but were forced out, absorbed, and enslaved by more powerful Maninka, Fulbé (qq.v.) and Tukulor neighbors.

KONDE-BIRAMA. A military leader of Upper Guinea (q.v.) who waged war against the Muslims of Bateh and the Futa Jalon (qq.v.) in the eighteenth century.

KONO. A Mandé-speaking people, a few of whom live in the very southeast corner of Guinea. The majority of this numerically small ethnic group live in Côte d'Ivoire and Liberia.

KONYA. An area between Upper Guinea and the Forest Region (qq.v.) inhabited by Maninka (q.v.) people with a very recognizable accent. Beyla-Jakolidugu (q.v.) is the main town in the Konya. Samory Touré (q.v.) was from this area.

KORA. A lute-harp or guitar which consists of half a large calabash used as the sound box and a long wooden pole that protrudes from its rim to form the neck. It usually has 21 metal or fiber strings. Such stringed instruments were usually played by individual *griots* (q.v.).

KOUMBASSA, SALIOU. A member of a Guinean family from the Boké (q.v.) region, Koumbassa was a high school principal, professor at the University of Conakry and the inspector general of education during the late 1960s. Many members of the family were jailed, executed, or exiled and Koumbassa was imprisoned for eight years for political reasons. He was freed in 1980, became the Guinean representative to the United Nations (q.v.) for three years and was later appointed minister of national education during the Second Republic.

KOUNDARA. A town and *préfecture* of the same name in Middle Guinea (q.v.) bordering on Guinea-Bissau and Senegal. A rather isolated region producing peanuts, cattle, rice, millet, and maize (qq.v.). Koundara still promises to become a major food-producing region in the future.

KOURANKO. A Maninka (q.v.) subgroup who live in the northern part of the Kissidougou (qq.v.) region. These peaceful cultivators were probably originally a "caste" group within the larger Maninka ethnicity and today maintain a separate ethnic identity out of pride and self-respect.

KOUROUSSA. A town and *préfecture* of the same name located in Upper Guinea between Kankan and Dabola (qq.v.). Located in what is largely a rice-producing area of little importance in pre-colonial times, the town originally grew as an administrative center. It has become important as a transportation center with the arrival of the railroad in 1911 due to its position on the Niger River (q.v.). When the railroad was pushed to Kankan, Kouroussa returned to its position as an administrative post with little other reason for existence.

KPELLE. The self-designation of the Forest Region ethnic group known in French as Guerzé (qq.v.).

- L -

LABE. A city and *préfecture* of the same name in Middle Guinea (q.v.) between the regions of Mali and Pita (qq.v.) with a northeast extension to the border of the Republic of Mali. Labé was an important commercial center in colonial times. The region produced coffee, oranges, and jasmine essences (for perfume). With a relatively large population it has continued to maintain an urban air, though commercial activities have declined in recent years and have not yet been replaced by any large-scale industrial operation. Architecturally and esthetically, it is one of the most pleasant towns in Guinea.

LABE PLOT. In February 1969 President Touré, apparently fearful of an army coup like that which had overthrown the government of Modibo Keita in Mali, accused the army garrison at Labé (q.v.) with fomenting plans to seize national power. More than 1,000 Guineans were arrested in this so-called "Labé Plot." Many were executed including high-ranking army and government officials. After this alleged coup attempt, the army's capabilities to act independently were severely curtailed and party control was expanded. See PLOTS.

LABOR. Figures on Guinea's labor force vary greatly, but the total labor force of more than three million persons age ten and over probably has less than 10 percent wage and salary earners. Until the military coup of 1984 most of these were employed by the government in administration or other government-sponsored activities. The structural reforms of the late 1980s and early 1990s reduced this employment considerably. The wage-earning sectors of the economy are largely concentrated in the bauxite-mining enterprises at Boké, Fria, and Sangaredi (qq.v.). Plantation employment has virtually ceased and subsistence agriculture (q.v.) has probably increased over the past 40 years. Since the reforms of the late 1980s, independent unions once more are beginning to operate. The production brigades of the type employed in the People's Republic of China (q.v.) are no longer used to mobilize the masses of the population in public works projects as they did under the Touré regime.

LABOR UNIONS. Independent labor unions, important before independence, did not exist in Guinea under Touré (q.v.). The Confédération National des Travailleurs de Guinée (CNTG) became a government union. It was headed by a cabinet minister with party militant holding all key posts at all levels. At the top the CNTG linked separate national craft unions and professional organizations. The same model was applied at the regional level. In theory independent unions were allowed after 1984, but a strong movement has yet to emerge. See CONFEDERATION GENERALE DU TRAVAIL.

LANDOMA (also Landouma, Cocoli, Tyopi, and Tiapi). A people speaking a Baga (q.v.) dialect living inland from the Nalou between the Rio Núñez (qq.v.) and the Fatala River to the West of Gaoual (q.v.) along the Guinea-Bissau border. Now largely integrated into the larger Susu-speaking (q.v.) populations of the coast. See BAGA.

LANGUAGE. The official language of Guinea is French but after independence eight of the country's major vernaculars were chosen as national languages. These are Poular, Maninkakan, Susu, Kissi, Guerzé, Toma, Konagi, and Bassari (qq.v.). Lack of funds hampered attempts to teach people to read and write in these languages. Only Susu, Maninkakan, and Poular challenge French as languages useful in all of Guinea. Under the present government French is once more being stressed. See FRENCH LANGUAGE.

LAWRENCE, ANTOINE. A supporter of David Soumah (q.v.) in founding the Confédération Française des Travailleurs Chrétiens (CFT) to compete with the Marxist Confédération

Générale du Travail (CGT), with which Sékou Touré (qq.v.) was affiliated.

LAYE, CAMARA. See CAMARA LAYE.

LEBANESE. An ethnic minority in Guinea that from the early colonial period filled the sociological and commercial role of intermediaries in the colonial system. Migrants from Lebanon and Syria (both called Lebanese locally) began arriving in Guinea in the 1920s and the flow increased through the 1920s and 1930s.

As European commercial firms expanded into the interior in the 1920s and 1930s, they frequently gave employment or credit preference to Lebanese retailers and middlemen over their Maninka and Fulbé competitors. Operating some small-scale coffee and banana (qq.v.) plantations, most moved their investments in the 1950s into real estate, transport, wholesale commerce, and some light industry. They also remained dominant as middle-level merchants. After independence, the Touré regime drove most of this entrepreneurial group out of business, allegedly because of their active involvement in smuggling (q.v.) into Sierra Leone, Liberia, and other countries.

LEGAL SYSTEM. For all practical purposes there was no autonomous legal "system" in Guinea under the Sékou Touré (q.v.) regime. What judicial authorities there were would seem to have been guided simply by the expedience of attempting to bring about the interests of the PDG (q.v.). The chairperson of the party unit at each level presided over courts at that level. At the *arrondissement* (q.v.) level these courts handled both civil and criminal cases. Such was also the case at the regional level, since there was an interlocking membership on these courts. A superior court in Conakry (q.v.) in theory, served as a final appeal in case of procedural questions, but this judicial body had no power to advise or judge constitutional questions and in practice did not function.

Since Touré convicted persons accused of crimes against the nation without trial, the "system" existed only on paper. The Supreme Revolutionary Tribunal, which condemned 92 persons to death after the November 1, 1970 attack on Conakry, allowed no defense testimony and performed the whole trial by audio cassette recorded in prison. This was perhaps more representative of the legal system which operated in Guinea under Touré than any description of a theoretical scheme.

In mid-June 1984, after a week-long Conférence National-ale de la Justice, the Conté (q.v.) government announced major reforms of the judiciary. Tribunals created under the Touré regime, over which PDG officials had presided, were abolished and their jurisdiction over civil and some criminal matters was transferred to newly created local courts and justices of the peace. The Supreme Revolutionary Tribunal, a court composed of members of the National Assembly with jurisdiction to try political cases, was also abolished. Its powers were transferred to the Haute Cour de Justice (High Court of Justice), a court which had not functioned in President Sékou Touré's time. In 1992 a new Supreme Court was also established. Its functions were expanded with the *loi fondamentale* (q.v.) enacted in 1990; the responsibility for the administration of prisons was returned from the Ministry of the Interior to the Ministry of Justice. All of these reforms have yet to be implemented.

LELE. A small ethnic group living on the Sierra Leone border in the Kissidougou (q.v.) region since colonial times. In recent years they have been almost completely absorbed into large surrounding groups such as the Maninka and the Kissi (qq.v.). There are other ethnic groups elsewhere in Africa identified by this name as well.

LEROUGE, RAYMOND. The Roman Catholic bishop of Conakry who founded a Guinean branch of the Confédération Française des Travailleurs Chrétiens (CFTC) to compete with the Marxist Confédération Générale du Travail (CGT [q.v.]).

LOCAL ADMINISTRATION. Under Sékou Touré (q.v.) the administration at the local level was made up of the executive council of the PDG (q.v.) whose president was also the mayor. This council was in charge of political, administrative, and some judicial functions. This local council was empowered to employ party members to help keep birth, marriage and death records, maintain roads, dispensaries and sometimes corporations. Above all, though, the local council's major duty was to mobilize all citizens for projects elaborated by higher ranks in the PDG hierarchy.

The Conté (q.v.) administration returned to a system more like the French colonial administration than the Touré model. The country is currently divided administratively into eight provinces headed by governors, who are directly responsible to the CMRN (q.v.). The provinces are divided into *préfectures, souspréfectures,* and districts known as "quartiers" in Conakry and the larger towns, in practice, extended family and traditional lineage authority figures seem to be reasserting their importance at the local level so that some local self-government may be evolving. See ADMINISTRATIVE ORGANIZATION; ARRONDISSE-MENT.

LOI CADRE. This act passed by the French National Assembly on June 23, 1956, offered some palliative reforms within the French colonial system. It proclaimed universal suffrage and extension of a single electoral college. Of primary importance for Guinea was a local executive council established in Conakry (q.v.) with certain powers to run the administration of the territory. Control of this territorial assembly became the immediate goal of the Guinean African political parties, which turned from the more illusive goal of participation in the politics of metropolitan France. Sékou Touré and his PDG (qq.v.) gained control of this *loi cadre* government. This gave the party the impetus to forge ahead and create a strong, united Guinean party ready for self-government. The law also helped ensure the creation of separate, independent nation-states in former French West Africa (AOF [q.v.]) rather than the creation of a unified confederation. Another *loi cadre* was passed in 1964 to target Saifoulaye Diallo (q.v.), but officially aimed at controlling illegal business by high-ranking public officials.

LOI FONDAMENTALE. A set of basic laws designed by the

Comité Transitoire de Redressement National (CTRN q.v.) in the early 1990s under the military government of Lansana Conté (q.v.) to guide in the writing of the Constitution of the Second Republic (q.v.) and in the creation of a democratic system of public governance.

LOS ISLANDS. See ILES DE LOS.

LOWER GUINEA. One of the four major topographic areas of Guinea, this coastal area is largely a plain, giving way at its eastern borders to low hills, cut by deep river valleys which in turn lead up to the higher escarpment of the Futa Jalon (q.v.). Lower Guinea stretches from 50 to 100 kilometers (30 to 60 miles) inland from the Atlantic Ocean. Marshy islands and peninsulas help form a coast which is deeply indented by brackish estuaries and dotted with mangrove swamps forming the mouths of many rivers. heavy rainfall and warm tropical temperatures make this area an excellent rice- and banana-producing (qq.v.) area.

- M -

MACENTA. A *préfecture* in the Forest Region between Nzérékoré and Guéckédou (qq.v.) on the Liberian border. A forestry-training center, a particle board factory, and a tea plantation have been developed since independence. The regional center is a pleasant town in rolling hills supplied with adequate agricultural production.

MAGASSOUBA, COLONEL LAMINE. Born in Siguiri (q.v.) about 1935, this former military officer was a member of the Comité Militaire de Redressement National (CMRN [q.v.]), served as head of the Gendarmerie Nationale in Conakry (q.v.) and was commander of the Guinean battalion sent to Liberia from 1989–1991. He was demoted and retired in 1992 and is currently living in Siguiri.

Magassouba, Dr. Moriba / 115

MAGASSOUBA, DR. MORIBA (ca. 1923–1971). Born in Siguiri (q.v.), he graduated from the William Ponty School (q.v.) and was a Parti Démocratique de Guinée (PDG [q.v.]) activist in Upper Guinea (q.v) in the early 1950s. Elected mayor of Kankan (q.v.) in 1956 he later served as head of police and internal security as well as minister of the interior. He was arrested and hanged in Conakry (q.v.) in 1971.

MAHDI. In Islamic theology an apocalyptic figure who will one day rule this world and bring about the universal true religion before the end of time. This teaching is not unknown among Guinean Muslims and could yet be a powerful force for socio-political change.

MAIZE (corn; *Zea mays*). A major subsistence crop throughout Guinea, it is especially important as a food crop in Middle and Upper Guinea (qq.v.). The regions of Mamou, Siguiri, Koundara, and Labé (qq.v.) grow the largest amounts but relatively little of this crop finds its way into the market system. Rather, self-consumption and relatively low yields make this food crop less important than it might be.

MALI. A town and *préfecture* north of Labé on the Senegal border between the Koundara and Tougué regions in the Futa Jalon (qq.v.). This region of 9,000 square kilometers (3,400 square miles) has tremendous potential. It is the major entry point from Senegal. The region has considerable limestone and could become a major producer of cement. The Mali region produces many cattle and is the major center of "Irish" potato production in Guinea. There are some indications that diamonds (q.v.) and even uranium may be found in the area. During the colonial area this relatively high-altitude region with its more temperate climate attracted European visitors and the area may someday attract tourists.

MALI EMPIRE. Mali is an Arabic form of the Maninka word "Mandé." Some areas of Upper Guinea (q.v.) were part of this famous West African empire. A Mandé-speaking ruler, Sundiata Keita (q.v.), emerged from a village based on the Niger River (q.v.) in present-day Guinea in the early 1200s. Sundiata defeated other contenders for the military and commercial hegemony of much of the west-central Sudan (q.v.). On the base of his conquests later rulers built the most powerful and richest African empire in the area. The empire lasted until the second half of the fifteenth century but the cultural influence and common sense of identity forged by this empire continued well into the twentieth century. See MANSA MUSA.

MALIKI LAW. The body of Islamic law most widely accepted in West Africa, including Guinea. It is based on the writings of the jurist Iman Mal-le ibn Anas of al-Madina (d. 795) and his school.

MAMOU. A *préfecture* and town of the same name south of Dalaba on the Sierra Leone border between Dabola and Kindia (qq.v.). Long an important trade center, its location on the crossroads of the east-west axis between Conakry and Kankan and the route north through Pita to Labé (qq.v.) enhanced the importance of this trading town in the colonial period. A center of fruit and vegetable production, the region also boasts an agriculture school and major meat and food-processing industry.

MANINKA (Malinké, Mandinka, Manding). A Mandé-speaking population who claims descent from groups which were once united in the Mali Empire (q.v.). Bearing clan names such as Camara, Condé, Diawara, Fofana, Kanté, Kourouma, Kouyaté, Soumaoro, and Traoré, this ethnic group is widespread in an arc of 1,300 kilometers (800 miles) from the mouth of the Gambia River in the northwest to the interior Côte d'Ivoire in the southeast. In Guinea, Maninka can be found in all regions but primarily in Upper Guinea (q.v.).

MANINKAKAN. The language of the Maninka (q.v.) people.

MANIOC (*Manikot utilissima*). Also called tapioca and cassava, manioc is a plant of American origin introduced to Africa by the Portuguese. Its roots are eaten by many Guineans when cereal grains are not available. The young leaves of the plant are sometimes also used as a vegetable. Though high in calories, this starchy food is poor in minerals, vitamins, and protein. It is filling though, and constitutes an important part of subsistence agriculture throughout much of the country especially in Upper Guinea.

MANO. A relatively small ethnic group living to the east of the Kpelle in the Nzérékoré *préfecture*. The majority of these Mandé-speaking people live in Liberia.

MANSA. A traditional Mandé title for the ruler of a kingdom.

MANSA MUSA (ruled ca. 1307–1332). Most famous of the kings of ancient Mali (q.v.) largely because of his pilgrimage to Mecca in 1324–1325. On this pilgrimage his lavish alms giving of the great wealth in gold from the Buré (q.v.) gold fields made a lasting impression on the Arabic chroniclers. Mansa Musa represented a "golden age" of ancient Mali, during which the literature of the western Sudan (q.v.) grew and Sudanic architecture flourished.

MARABOUTS. Muslim religious teachers who in some areas of Guinea came to exercise considerable political and economic influence. In the households of African rulers who had accepted Islam (q.v.) there was usually at least one marabout whose responsibilities in normal times were to pray for the ruler, give advice, and handle correspondence. In colonial times, the term came to apply to anyone claiming a modicum of Koranic learning and/or Arabic literacy.

MARTIN, MARCEL. Brother of Jeanne Martin Cissé (q.v.), he was born in Kankan (q.v.) and graduated from the University of Paris Law School. He served as prosecutor in Conakry (q.v.), chief justice of the court of appeals, and ambassador to France from 1989–1993.

MEDICAL EDUCATION. The French began to train African

doctors (*médecins Africains*) and African pharmacists for all of French West Africa (AOF [q.v.]) in Dakar in 1918. Candidates followed a special science curriculum in the last years of the *lycée* and then received four years of medical education. A total of 481 *médecins Africains,* including a number of Guineans, graduated in the next 35 years. Until 1954 training as full physicians (a six-year post-secondary curriculum) was available only in France. The current lack of appropriately trained physicians and pharmacists in Guinea can be traced to the decline of the *médecins Africains* training program after independence.

METIS, METISSE. An individual of mixed European and African ancestry. In colonial Guinea the mixed community was a small, self-conscious local elite on the coast and in some of the large regional towns.

MIDDLE GUINEA (Moyenne Guinée). One of the four reasonably clearly marked topographical regions of Guinea. The region is made up of a relatively high plateau called the Futa Jalon (q.v.). Varying in altitude from 450 to 1,350 meters (1,500 to 4,500 feet), most of the plateau is savanna (q.v.) covered with short grass, interspersed with occasional clumps of brush, baobabs (q.v.), and even pines. Rainfall is less here than on the coast so the only heavily forested areas are in the river valleys, which cut through the plateau in all directions. The Dalaba, Gaoual, Koubia, Koundara, Labé, Lelouma, Mali, Pita, and Tougué (qq.v.) *préfectures* are all found in Middle Guinea.

MIFERGUI (Société des Mines de Fer de Guinée). This proposed multi-national project for mining the rich iron ore deposits of the Nimba-Simandou mountain ranges included Algeria, Nigeria, Zaire, Japan, Spain, and Yugoslavia and possibly Romania as partners with Guinea. This project also envisaged the construction of 1,000-kilometer (620-mile) trans-Guinean railroad from these mines to a proposed deep water ore port at Conakry (q.v.) for a minimum cost of US $550 million. See MINING.

MIGRATION. Until the early 1960s farmers from Upper Guinea

(q.v.) migrated to work on the peanut harvest in the Gambia and Senegal. Some migration from Guinea to Sierra Leone and Liberia also took place, with young men going to work for cash wages for a period and then returning home. Within the country Maninka merchants regularly went from Upper Guinea to the Forest Region (qq.v.) to engage in small-scale trading in rice and other goods, while Fulbé (q.v.) cattle raisers moved from valley pasturage in the rather large-scale shift in population from rural areas to urban and mining areas has also gone on since independence. Finally, political disillusionment and economic pressure have induced over two million Guineans to leave their country in search of better living conditions in Senegal, Côte d'Ivoire, and elsewhere. A large number of such exiles are also found in Sierra Leone, Liberia, Mali, the Gambia, and France.

MILICES POPULAIRES. Beginning with Jeunesse de la Révolution Démocratique Africaine (q.v.) volunteers who sought out "opponents" of the party in the early 1960s, this popular militia was made an organized civil service organization composed of young men and women between the ages of 17 and 30 in the late 1960s. By 1969 the militia was given small arms and military training and had a role equivalent to the army. In 1974 this militia was organized as a reserve force at several levels throughout the country for national defense. In Conakry (q.v.) it became a full-time regular force and, throughout the nation Milices Populaires, organized in both combat units and as staff and cadre for reserve militia units at the village and school levels, were granted a status superior to the military and police. In effect this second police force was an attempt to lessen the possibility of a military coup d'état. After the military coup on April 3, 1984, elements of this militia were integrated into the national army.

MILLET (*Panicum miliaceum* and others). A number of drought-resistant cereal grains with small round seeds enclosed in a hard outer coat which occur in large numbers on short stalks at the top of the stem. Of little commercial value most of the cereals are grown widely in Middle and Upper Guinea (qq.v.) on land too poor for maize. They are a good source of starch, but aside from some useful mineral salts, contribute little more than bulk to the human diet.

MILO RIVER. An important tributary of the Niger River in Upper Guinea rising in the Simandou Mountains just southwest of Beyla and emptying into the Niger about 30 kilometers (20 miles) south of Siguiri (qq.v.). Navigable by shallow-draft barge from Kankan (q.v.) to the Niger, in colonial times the river was a rather important avenue of trade and commerce since it helped connect the railheads of Kankan and Bamako. With independence the interregional flow of traffic has declined on the Milo. Milo is also the name of the Guinean-made cigarette.

MINING. The most important mining operation is the Boké bauxite project (q.v.), which began in 1973. This project operates under the authority of the Compagnie des Bauxites de Guinée jointly owned by Guinea (49 percent) and a consortium of European and American companies. Three other bauxite projects at Dabola, Kindia, and Tougué (qq.v.) are also planned. The government of Guinea also controls 49 percent of the Fria (q.v.) mining industry, which had operated as a private enterprise until 1973. A multinational project called MIFERGUI (q.v.) for mining the rich iron ore of the Nimba-Simandou (qq.v.) mountain ranges was also planned in the mid-1970s. Diamond-bearing gravels as well as diamond-bearing pipes in the area encompassed by Macenta, Kerouané, and Beyla (qq.v.) produced both industrial and gem stones. Only one major gold-mining operation is apparently now functioning run by a Canadian firm, the Société Minière du Québec. Despite major policy changes following the 1984 military coup d'état, the mining situation of Guinea has not improved much. A persistent lack of electric power and poor road and railroad infrastructures have proven to be strong impediments to any significant improvements in the mining sector.

MINISTRES IMPORTES. Some of the *diasporé* (q.v.) technocrats who were called upon to help implement the economic and political reforms initiated by the Conté (q.v.) regime.

The best known were Bassirou Barry who ran the Ministry of Justice, Edouard Benjamin who was minister of planning, cooperation and finance, Banah Sidibé, minister of housing, Jean-Claude Diallo, minister of communications, Dr. Ousmane Sylla, minister of natural resources, Dr. Kerfalla Yansané, governor of the central bank, and Dr. Salif Camara, president of the University of Conakry and, later, minister of justice. Most of these persons were unable to overcome the tremendous resistance to the structural reforms and either quit or were reappointed to less prominent positions.

MISE EN VALEUR. A term employed in Guinea under Sékou Touré (q.v.) and still used to mean "development" or "a realization of potential." Wide usage of the term dates to 1923, when the then colonial minister of France, Albert Sarrant, laid down the French colonial policy of planned economic development. Initially the term implied the role of raw materials sources for the colonies and manufacturer for France. The goal of this policy was to set up a close interdependence on the economic level between France and its African colonies.

MOUNT LOURA. This highest mountain (1,573 meters; 5,100 feet) of the Futa Jalon (q.v.). Spectacular vistas of Senegalese towns can be viewed from this mountain. Located outside the town of Mali (q.v.) with a rock at the summit resembling a woman's head and shoulders, Mount Loura has long been appreciated by local residents.

MOUNT NIMBA. The highest mountain in Guinea, located very near the border with Liberia and Côte d'Ivoire. It is 1,724 meters (5,600 feet) high. See NIMBA MOUNTAINS.

MOUVEMENT SOCIALISTE AFRICAIN. See DEMOCRATIE SOCIALISTE DE GUINEE.

- N -

NABE, MAMADI. A university professor, he held several positions including dean of the Faculty of Administrative Sciences, rector of the University of Conakry, inspector general of education, ambassador to Senegal, counselor to the Ministry of Education, and ambassador to the U.S. Dr. Nabé was among the people who shaped the Guinean educational system's outlook in the 1970s. He was one of the main editors of the university journal *Miriya.*

NAFADJI. A town on the Milo River (q.v.). Ancient official capital of the Kingdom of Bateh (q.v.).

NAFAYA. A state-run retail general store in Conakry during the Touré (qq.v.) era. See SABOUYA.

NALOU. A small ethnic group which in colonial times lived on the lower Rio Núñez and on the Tristão Islands (qq.v.). They probably represent a remnant population driven from the Futa Jalon by more organized Fulbé immigrants.

NAVETAN (*navetane*). Wolof (the dominant Senegalese ethnic group term for migrant farm laborers. During the colonial period large numbers of *navetan* journeyed from Guinea to farm in the peanut-growing areas of Senegal. The word comes from the Wolof (or possibly pidgin) term for the rainy season.

NDAMA (N'dama). A small village in the Gaoual (q.v.) *préfecture* which has given its name to the local Guinea, perhaps West Africa, cattle. These small, prolific, and tse-tse fly-resistant (q.v.) cattle are highly prized throughout West and Central Africa. With proper management and stock-breeding techniques, this variety could become a valuable asset for African development.

NDIAYE, BOBACAR. Born in Conakry (q.v.) in 1939, he graduated from the Ecole Nationale des Sciences Politiques in Paris. The chief accountant, financier, and administrator at the African Development Bank in Abidjan, Côte d'Ivoire, he served as president and chief executive officer of this same multinational bank from 1986 on.

NENEKHALY-CAMARA, CONDETTO. A poet and playwright

who published a small volume of poems in France in 1956. His two plays, *Continent Afrique* and *Amazoulou,* were published in France in 1970. *Amazoulou* is an epic drama of the Zulu King Shaka and shows the strong bias toward historical African themes in government-approved artistic works in contemporary Guinea. The Pastoria center at Kindia (q.v.) has been renamed after him.

NEWSPAPERS. See PRESS.

NIANE, DJIBRIL TAMSIR. A Guinean author and historical scholar. His *Soundjata où l'Epopée Mandingue* (Paris, 1960), translated into English in 1965 as *Sundiata* (q.v.), is an account of the founder of the Mali Empire (q.v.) based on oral traditions still extant in Guinea and modern Mali. Niane collaborated with Jean Suret-Canale in writing a history of West Africa in 1961. He also contributed a number of articles to the scholarly journal, *Recherches Africaines* in Conakry (q.v.) during the early 1960s. A volume with two plays by Niane, *Sikasso* and *Chaka,* was published in France in 1971. Jailed in 1962 for his role in the Guinean teacher's union, he lived in exile as executive secretary of the Léopold Sédar Senghor Foundation in Dakar, Senegal in the 1970s and early 1980s. Since 1989, he has been a librarian and editor in Conakry.

NIANI. A town in Upper Guinea (q.v.). One of the capitals of Sundiata Keita (q.v.) in the thirteenth century.

NIGER RIVER. The fan-shaped drainage system of the headwaters of this great river, known at the Joliba in Maninkakan, which originates in the Guinea highlands, drains over one-third of the country's total area including most of Upper Guinea and the Forest Region (qq.v.). The fertile valley of this river has long been an important agriculture-producing area of this part of West Africa, but the massive flood control projects, which would makes these plains fully productive, have scarcely been started. Some few shallow-draft barges are used from Kouroussa to Bamako, Mali on this river.

NIMBA MOUNTAINS. Located southeast of Nzérékoré (q.v.) on

the border with Côte d'Ivoire and Liberia, this mountain range is part of the larger Guinea highlands stretching all across the Guinea forest zone. Major deposits of magnetite (an iron ore) are located here and are being mined on the Liberia side of the mountain range. In the center of this range is Guinea's highest mountain, Mount Nimba (q.v.) at 1,724 meters (5,600 feet).

NYAMAKALA. A Manikakan word referring to the members of a large social group characterized by caste-like features. The clans (q.v.) which belong to the *nyamakala* have professional specializations such as jewelry making, blacksmithing, leather working, wood carving, and music. They are endogamous. Although part of the free communities and although close to the aristocracy, they historically occupied lower social positions. See CASTE and CLAN.

NZEREKORE. A *préfecture* in the Forest Region between Beyla and Yomou (qq.v.) on the border with both Côte d'Ivoire and Liberia. Long isolated in the forest, the town of Nzérékoré grew as an administrative, mission, and trading center after World War II. Today the region boasts a sawmill and plywood plant as well as a growing population. The region has a relatively dense population and could produce a considerable agricultural surplus. The future exploitation of the rich iron deposits of the region may someday make Nzérékoré a major industrial area.

- O -

OFFICE DE COMMERCIALISATION AGRICOLE (OCA). An institution created in 1970 to handle the selling of rural agricultural produce properly. The OCA bought agricultural produce from the farmers through the Pouvoir Révolutionnaire Local (q.v.) at fixed prices set by the government. Then the OCA sold these goods to Importex (q.v.), the government agency charged with all import and export trade.

OFFICE NATIONAL DES CHEMINS DE FER DE GUINEE

(ONCFG). A national railway corporation which took over the nation's only railroad at independence. This road from Conakry to Kankan (qq.v.) was in poor repair and had been scheduled to be closed by the colonial administration. By 1967 only 140 of the 662 kilometers (87 of 410 miles) from Conakry to Kankan had been repaired. Service was cut to one passenger run a week from Conakry and freight greatly reduced except for a few trains at harvest time for the bananas of Coyah, Kindia, and Mamou (qq.v.). A commuter shuttle continued to operate between Conakry and the suburb of Dixinn. Without substantial changes in maintenance and management, the ONCFG continued to operate at a greater deficit each year. In 1991 it ceased operation.

OLIVIER, AIME (Comte de Sanderval). A French adventurer regarded as the explorer of Lower and Middle (qq.v.) Guinea. Born in 1840, he lived many years in the Labé and Timbo regions of the Futa Jalon (qq.v.). He was a resolute adversary of English colonial ambitions toward the Futa. He later settled in Conakry (q.v.) in an area (*quartier*) that took his name. He often opposed the French administration and was long remembered in Conakry.

ONCHOCERCIASIS (river blindness). A disease carried by the simulium fly or blackfly. This fly breeds in the waters of a number of rivers in Upper Guinea (q.v.). River blindness is a serious health problem in Guinea. In 1975 the World Bank and World Health Organization established a fund to provide money for a control program to destroy the larvae of the simulium in the Sahel by aerial spraying. Guinea was not included in the coverage area.

ORGANISATION DES ETATS RIVERAINS DU SENEGAL (OERS). Multinational union created by Senegal, Mauritania, Mali, and Guinea in 1968 to politically coordinate the development of the Senegal River Basin. Its headquarters were in Dakar. In 1969 a quarrel between Guinea and Mali occupied much of its effort and in 1972 a dispute between Guinea and Senegal finally led to Guinea's withdrawal. The remaining three states organized themselves into the Organisation Pour La Mise en Valeur du Fleuve Senegal (q.v.) which has continued the search for riverine development project funding.

ORGANISATION POUR LA MISE EN VALEUR DU FLEUVE GAMBIE (OMVG). This organization was founded in 1978 by Senegal and Gambia to coordinate the development of the Gambia River Basin. The tentative development plan called for salt intrusion dams on the lower reaches of the river and at least one hydroelectric and irrigation dam in Senegal on the upper river. After a brief disagreement, studies have continued as to whether a simple bridge on the Senegalese trans-Gambia highway at Farateni or a more expensive bridge-dam, as the Gambians insist, ought to be built. OMVG headquarters are in Kaolack, Senegal, and both Guinea-Conakry and Guinea-Bissau are now members of the organization. Plans for a dam in Guinea are held up for lack of funds.

ORGANISATION POUR LA MISE EN VALEUR DU FLEUVE SENEGAL (OMVS). This organization was created in 1972 by Mali, Mauritania, and Senegal to coordinate planning and political questions surrounding the Senegal River after Guinea left the Organisation des Etats Riverains du Sénégal (q.v.), the initial group. (Guinea has since rejoined.) Beginning with colonial plans dating to the 1920s included now, in order of priority, are a salt-intrusion dam at Diama in the delta of the river; a hydroelectric and flow-regulating dam at Manatali, Mali; irrigated perimeters in Senegal, Mauritania, and Mali; plans to make the river navigable as far as Kayes, Mali; and new port facilities at Saint-Louis, Mali, and Kayes. Funding for these projects has been slow and sporadic from OPEC, European, and American sources. The Diama and the Manatali dams and the irrigated perimeters have been completed though their long-term value and human and environmental impact cannot yet be predicted.

ORGANIZATION OF AFRICAN UNITY (OAU). In this pan-African body, founded in Addis Ababa in May 1963, Guinea has always been an active member. Under the secretary-generalship of Guinean Diallo Telli (q.v.) from July 1964 to June 1972, it has led the African fight against colonialism and apartheid. It also sought to improve living conditions for refugees in Africa and settled some border conflicts. Under Telli the OAU was involved in attempts to resolve the Nigerian-Biafran conflict.

OUASSOULOU. See WASSULU.

OUROUKORO. A small village between Kissidougou and Kérouané in the Forest Region where diamonds (qq.v.) are mined in considerable numbers.

- P -

PALM OIL. One of Guinea's principal cooking oils. Growing wild along the coast, oil palms are spared and helped to multiply. Serious plantation cultivation is not very widespread and most palm nuts are simply gathered from scattered trees when the price warrants the hazardous task of climbing them. Most oil is locally consumed while a relatively small number of palm kernels are exported.

PARK, MUNGO (1773–1805). Scottish explorer, sponsored by the African Association in 1795–1798 to investigate rumors concerning the Niger River (q.v.). He traveled to the Niger near Ségou in present-day Mali and obtained some knowledge of the Mandé-speaking populations in Upper Guinea (q.v.). He probably drowned on a second expedition to the Niger in 1805 but he represented a tangible beginning of the European drive to open up the interior of West Africa. His book is an important source for nineteenth-century history of the region.

PARTI DE L'UNITE ET DU PROGRES (PUP). See CONTE, GENERAL LANSANA.

PARTI DEMOCRATIQUE DE GUINEE (PDG). Founded as an branch of the Rassemblement Démocratique Africain (q.v.)

in June 1947, this party became the sole legal party in Guinea after independence in 1958. Beyond that it, in effect, became the government of Guinea. During the first few years of independence the ideal of the PDG as the party of the entire Guinean people was somewhat real. What actually existed by the 1970s was an oligarchy of party elite which struggled for power within the confines of an increasingly autocratic control by the president, Sékou Touré (q.v.). This party was abolished in 1984, though El-hadj Ismaëla Ghussein (q.v.) was the leader of a party with the same name in the early 1990s.

PARTI DU RENOUVEAU ET DU PROGRES (PRP). See DIALLO, SIRADIOU.

PARTI-ETAT. Term used when referring to the nation or the government. As President Touré (q.v.) explained it, at first the people commanded the party, and the party controlled the state. Finally, the party became identical to the state, or was the state.

PARTI GUINEENNE DU PROGRES (PGP). See DIALLO, ABDOULAY.

PARTI PROGRESSISTE DE GUINEE (PPG). This party was an outgrowth of the Group d'Etudes Communistes, founded by a small group of French-education bureaucrats and teachers. It was created in 1946 and dissolved in 1947. Sékou Touré belonged to it.

PARTIDO AFRICAO DA INDEPENDENCIA DA GUINE E DO CABO-VERDE (PAIGC). The party founded by Amilcar Cabral (q.v.) which, in 1975, achieved the independence from Portugal of Guinea-Bissau. This party received support from the government of Guinea throughout the 1960s and early 1970s, despite rumors of tension between Cabral and Touré.

PASTORALISTS. This social science term applies to peoples whose economic and social institutions center on livestock, cattle, sheep, and goats. Few were actually nomadic, with young men or small family groups traveling in transhumant (see TRANSHUMANCE) cycles from dry season to rainy season pastures. Most Guinean pastoralists today are settled quite permanently along the market roads and permanent water sources, combining farming with raising livestock. Though originally virtually a Fulbé (q.v.) monopoly, the mixed herding and farming populations of Guinea are now of almost any ethnic origin.

PASTORIA. A bacteriological research center near Kindia (q.v.) established by the French during the colonial regime which became world famous for anti-snake venom vaccine preparation. Renamed Nenekhaly Condetto and much enlarged by Soviet assistance, this center is a major focus for research in Guinea.

PATERSON-ZOCHONIS (PZ). A British-owned firm which, along with other European import-export firms, dominated commercial life in Guinea during colonial times. These firms controlled the import-export trade, wholesale trade, and some aspects of the retail trade until state-controlled enterprises severely curtailed their operations after independence.

PEANUTS (groundnuts). A spreading, fuzzy-stem annual legume (*Archis hypogosa*) grown in many areas of Guinea. The plant was brought to Europe in the sixteenth century from Brazil and later introduced to Guinea by Europeans seeking a cash crop to exploit. Peanuts are grown in all regions of Guinea in large fields as well as in subsistence plots. A small surplus is marketed but peanuts do not represent an important source of cash income in Guinea as they do elsewhere in West Africa. A peanut oil factory was built in Dabala at the Tinkisso border by the People's Republic of China (qq.v.) in the mid-1970s.

PEDDIE, JOHN. A British officer who journeyed to Rio Núñez (q.v.) in December 1816 as part of that nation's expansion plans when Portuguese and African control of the coast weakened with the decline of the Atlantic slave trade.

PEROZ, COMMANDANT ETIENNE. French military officer who, with Colonel Guy Humbert, fought Samory's (q.v.) forces in French Soudan (Mali) and Upper Guinea (q.v.) during the 1890s. Author of *Au Niger: Récits de campagnes* (1895), an informative book which showed some respect for Samory's military strategy and operations.

PERSON, YVES. One time French administrator in Kissidougou (q.v.) and later professor at the University of Dakar and the University of Paris I (Sorbonne). He wrote a monumental three-volume work, *Samori, une révolution dyula* (1968).

PETROLEUM. One of Guinea's major import needs is petroleum products. Oil deposits in Lower Guinea (q.v.) near the border of Guinea-Bissau have been discovered and Guinea's broad continental shelf, parts of which extend over 160 kilometers (100 miles) out to sea, show considerable promise as an oil-bearing area.

PEUL. See FULBE.

PINEAPPLE (*Ananas comosus*). A plant of Central American origin which grows a juicy mass of 100 to 200 separate fruits at the apex of a cluster of long, thin leaves with sharp edges. Planted from shoots it represents a potentially very important export crop for Guinea. Most pineapples for export are grown on the coastal plains since plantations in the interior face severe transportation problems. A pineapple juice factory (Solquidia) was built in Kindia (q.v.) in the mid-1970s to produce juice for national use.

PITA. A town and *préfecture* located north of Kindia and south of Labé, between Dalaba and Telimélé (qq.v.). This heavily populated region possesses a major hydroelectric-producing facility at Kinkon gorge on the Kokulo River (q.v.) just below the town.

PLAN COMPTABLE NATIONAL. Plan to enforce socialism in each sector of the economy by requiring strict accountability. It covered industry, commerce, agriculture and cattle-raising, banking, and transportation (qq.v.).

PLAN QUINQUENNAL (1973–1978 and 1978–1985). Third and fourth national economic plans. These five-year plans followed the Three-Year Plan, 1960–1962 and the Seven-Year Plan, 1964–1970. These Five-Year plans focused on the production of material goods needed for national well-being, especially agricultural development and the formation of state-private enterprises. Party activists played a major role in producing the plan which called for a large degree of mass participation in the form of 200 work brigades in 1974, 3,000 in 1975, 4,500 in 1976, 5,500 in 1977, and 7,125 in 1978. The Deuxième Quinquennal (1981–1985) was much the same.

PLANNING. Guinea has attempted since 1960 to operate under a centrally planned economy. The first plan, the Three-Year Plan, 1960–1962, was prepared by a team of French experts. Its major decision was to create an independent Guinean currency (q.v.). Lacking adequate administrative machinery, this first plan had little effect. The second plan, the Seven-Year Plan, 1964–1970, was based on lists of needs compiled throughout the country by party institutions. Economic analysis was lacking and most of the projects listed proved unfeasible. Neither the third *Plan Quinquennal* (1973–1978 [q.v.]), nor it successor the *Deuxième Quinquennal* (1981–1985) was overwhelmingly successful though they did attempt to involve both party institutions and obtain adequate technical advice.

In July 1985, the Conté (q.v.) government's national planning commission issued an outline of the strategy to be incorporated in the Plan Intérimaire de Redressement National (PIRN), the short-term economic plan covering the period 1985–1987. This plan stressed the role of rehabilitation and reorganization, rather than new investments. It assigned priority in general to projects that would provide an early return and to rural development, particularly food production, and infrastructure improvements. This detailed program and project preparation, as well as the system for plan implementation and control, were drawn up by Guinean officials with support from the World Bank, the French government, and the United Nations Development Program. There are indications that these internationally supported programs and projects have resulted in a better understanding of the country's needs and limitations. Another noticeable impact is the development of more efficient management systems throughout the country especially with government-sponsored programs. However, mismanagement of public funds and the overreliance of many programs on foreign funds and expertise are still major problems.

PLOTS. A special dimension of Guinea politics under Touré is what Guinean leaders referred to as the "permanent plot." According to this view, since independence in 1958 there was a permanent plot against the PDG-led (q.v.) government of Guinea. From the first alleged plot in April 1960, which was said to have been led by French troops, to the Portuguese invasion (q.v.) in November 1970, the Guinean regime expressed fear of "imperialist" and "neo-colonial" schemes to overthrow the government. Some of these fears may simply have been an attempt to mobilize mass support, but some fears might have been well founded. More than two million Guinea exiles live in neighboring countries and elsewhere.

POLITICAL PARTIES. Until War World II political activity in Guinea was largely confined to small groups concerned with local or self-interest issues. In late 1945 organizations made up of French and local African elites that had relations with parties in France and local organizations that were basically ethnic and regional dominated the scene. The affiliate of the French Socialist Party called the Démocratie Socialiste de Guinée (DSG [q.v.]) headed by Yaciné Diallo (q.v.) was one of the former and the latter included Comité de la Basse-Guinée (dominated by Susu [q.v.]), Amicale Gilbert Vieillard (largely Fulbé [q.v.]), Union du Manding (mostly Manikakan peoples from Upper Guinea [q.v.]), and Union Forestière (combining various ethnic groups from the Forest

Region [q.v.]). After independence only one party remained, the Parti Démocratique de Guinée (PDG-RDA [q.v.]). This party had replaced the others by building a base in labor unions (q.v.), youth groups, women's organizations, and even veterans groups and represented the whole territory of Guinea including the great "peasant" mass. The outspoken call for colonial reform which the PDG made throughout the 1950s gave it broad support which the other parties could not muster. This, coupled with a far greater skill at mobilizing all segments of the Guinean society and finally the decision to vote for independence from France on September 28, 1958, left it the only viable party on Independence Day, October 2, 1958. From 1989 through the elections of December 1993 political parties proliferated, though only a dozen or so had any real following.

POPULATION. An official government census in 1972 fixed Guinea's population at 5,143,284. United Nations figures and foreign governmental organizations placed the total between 4.1 million and 4.2 million in 1972. The larger figure would seem to include Guinean-born persons who were not actually residing in the country as of December 31, 1972. The best estimate in the early 1990s placed the figure at about 7.3 million.

PORTS. Only two international ports of entry exist in Guinea. The facilities at Conakry (q.v.), though poorly maintained and managed, are probably sufficient for the nation's present needs. The harbor itself is one of the best in West Africa but is badly subject to silting. One ore-loading dock maintained by foreign technicians functions quite well. A second subsidiary port has been developed at Kamsar (q.v.) in recent years to handle the export and import requirements of the Boké project (q.v.), a bauxite industrial unit. Smaller coastal ports, which once carried on some trade, are now of little importance.

PORTUGUESE. Portuguese merchants and explorers under Prince Henry the Navigator's sponsorship made the first European maritime contacts with Guinea. After reaching various African peoples to the north, the Portuguese established trading bases on the coast of Guinea from which coastal agents or *lancados* served as intermediaries in the Atlantic slave trade before the late sixteenth and seventeenth centuries. By the eighteenth century English and French competition had taken away most of this trade, though the Portuguese retained trade contact with some parts of the Guinea coast through a former Portuguese settlement on the Cape Verde Islands. Portuguese names, terms, clothing, and a syncretic form of Catholicism found among some Guineans in the Boké (q.v.) area and elsewhere attest to remainders of Portuguese influence even into the 1960s.

PORTUGUESE INVASION. A dozen or more plots and alleged attempts to overthrow the government of Guinea had been part of an atmosphere of perennial conspiracy from independence on. Beginning with the abortive November 1970 Portuguese invasion of Conakry, Sékou Touré's (q.v.) supporters ushered in a decade of massive arrest of Guineans of all backgrounds and conditions and more generalized repression. Guinea became a veritable police state.

POULAR. The language of the Fulbé (Fulani) (q.v.) people.

POUVOIR REVOLUTIONNAIRE LOCAL (PRL). Refers to the local organization of party and government officials who directed economic, political, social, and cultural affairs at the village level under President Touré (q.v.). He called the PRL real socialism because the power of decision over all services and goods was theoretically in the hands of the people at the local village level.

PRE, ROLAND-JOANES-LOUIS. French administrator from 1937 to 1939 in Guinea, Pré was secretary-general of the Federation of Buildings and Public Works, and from 1940 to 1942 the director of the Federation of Buildings and Public Works in France. During the Vichy period he was active in the resistance and was a strong supporter of de Gaulle after 1944. He was named governor of Gabon 1946–1947, of French Guinea 1948–1950, of Upper Volta 1952–1953, of

French Somalia 1954, and high commissioner of Cameroon, 1954.

PREFECTURE. Since 1984 the name used for administrative regions.

PRESS. Printed media in Guinea under the colonial regime were limited. At independence only a half-dozen newspapers and periodicals were published. Under Touré only the party daily, *Horoya* (q.v.), the party weekly, *Horoya-Hebdo,* and the government *Journal Officiel de la République de Guinée* appeared on anything approaching a regular basis. The Agence Guinéenne de Presse (AGP [q.v.]), Xinhua (People's Republic of Guinea), Tass, and Novosti Press Agency were the only press bureaus in operation under Touré by the early 1980s. Since April 3, 1984, other western press agencies have operated in Guinea from time to time and dozens of newspapers and journals are now published on a regular and irregular basis.

PROTESTANT MISSIONS. Protestant missionary activities in Guinea were rather limited even in colonial times. Today no more than 1,000 converts of a few American missionaries and a few Anglicans make up the entire Protestant community. The Church Mission Alliance operations in Guinea, which once included a boarding school for children of missionaries near Mamou and a vocational education center near Kissidougou (qq.v.), were terminated in the late 1960s. There are six Protestant mission centers active in Guinea at present. Four are British (Anglican) and two are affiliated with U. S. mission societies.

- Q -

QADIRIYYA. The dominant Muslim *tariq* (literally, way), sufi order, or brotherhood in Western Africa in the nineteenth century. In the fifteenth century it was the first such *tariq* to arrive in West Africa, having originated in Baghdad with Sidi Abd-el-Qadir el Jilal (1079–1166). It became popular in

West Africa after having been introduced by a Touatiy scholar, Mohammed ibn Abd el Karim el-Maghili and his disciple, Sidi Ahmed el Bakkai el Kunti. The Qadiriyya remains important among the Muslim elite in Touba, the Futa Jalon, and Kankan (qq.v.).

QUELAN BIRDS (*Quelea quelea*). These birds pose a major problem to the subsistence farmers of Guinea. There are millions of them, and they consume much of the cereal crop each year.

QUININE. A drug obtained from the bark of the cinchona tree. Once a relatively important substance for the suppression of malarial attacks, the production of quinine in the Forest Region (q.v.) of Guinea is now practically abandoned.

QUINZAINES ARTISTIQUES. An annual arts festival lasting two weeks, which, since its founding in 1964, the PDG (q.v.) used in an attempt to develop a unified national cultural heritage as part of national development. Theater, traditional music, modern music, painting and decorative design, and folklore supported by party institutions from all over Guinea were judged on the basis of their contribution to party ideology and artistic excellence. After 1969, the festival attracted increasing numbers of foreign delegations. In 1973 the competitions were observed by delegates from Liberia, Gambia, Zaïre, and many Eastern-bloc countries. After 1979, the Festival National des Arts et de la Culture declined in international importance as Guinea became an increasingly closed society under Touré. After his death in 1984 and the abolition of the one-party system, Quinzaines Artistiques and most other party-sponsored cultural programs disappeared from Guinean public life.

- R -

RAILROADS. The railway line linking Conakry with Kankan is badly in need of upgrading beyond Kindia (qq.v.). The line to the bauxite works in Fria (qq.v.) is in reasonable repair.

The 135-kilometer (84-mile) line which links the Boké bauxite deposits with the new deep-water port at Kamsar (qq.v.) has an excellent heavy gauge roadbed and should prove quite durable. The projected 1,200-kilometer (800-mile) Conakry-Mount Nimba (qq.v.) railroad for iron ore export seems unlikely to be built in the near future. The only railway lines actually functioning in Guinea today are those owned by the mining companies. The Conakry-Kankan line has ceased functioning. See OFFICE NATIONAL DES CHEMINS DE FER DE GUINEE.

RAINY SEASON. See HIVERNAGE.

RASSEMBLEMENT DEMOCRATIQUE AFRICAIN (RDA). The first inter-territorial political party in the sub-Saharan territories of France, it served as an umbrella organization for all the African political parties struggling against French colonialism. Founded in Bamako, Sudan (present-day Mali), by Félix Houphouët-Boigny and his associates in October 1946, the party was allied with the French Communist Party from 1946 to 1955. The RDA manifesto demanded the constitutional confirmation of the rights of all people in the French overseas possessions. It also called for the peaceful, parliamentary elimination of colonialism throughout the world. Originally part of the RDA, the Parti Démocratique de Guinée (PDG [q.v.]) completely severed its ties with the parent organization in the late 1960s. The process of estrangement began with Guinea's 1958 rejection of the Constitution of the Fifth French Republic (q.v.) and went against the idea of a closer union with France which many RDA leaders had adopted as expedient.

RASSEMBLEMENT DU PEUPLE GUINEEN (RPG). See CONDE, ALPHA.

RAY, AUTRA (Mamadou Traoré). A teacher, graduated from the William Ponty School (q.v.), he was very active in the early Parti Démocratique de Guinée (PDG [q.v.]) politics in Conakry, Mamou, and Nzérékoré (qq.v.). As one of the major writers in the first journals of the PDG he was very critical of the colonial system and adopted the pen name "Ray Autra." With other teachers and bureaucrats, he contributed to making the PDG section of Mamou the most radical one in the 1950s. After 1960, he denounced the PDG leadership for its lack of democracy and its "bourgeois" tendencies. Jailed with the other leaders of the teacher's union in 1962, he lived in exile in Dakar, Senegal from 1978 to 1984. He died in Abidjan, Côte d'Ivoire in 1991.

RECHERCHES AFRICAINES. A quarterly journal of the Institute National de Recherches et de Documentation (q.v.). This "in-house" publication offers a means for the organization's small research staff and the few other Guineans engaged in social and natural science research in Guinea to publish their works. It is a successor to *Etudes Guinéennes* (q.v.).

REFUGEES. The increasingly repressive measures adopted by the government of Guinea in the 1970s continued to swell the ranks of those who had already left the country for political and economic reasons in the 1960s. There were more than one million persons of Guinean origin living in exile by 1984. (Some sources suggest figures as high as two million.) A great majority of these people were living in the countries immediately bordering Guinea. But substantial numbers, especially those with higher education and skills, could be found in France and elsewhere outside of Africa. Several opposition movements, including the Front pour la Libération Nationale de Guinée (FLNG) and the Regroupement de Guinéens à l'Etranger (RGE) existed among the exiled Guineans, but none of them posed much real threat to the Sékou Touré (q.v.) regime. Since April 1984, some of these refugees have been returning to Guinea. The civil war in Liberia and the violence in Sierra Leone have created other refugees, thousands of whom are now residing in Guinea.

REGIONAL ADMINISTRATION. Guinea under Touré (q.v.) was divided into 30 administrative regions. Each of these regions was under the authority of a governor appointed by the president. Each governor had three secretaries general:

one for economic affairs, one for social affairs, and one for fiscal control. In theory each of these administrative regions had a party-elected council which approved the regional budget. It would appear that this regional level of government was where most central governmental controls were exercised and most services dispensed. In 1984 administrative regions were renamed *préfectures.*

RICE *(Oryza glabberima* or *Oryza sativa).* This is the most important cereal grain grown in Guinea. In Upper Guinea (q.v.) *Oryza glabberima* probably evolved from a native species called *Oryza barthii.* Today, an Asiatic type, *Oryza sativa,* is grown very widely. An annual plant of the grass family, it is a good producer, especially in the paddy variety, but Guinea continues to suffer from a chronic shortage of this important food crop. With little use of large scale irrigation and either animal or mechanical traction, none of the ricelands of Guinea produce to their full potential.

RIO NUNEZ. A short river in northeastern Guinea flowing past Boké (q.v.) into a large estuary from which ivory and slaves were shipped by the Portuguese (qq.v.) in the 1500s. French ships bombarded Boké, the Landoma (q.v.) center, in 1849 and forced local acceptance of French sovereignty. Slaving continued on this navigable river into the 1840s.

RIVER BLINDNESS. See ONCHOCERCIASIS.

RIVIERES DU SUD. Initially all French settlements in West Africa were under the authority of Senegal, but in 1845 French possessions were divided into Senegal (having its administrative center in Saint-Louis), and Rivières du Sud, with headquarters on Gorée Island. From there a naval commander-in-chief had authority over all French centers (at that time coastal only in nature) south to Gabon. From 1859 to 1882 Senegal assumed direct administrative control over the Rivières du Sud colony, and in 1882 the Rivières du Sud again became a separate political unit with a lieutenant governor subordinate to the governor of Senegal. In 1889 the lieutenant governor was granted a separate budget and staff (located in Conakry) with direct access to the government in Paris. At that time Dahomey (Benin), Côte d'Ivoire, and the Futa Jalon (q.v.) protectorate were part of the colony. In 1891 an independent governor was authorized and the colony was renamed French Guinea and the Dependencies. Dahomey (Benin) and Côte d'Ivoire were separated from Guinea in 1893.

ROADS. Like most West African countries, Guinea has a rather incomplete road system. There are more than 30,000 kilometers (19,800 miles) of roads and tracks in the country but less than 14,000 kilometers (9,500 miles) of them are passable by regular vehicular traffic at all seasons. Only about 1,000 kilometers (700 miles) of road are hard surfaced and even these are not always in good repair. Motor vehicles are relatively few in number and often in poor repair throughout Guinea, because of initial cost and poor maintenance facilities.

- S -

SABOUYA. A state-run retail general store in Conakry (q.v.). See NAFAYA.

SACKO, BIRAM. Writer very involved in journalism in Conakry (q.v.) in 1993. He wrote the novel *Dalanda* (1975).

SAGNO, MAMADI. A teacher in Nzérékoré (q.v.) who served as federal secretary of the Parti Démocratique de Guinée (PDG [q.v.]), as governor successively of Nzérékoré, Conakry, and Kankan (qq.v.), and as minister of defense and minister of education. He was arrested in 1971 and died in detention in Conakry.

SAHEL. The border of the Sahara Desert. The Sahel, properly speaking, does not include Guinea, but those areas with fewer than 500 mm (20 inches) of rain annually, northeast of Siguiri (q.v.) are generally included in the region.

SAINKOUN, MARIUS. A supporter of David Soumah in founding the Confédération Française des Travailleurs Chrétiens (CFTC) developed to compete with the Marxist Confédération Générale du Travail (CGT) with which Sékou Touré (qq.v.) was affiliated.

SAKO, LANSANA. Born in Kankan (q.v.) in 1939, he studied in France and graduated from Columbia University in New York. As a civil administrator he specialized in finance and was the executive director of the office of prime minister in the 1970s. He served as ambassador to West Germany from 1979–1984 and was advisor at the ministry of mining in 1993.

SALIFOU, DINAH. King of the Nalou (q.v.) in 1887, he was considered to be a "friend of the French" and invited to the Exposition of 1889 held in Paris. Arrested by the French "commandant" of Boké (q.v.) in November 1890 for what was termed "insubordination," and exiled to Senegal, he died in 1897.

SAMBEGU, IBRAHIMA. Better known as Karamoko Alfa, this Muslim cleric launched a multi-ethnic *jihad* (q.v.) in the Futa Jalon (q.v.) in 1725 against rulers whom he considered to be incompletely Muslim. He died in 1751 but the *jihad* continued under the military leadership of his cousin Ibrahima Sori (q.v.) and one of his descendants as almamy (q.v.). See ALFAYA; SORIYA.

SANGARE, KADER. Son of Toumany Sangaré (q.v.), he graduated from the University of Conakry and was a civil administrator in finances. He was jailed along with his father, his mother, and an uncle, Nfaly Sangaré (q.v.), in 1984. He has very popular among Guinean youth because of his support of soccer teams, especially the Hoffiya Club of Conakry (q.v.). Elected mayor of Kankan (q.v.) in 1990, he was appointed governor of Upper Guinea (q.v.) in 1992. In December 1992 he became the adviser to the minister of internal affairs.

SANGARE, NFALY. Born in Kankan (q.v.) in 1935, this graduate of the Paris law school was Toumany Sangaré's brother
(q.v.) and married to Sékou Touré's (q.v.) sister-in-law.
Sangaré was the governor of the Guinean central bank for
many years before becoming the ambassador to the European Community (EC) in Brussels. From 1980 to 1985 he
held a position with the International Monetary Fund (IMF)
in Washington, D.C. He was arrested with his nephew Kadar
Sangaré (q.v.) and brother Toumany Sangaré on April 3,
1984. Released with the help of IMF, he lives in exile in
Dakar, Senegal.

SANGARE, TOUMANY. Born in Kankan (q.v.) about 1930, he
was a teacher who graduated from the William Ponty School
(q.v.). A key figure in the establishment of the Parti
Démocratique de Guinée (PDG) in Guéckédou in the Forest
Region (qq.v.), he was a member of the Guinean territorial
assembly and the PDG central committee. He was a popular
and successful organizer, builder, and administrator and held
many key ministerial positions in the 1960s and 1970s. He
was arrested on April 3, 1984 and released a few months
later only to be arrested again and executed in Kindia (q.v.)
in July 1985.

SANGAREDI. The site of one of Guinea's five or six major
exploitable bauxite (q.v.) mines. Mining operations began at
this location on the Kogon River in the Boké region in
August 1973. The government of Guinea hoped to export
nine million tons of bauxite a year from this location when
full production was reached. This goal has yet to be reached.

SANKARAN. A Maninka region in Upper Guinea to the west of
Kankan (qq.v.) which was very important in nineteenth-
century politics. The musical tradition of the region is
particularly rich.

SANO, MAMBA (ca.1905–1985). Born in Kissidougou (q.v.), he
graduated from the William Ponty School (q.v.) and became
a school teacher. Elected *député* to the French National

Assembly in 1946 with Yaciné Diallo (q.v.), he was defeated in 1956.

SATIYO-TIYO. Village head, a Maninka (q.v.) title which literally means owner of the land. This man was normally the eldest member of a lineage recognized as having titular rights to this office.

SAVANE, MORIKANDIAN. An administrative clerk who served Sékou Touré as governor of Macenta (qq.v.), director of information services, and minister of transport. He was arrested in Conakry in 1971 and died in detention.

SAVANNA. A tropical grassland region where rainfall is seasonal and there is one long, dry season. A number of grasses form the main vegetation along with trees and shrubs that vary in kind and number according to the climate and soil. The Guinea savanna ranges from the rain forest along the coast and the forest region to the northwest borders with Mali and Senegal where only scattered baobab (*Adansonia digitata* [q.v.]) and acacia (*Acacia senegal* [q.v.]) trees break up the carpet of grass (*Cherchrus biflorous*).

SECTION FRANCAISE DE L'INTERNATIONALE OUVRIERE (SFIO). This French socialist group gave considerable support to African politicians in the early 1940s. This support was never as important in Guinea as it was in neighboring Senegal.

SENEGAL COMPANY. A short-lived, but important commercial company established by the French in 1672. In 1677 a French fleet captured Gorée, an island just off Cape Verde in Senegal, from the Dutch. Using this as the main base of operations, the company, in conjunction with French naval vessels, harassed the shipping of the British Royal African Company. The company established some posts south toward Guinea but war in 1689 caused it to give up its monopoly, first to the Guinea Company and finally in 1696 to the Royal Senegal Company.

SHEA-BUTTER TREES (*Butyrospermum parkii*). A semi-cultivated tree which grows in the Upper Guinea savanna (qq.v.). The shea tree produces a large, white kernel which is rich in oil, or shea butter. When palm and peanut (groundnut) oil are lacking or too expensive, shea butter is used throughout Upper Guinea (q.v.) for cooking, making candles, ointments, and soap.

SHOPKEEPERS' PLOT (Traders' Plot). One of some dozen or so alleged attempts to overthrow the Touré (q.v.) government. Plots such as this, whether real or imaginary, were used as occasions for arousing the patriotism of the Guineans masses in support of the regime. In this particular case merchant groups who were unhappy with trade restrictions and nationalization of retail and wholesale trade were accused in 1965 of seeking to replace President Touré's government with a French-oriented one. Some external support from French commercial and governmental interests may possibly have been involved.

SIDIBE, BANAH. Born in Kankan (q.v.) in 1938, he studied architecture in France and Italy and became a member of the School of Architecture of Dakar, Senegal. An active member of the radical wing of the student and opposition movement he became minister of housing and urbanism from 1988 to 1992 in the government of President Lansana Conté (q.v.).

SIDIME, LAMINE. Born in Mamou of Maninka (q.v.) parents, he was a jurist "agrégé," and professor of law at the University of Dakar until he returned to Guinea in 1988. A key legal adviser to President Lansana Conté (q.v.), he was technical director of the constitutional committee that drafted the *loi fondamentale* (q.v.). He was a prominent member of the Comité Transitoire de Redressement National (CTRN [q.v.]) and was appointed chief judge of the Guinean Supreme Court in 1992.

SIFFRAY, FRANCOIS JOSEPH. French engineer who directed part of the construction of the Conakry-Niger Railroad in 1907 and 1908.

SIGUIRI. A town and *préfecture* in Upper Guinea (q.v) on the border with Mali. Bordering on the regions of Kankan, Kouroussa, and Dinguiraye (qq.v.), this area was historically an important gold-producing center. The French colonial regime planned to use the extensive Upper Niger plains in the Siguiri region as a major rice-producing area but since independence such plans have languished.

SIMANDOU MOUNTAINS. A range of mountains running north and south between Beyla and Kérouané (qq.v.) in the southeastern Guinea highlands. These mountains contain major deposits of magnetite, a rich iron ore which may eventually make Guinea a leading exporter of iron ore if transportation and capital costs can be met.

SLAVE TRADE. Domestic servitude was an indigenous institution among most peoples of Guinea. It was converted by the Atlantic slave trade into a much larger and mutually profitable business for some Africans and Europeans. The Portuguese (q.v.) in their earliest voyages captured slaves, but not until the plantation economies of the Western Hemisphere developed in the sixteenth century did the slave trade achieve major importance. The earliest English and French traders to Guinea were not interested in slaves, but in the eighteenth century fairly large numbers of slaves were shipped from areas on the Guinea coast. British abolition in 1807 dealt a major blow to the Atlantic slave trade, though some slave ships called in the area for the next 20 years. The British presence at Victoria and the Iles de Los (q.v.) was part of the British anti-slavery movement in the early nineteenth century, which declined after 1850. Domestic servitude of various forms continued in Guinea until well into the twentieth century.

SMUGGLING. Under Touré the Guinean currency (qq.v.) was nonconvertible. The regime set fixed prices on agricultural goods and basic necessities were often unavailable; therefore, smuggling constituted a continual problem after independence. Agricultural products produced in Guinea were sold in Mali, Senegal, Liberia, Sierra Leone, and Côte d'Ivoire for reasonably high prices in convertible currency. Consumer goods were in turn smuggled in to be sold at high profits which in turn were used to buy more agricultural goods. Guinea's long, permeable borders thwarted governmental attempts to stop such clandestine traffic. Since 1984 the situation has improved, and some agricultural goods from Sierra Leone are now smuggled into Guinea for higher "free" market prices.

SOCIETE AFRICAINE DES PECHES MARITIMES (Afrimar). A mixed enterprise fishing venture begun in 1973. KLM, a Dutch airline, furnished the capital for this venture and retained 51 percent ownership while taking 35 percent of the profits. The Guinean government held 49 percent of ownership and took 65 percent of the profits. This company was managed by a United States fishing firm.

SOCIETE COMMERCIALE DE L'OUEST AFRICAIN (SCOA). One of the most important of the foreign firms which dominated commercial life in Guinea during colonial rule. Firms like this one largely controlled the import-export trade and wholesale trade of the colonies. This company was largely Swiss owned. Since 1984, this company has been reestablished in Guinea (see COMPAGNIE FRANCAISE DE L'AFRIQUE OCCIDENTALE).

SOCIETE DES PECHES DU KAMSAR (SOPEKAM). A U.S.-Guinean joint venture fishing company established in 1985. Having begun operation in 1987, SOPEKAM concentrates mainly on catching shrimp, lobster, and shark for the export market and supplying some fish for the Guinean market.

SOCIETE DES PECHES INDUSTRIELLES DU KALOUM (PECHIKA). The Guinean government entered into a 25-year agreement in April 1985 that established a Franco-Guinean fishing venture. The new company is owned 51 percent by the Guinean government, with Euratec, a French engineering company, owning 49 percent. The agreement provided that eventually the partners will reduce their share to 40 percent each, with the remaining 20 percent being owned by private Guinean interests. PECHIKA plans to eventually produce 25,000 metric tons of fish for the domestic market and 15,000 metric tons for export. The short-term plan called for the company to acquire a fleet of six 35-meter (100-foot) trawlers, involving an investment of about $12 million, and to catch about 10,000 metric tons a year. Ultimately the fleet is to have some 25 vessels. The initial six vessels were due to be delivered in mid-1986, but operations were instead started on a limited basis using rented trawlers.

SOCIETE GUINEENNE DE PETROLE (SOGUIP). A joint enterprise created in June 1974 with the American oil company, Buttes Resources International, which was to prospect for oil in a 44,000-square-kilometer (17,000-square-mile) area of the Guinean offshore continental shelf. The Guinean government held 49 percent of the shares and the American firm held 51 percent while Guinea was to receive 63 percent of the eventual oil profits.

SOCIETE GUINEO-KOWEITIENNE DE PECHE (SOU-GUIKOP). A mixed enterprise fishing venture started in 1973 with two trawlers. The Guinean government received 49 percent ownership and 65 percent of the profits in return for fishing rights in its coastal waters. The government of Kuwait furnished the capital in return for 51 percent ownership. See SOCIETE NIPPO-GUINEENNE DE PECHE.

SOCIETE INDUSTRIELLE ET AUTOMOBILE DE GUINEE (SIAG). One of the French trading firms which literally controlled Guinean commercial life during colonial times. Specializing in Renault cars and trucks, SIAG had a large operation in Kankan (q.v.) where many Renault models were tried and adapted to the African environment before being sold.

SOCIETE NATIONALE D'ASSURANCE (SNA). One of the many national financial institutions created after independence to replace the French-controlled institutions which existed in colonial times. This national insurance enterprise became the sole insurance-granting institution in independent Guinea.

SOCIETE NIPPO-GUINEENNE DE PECHE (SONIGUE). Another mixed enterprise fishing venture which operated prospecting boats, two fishing boats, and a refrigerator ship. The Guinean government received 49 percent ownership and 65 percent of the profits in return for fishing rights in its coastal waters. Japanese capital supplied the ships and technical management. See SOCIETE GUINEO-KOWEITIENNE DE PECHE.

SOCIETE NOUVELLE D'ASSURANCE ET DE RE-ASSURANCES DE GUINEE (SONAG). This is one of the two major insurance companies (see UNION GUINEENNE D'ASSURANCE ET DE RE-ASSURANCE, UGAR) that have replaced the failing national company of Touré's era. SONAG is affiliated with a French company.

SOCIETES INDIGENES DE PREVOYANCE (SIP). Pseudo-cooperatives organized by the French government in the 1930s as a means of improving agricultural productivity. The full title of these "cooperatives"—Sociétés Indigènes de Prévoyances de Secours et des Prêts Mutuels Agricoles—more clearly reveals their intent. They were governmental commodity credit associations with little if any cooperative aspects.

SOFA. A Maninka word meaning "guardian of the horses" and infantrymen with firearms in the regular army of Samory Touré (q.v.).

SONGHAY. An empire that had origins along the banks of the Niger with Gao near the present-day Malian city of the same name. It first existed as state from the ninth through the fifteenth centuries. Songhay became a de facto vassal state of Mali (q.v.) in the early fourteenth century. From 1335, when Sonni (meaning "savior") Ali Kolon became king, to 1492, when Sonni Bakari was overthrown by Askia Mohammed Touré, there were 20 Sonni kings. By far the most important was the next to the last, Sonni Ali Ber, who ruled from 1456 to 1492. He transformed Songhay from a small riverine state to an empire which included parts of the Mali

Empire. Eleven *askias* ruled Songhay from Askia Mohammed's accession to power in 1492 until the Moroccans
invaded Songhay in 1591. The empire reached its greatest
extent under Askia Daoud (1549–1583) and at that time had
an influence on affairs of present-day Guinea.

SONINKE (Sarakolé). The ethnic group which constituted the
basic population of the ancient empire of Ghana. Many
devout Maninka-speaking Muslim scholarly lineages in
Guinea claim to be descended by Soninké ancestors. In
Upper Guinea (q.v.), the term applies primarily to non-
Muslin Maninka (q.v.) people.

SORGHUM (varieties of *Sorghum vulgare*). This cereal grain
plant, also called giant millet, Guinea corn, or durra, is an
important human food crop in Guinea. Almost impervious to
disease and insects, it is planted with the earliest rains and
harvested before the rice in the "hungry period" of the year.

SORI, IBRAHIMA. This secular military leader succeeded Karamoko Alfa (Ibrahima Sambegu [q.v.]) as leader of the Fulbé
Islamic state in the Futa Jalon (qq.v.) about 1751. Ibrahima
Barry (his given name, Sori, "early riser," simply refers to
his habit of conducting most of his military operations
before dawn) managed to establish Fulbé control firmly over
the Futa and some surrounding territories by the late 1770s.
When he died in 1784 the clerical supporters of Karamoko
Alfa (whose given name was also Barry), the Alfaya (q.v.)
and the military party, the Soriya (q.v.) which supported
Ibrahima Sori's descendants, kept the Futa divided in civil
war until the French occupation in 1897.

SORIYA. After the death of the successful *jihad* leader, Karamoko Alfa, in the mid-eighteenth century Futa Jalon (qq.v.)
two rival factions developed. The military party favored the
descendants of the war leader Ibrahima Sori (q.v.). This
group was called the Soriya. The clerical supporters of the
family of Ibrahim Musa were called Alfaya (q.v.). These two
groups contended for the position of almamy (q.v.) in the

Futa Jalon until well into the twentieth century, though succession was in theory fixed by the French after 1897.

SOUMAH, DAVID. The leader of the Guinean branch of the Confédération Française de Travailleurs Chrétiens (CFTC) which the Catholic Bishop Raymond Lerouge (qq.v.) had reluctantly allowed to be established in 1946. The CFTC was formed in opposition to the Marxist Confédération Générale du Travail (CGT), with which Sékou Touré (qq.v.) was associated.

SOUS-PREFECTURE. Since 1984 the name used for *arrondissement* (q.v.).

SOW, OUSMANE. Colonel Sow was a founding member of the Comité Militaire de Redressement National (CMRN [q.v.]) and an important figure in Lansana Conté's (q.v.) first government. During his tenure on the CMRN he held several key positions including minister of defense and army chief of staff. Sow played a decisive role in July 1985 while President Conté was out of the country during the alleged coup attempt by Diarra Traoré (q.v.). He was later compelled to retire.

SUDAN. The Bilad as-Sudan of Arab writers literally means "land of the blacks." This term has generally been applied to the vast area of the savanna (q.v.) stretching from the Atlantic to the Red Sea between the Sahara Desert and the tropical rain forest to the south, but more especially that part west of Lake Chad where Islam (q.v.) and large-scale states were long known to writers in Arabia. Much of Upper Guinea (q.v.) is part of the western Sudanic world.

SUJETS INDIGENES. So-called "native subjects" in colonial times. This status denied Africans the right to vote, made them subject to disciplinary measures without trial for "disrespect" or refusal to perform minimal tasks for white administrators. All but a very few Africans remained in this status during French colonial rule. See ASSIMILES; EVOLUES; INDIGENAT.

SUNDIATA KEITA. See KEITA, SUNDIATA.

SUSU (also spelled Sosso or Sousou). A Mandé-speaking people whose culture has gradually supplanted those of other ethnic groups in the coastal areas of Guinea in the past 300 years. Susu is now the lingua franca of most residents of Lower Guinea (q.v.). The Susu, who are still predominantly cultivators and traders, probably originated in the savanna of present-day Mali and Upper Guinea (qq.v.). The Susu are now one of the three major ethnic groups in Guinea. Also the name of the powerful kingdom that had emerged upon the disintegration of the Ghana Empire. The Susu leader, Sumanguru Kanté (q.v.), was defeated by Sundiata Keita (q.v.), the founder of the Mali Empire (q.v.) in 1235.

SYLI. The name means elephant in Susu (q.v.) and was the official party emblem of the PDG and became the nickname of Sékou Touré (qq.v.). This name was given to the basic unit of Guinean currency (q.v.) from October 2, 1972 until January 20, 1986. One syli was originally equivalent to ten of the then existing Guinean francs and was made up of 100 couris (cowries). With an original official rate of 20.46 sylis to one U.S. dollar, the clandestine rate of exchange approached 180 per dollar in the mid-1970s. After January 20, 1985, the new Guinean franc (GF) replaced the syli.

SYLIART. A civil society created by the government of Guinea in July 1971 to subsidize and regulate the works of authors and producers in the Republic of Guinea. Granted a capital of two million Guinean francs, this society was to operate on revenue derived from authorship rights, receipts from productions, artistic and cultural shows, and state grants. It was also to provide pensions for retired artists. In May 1973 Syliart was replaced by the Agence Guinéenne de Spectacles (q.v.), a public institution under the Ministry of Youth, Arts, and Sports.

- T -

TALL, AL HAJJ UMAR (1794–1864). Founder of the Tukulor Empire, he was a Muslim cleric who led a series of religious wars (*jihad* [q.v.]) against the traditional nobility of the Senegal-Niger region, and the French, and established Qadiriyya (q.v.) theocracies. His conquests spread the Tijaniyya (q.v.) Sufi order more widely in the western Sudan (q.v.). Born at Halwar in the Futa Toro of present-day Senegal, by 1825 he was widely respected as a learned cleric. In 1826 he traveled overland to Mecca, spending seven months with Mohammed Bello, the *khalifa* of Sokoto among the Hausa. Invested in Mecca by Mohammed el Ghali Abu Talif as *khalifa* of the Tijaniyya for the western Sudan, he returned to West Africa by way of Sokoto where he remained for seven years and married one of Bello's daughters. Returning to the Niger-Senegal area with many followers he established a religious and military base. In 1846 he began touring the Futa Jalon (q.v.) and Futa Toro, preaching and gathering followers. Breaking with the almamy (q.v.) of the Futa Jalon he fled on a *hijra* (a pre-*jihad* retreat) to Dinguiraye (q.v.) in present-day Guinea. In 1852 he launched the *jihad* against the "pagan" Bambara kings of Ségou and Kaarta and by 1863 he controlled the territory from the upper Senegal River to Timbuctoo. French opposition and internal dissension kept him from creating a permanent Muslim state at the Niger-Senegal headwaters. After his death in 1864 the empire that Umar had left broke up into numerous small states with only tenuous allegiance to his son, Amadou Tall.

TAMARIND (*Tamarindus indica*). A valuable food crop of the pea family grown in Upper Guinea (q.v.). The fruit or pod of this plant has an acid pulp used as food, as a laxative, for flavoring drinks, and as an antidote for fever. Ashes from its wood and pulp are used for tanning and dyeing goat skin. In some areas of West Africa the tree is a host for nests of wild silkworms and whole silk was once spun into thread to make cloth.

TARIQ. Literally, the "way." A group of individuals who subscribe to a common Muslim philosophy and ritual. The two most celebrated in Western Africa were the Qadiriyya and the Tijaniyya (qq.v.). The latter, founded in 1781, was a far more proselytizing group which called forth more active application of Muslim principles and hence helped mobilize large numbers of followers in Upper Guinea (q.v.) in the nineteenth century.

TATA. Garrisoned forts, traditionally built by Maninka rulers adopted by others during the slave trade and the nineteenth-century *jihads* (qq.v.). The earthen walls usually surround an inner enclosure made of sun-baked brick walls more than one meter (three feet) thick. Tatas were very effective against traditional cavalry and even cannons, but when exploding mortars were introduced in the latter part of the nineteenth century, they fell easily. The remains of some built by Samory Touré in Upper Guinea (qq.v.) can still be traced.

TCHIDIMBO, RAYMOND. The Roman Catholic archbishop of Conakry (q.v.) since 1961 when the French archbishop was expelled. Tchidimbo's mother was Guinean, while his father was Gabonese. Tchidimbo was accused of involvement in the coup of November 22, 1970, against Sekou Touré (q.v.) and condemned to life in prison. He was later released as a human rights goodwill gesture under Amnesty International and Vatican pressure. See PLOTS.

TEACHERS' PLOTS. An alleged plot against the government announced by Guinean leaders in November 1961. Basically teachers were complaining about working conditions, but some of the documents presented by the pupils demonstrating in support of the teachers contained left-wing ideological criticisms of the government. Among these statements were those suggesting that Guinea had to choose between Eastern-bloc and Western-bloc support. Touré ordered the expulsion of the then Soviet ambassador suggesting that the ambassador was supporting teachers' demands that the Guinean government become a member of the Eastern bloc. The Soviet role in the strike has never been verified but five members of the teachers' union were executed and others fled or were imprisoned. See PLOTS.

TELECOMMUNICATIONS. In 1971 there were about 7,000 telephones in the country but upkeep of lines was poor.

Telegraphy linkages between regional capitals were also erratic since communications personnel often were forced to leave their work to search for food and other necessities due to the chaotic state of commercial distribution networks throughout the country. In February 1974 the African Development Bank granted Guinea a loan equivalent of $4.8 million to upgrade telecommunications throughout the country according to a plan drafted with the help of the International Telecommunications Union. The project included installation of microwave relays south toward Sierra Leone and throughout the country. This plan also provided for the expansion of the automatic telephone exchanges of Conakry, Kankan (qq.v.), Kassa, and Sonfonya. Progress on the projects has been very slow. As late as 1985 little improvement could be noted with the exception of the Kindia-Labé and Conakry-Boké-Gaoual-Koundar (qq.v.) radio-links.

TELIMELE. A *préfecture* and town between Pita and Boké on the western slopes of the Futa Jalon. The town of Telimélé had been a small village in 1959 but by 1967 had grown to 12,000 as a *préfecture* capital. With cattle raising as its major industry the region is of relatively little economic importance.

TELLI, BOUBACAR DIALLO. See DIALLO, BOUBACAR TELLI.

TENDA (also Tanda). A cluster of ethnic groups (numbering about 30,000 people today) including the modern Bassari and Konagi (qq.v.) living in northern Guinea and neighboring Senegal and Guinea-Bissau. Once they were fairly widespread throughout southeastern Senegal but were raided as slaves (q.v.) by their more powerful neighbors from the fourteenth century on, particularly by Muslim rulers of the Futa Jalon (q.v.) in the eighteenth and nineteenth centuries. They took refuge in the hills and mesas of north central Guinea, Guinea-Bissau, and southeastern Senegal.

TIJANIYYA. A Muslim *tariq* (q.v.) or voluntary brotherhood, founded in the late eighteenth century in North Africa. A far more popular and active form of Islam (q.v.), it generated large followings in the nineteenth century and formed the ideological basis of Al Hajj Umar's (q.v.) theocratic state in the 1850s.

TIMBER. Less than four percent of Guinea is covered with valuable woodlands, and species like teak and ebony have almost totally disappeared. Without massive replanting and careful management it is unlikely that Guinea will ever produce very much timber.

TIMBO. The historical capital of the Fulbé state in the Futa Jalon (qq.v.). Located between Mamou and Dabola (qq.v.) today it is a *sous-préfecture* of Mamou.

TINKISSO RIVER. Rising in the Futa Jalon between Dabola and Mamou this river is one of Guinea's main tributaries of the Niger River (qq.v.). It flows into the Niger at Siguiri (q.v.). It is a potential source of much hydroelectric (q.v.) power and its lower flood plains could become a major source of rice (q.v.) if flood control and irrigation projects begun by the French in the colonial period are ever realized.

TIRAILLEURS. Local troops often recruited in the areas of present-day Mali and Senegal, used by the French during the colonial period.

TOBACCO (*Nicotiana tobacum*). Successive development plans have sought to achieve self-sufficiency in tobacco which is grown widely as a subsistence crop throughout much of Guinea. Before independence there was a private French tobacco estate near Nzérékoré and the French tobacco monopoly had a tenant estate near Beyla (qq.v.). To supply the cigarette factory built by the People's Republic of China (q.v.) at Wassa-Wassa in 1966, tobacco continues to be imported since Guinean production has diminished to practically nothing since independence.

TOMA (Loma). An ethnic group living to the east of the Kissi in the Macenta (qq.v.) administrative region. Unrelated to their Kissi neighbors, they probably represent an early incursion of savanna peoples into the forest zone some 500 years ago. In Guinea they are gradually being assimilated into larger Maninka (q.v.) populations.

TORON. A region of Upper Guinea (q.v.) located southeast of Kankan (q.v.).

TOUGUE. A town and *préfecture* in the Futa Jalon between Dinguiraye and Labé (qq.v.) on the border of the Republic of Mali. The region has some bauxite deposits and 28 square kilometers (11 square miles) of plains suitable for mechanized rice (qq.v.) cultivation. Currently it remains a relatively non-urban and non-industrialized region.

TOUNKARA, TIBOU. An inspector of primary education, Tounkara served as ambassador to France and Senegal, minister successively of national education, of information, and of agriculture, and minister-delegate of the Forest Region (q.v.). He was arrested in Conakry in 1971 at approximately 45 years of age. Detained in Kindia (q.v.) without benefit of a trial, he died in prison.

TOURE. A Soninka (Sarakolé [q.v.]) Muslim patronym very common in West Africa primarily among people of Maninka (q.v.) ancestry. The founder of the Askiya dynasty in Songhay, Askiya Mohammed I, who ruled from 1492 to 1528, was a Touré.

TOURE, DR. EL-HADJI ABDOULAYA. Born in Kankan (q.v) about 1920, he was the grandson of Samory Touré (q.v.) and graduated from the William Ponty School (q.v.). He served as a physician in Sudan (Mali) and Kankan in the 1950s. He was active in the Parti Démocratique de Guinée (PDG [q.v.]) in Kankan and served as ambassador to Mali and to the United Nations in the 1960s. He held many ministerial positions including that of foreign affairs during the last years of Sékou Touré's (q.v.) regime. He was arrested on April 3, 1984, and executed in Kindia (q.v.) in July 1985.

TOURE, AHMED SEKOU. The president of the Republic of Guinea from 1958 to 1984. Sékou Touré was born on January 9, 1922, at Faranah (q.v.). Expelled from George Poiret Teacher's College after one year in 1937, Touré became involved in union activities while serving as a clerk, first with the Niger Français, then with the post office and finally with the treasury department. After having taken part in the organization of the Rassemblement Démocratique Africain (RDA [q.v.]) in Bamako in 1946 he continued his trade union (q.v.) activities rising to importance not only in Guinea but throughout French West Africa (AOF [q.v.]).

In 1952 Touré become secretary general of the Guinea branch of the RDA, was elected to the Territorial Assembly of Guinea, and became mayor of Conakry (q.v.) in 1957. In March 1957 he became vice-president of the Government Council of Guinea. By September 1957 the debates over the disintegration of French West Africa led to disagreements with some RDA members and by September 28, 1958, only Guinea, under Touré's leadership, voted no to de Gaulle's (q.v.) referendum on the Constitution of the Fifth Republic of France (q.v.).

Touré remained in office, in spite of attempted and alleged coups (q.v.), through repression and manipulation. Plots (q.v.) and counterplots became the hallmarks of his regime. Internally, smuggling (q.v.), profiteering, and corruption were a constant challenge to the success of Touré's regime while a certain paranoia always plagued its international relations. He ruled through the Parti Démocratique de Guinée (PDG) in what became a *parti-état* (qq.v.).

A plot in January 1960 in which more than a dozen death sentences were issued was partially blamed on the French. Many French teachers and technicians were expelled from Guinea at this time as was the French archbishop of Conakry. In October 1965 a number of high officials were arrested and executed following alleged French-backed anti-government activities. The "Labé Plot" (q.v.) linked to

French "imperialism" was uncovered in February 1969. Following this, Touré purged the army and ordered the execution of at least 13 people. Though Touré was often accused of being a Soviet puppet by many Westerners, his actions did not bear this out. In November 1958 Kwame Nkrumah and Touré formed a loose Ghana-Guinea union, in December 1960 a union of Ghana, Guinea and Mali was proclaimed by the three heads of state, and Touré was consistently interested in the all-African Peoples' Conferences which led up to the establishment of the Organization of African Unity (OAU [q.v.]) in Addis Abba, Ethiopia in May 1963. During the so-called "teachers' plot" (q.v.) of November 1961, Touré accused Soviet Ambassador Daniel Solod of complicity and expelled him.

In 1962 Touré accused the Ghanaian government of ordering the assassination of Togo's President Olympio on January 13 of that year. On March 2 he welcomed to Guinea the exiled president of Ghana, Kwame Nkrumah as his "co-president."

In 1963 widespread arrests and purging of the PDG followed the "shopkeepers' plot" (q.v.). In April 1967 Touré ordered a wave of arrests to avert an alleged coup d'état and again purged the PDG in 1968. Ministerial shakeups, impassioned harangues, and constant purges of the party became common practice.

On June 24, 1969, Touré apparently narrowly escaped an attempt on his life during a visit from President Kenneth Kaunda of Zambia. On November 2, 1970, dissident Guineans, mercenaries, and Portuguese army elements failed in an attack on Conakry. Following this, Sékou Touré ordered a "people's trial" which condemned close to 100 people to death. In April 1971 another supposed attempt on his life was uncovered, apparently supported by a large percentage of the Guinean people.

His rather unexpected death on Monday, March 26, 1984, at the Cleveland Clinic Foundation in Cleveland, Ohio, U.S.A., opened the way for change. The military coup of April 3, 1984 ended the Touré era in Guinean history.

TOURE, AMARA. Sékou Touré's older half-brother who was

secretary-general of the party in Faranah and played an important role as clan (qq.v.) head both in family and national affairs. Following the April 1984 military coup he was arrested and jailed in Kindia (q.v.). He was executed there in July 1985.

TOURE, AMINATA. Sékou Touré's (q.v.) daughter by his first wife. Jurist and magistrate, she married the well-known soccer player, Maxime Camara (q.v.).

TOURE, COLONEL FACINET. Born in Forécariah (q.v.), he was a officer in the Guinean army during the Parti Démocratique de Guinée (PDG [q.v.]) era. A prominent member of the Comité Militaire de Redressement National (CMRN [q.v.]) after April 1983, he served as minister of foreign affairs, governor of Nzérékoré (q.v.), minister of transportation, and minister of justice. Demoted by Lansana Conté (q.v.) he retired from the army. He led the Union Nationale pour la Prosperité (UNP), a party critical of President Conté.

TOURE, ISMAEL. Sékou Touré's (q.v.) half-brother, he studied engineering in Paris. Returning to Guinea in 1950 he headed the Kankan (q.v.) weather station where he was elected to the Municipal Council of Kankan and to the Territorial Assembly from Faranah (q.v.) in 1956.

Sékou Touré appointed him minister of public works in his first cabinet. He was successively minister of posts, telegraph and transport, of public works and transportation, of economic development, and of finance. In June 1972 he was appointed minister of the Super Ministry of Economy and Finance in charge of industry, mining, power, banking, development, and public works.

As long as Sékou Touré maintained power, Ismaël Touré had a place in the government but following the April 1984 coup he was arrested and jailed in Kindia (q.v.). He was executed there in July 1985.

TOURE, KEME-BOUREMA. The younger brother of Samory Touré (q.v.) and his head of state. Remembered for his military prowess and many victories, he was killed at the siege of Sikasso. His name is the title of an acclaimed epic by Sory Kandia Kouyaté (q.v.).

TOURE, MOHAMED. Sékou Touré's son. A graduate in economics from Gamal Abdel Nasser Polytechnical Institute in Conakry (qq.v.). He later studied in the United States.

TOURE, MOHAMED LAMINE. Born in Kankan (q.v.) about 1928 this graduate in civil engineering from Paris was a several-time minister with various positions in the Sékou Touré (q.v) government. Following the April 1984 military coup he was arrested and jailed in Kindia (q.v.). He was executed there in July 1985.

TOURE, MOHAMMED (Petit-Touré). Born in Kérouané (q.v.) about 1925, he was Samory Touré's (q.v) grand-nephew. A business manager and private businessman in Bouaké, Côte d'Ivoire, he became active in the Parti Démocratique de Côte d'Ivoire-Rassemblement Démocratique Africain (PDCI-RDA) and returned to Guinea in 1958. He was a very influential director of the Guinean trading company, Comptoir Commercial. Critical of the one-party system in 1964, he submitted a proposal to the government for a second party in 1965. Arrested along with his two brothers, his wife and other prominent Guinean political figures, he was executed at Camp Boiro in Conakry (q.v.) in 1967.

TOURE, NOUNCOUMBA. Sékou Touré's (q.v.) sister, she was married to Cherif Sékou (q.v.) who was once minister of the interior. Following the April 1984 military coup she was arrested only to be released after a few months. She later went to live in Côte d'Ivoire.

TOURE, SADAN MOUSSA. Born in Kankan (q.v.) and graduated from the William Ponty School (q.v.), he was a distant cousin of Sékou Touré (q.v.) and served as a justice clerk at the court of appeals of Dakar from 1947–1954. He served as a notary in Kankan (q.v.) from 1955–1958 and then was prosecutor in Conakry (q.v.) and, later, head of security services. He was ambassador to Egypt, Senegal, and the United States. He died in Conakry in 1988.

TOURE, SAMORY. Born about 1830 near Sanankoro, Guinea, he became a trader at the age of 17 and later served in the army of a Maninka (q.v.) war leader. By 1879 he had established an independent state stretching from near Bamako, Mali, to the Liberian forest and including Kankan, the trading center of present-day Upper Guinea (qq.v.). He resisted the French from 1882 until his capture in 1898. He ultimately died in exile in 1900 in Gabon. Sékou Touré (q.v.) claimed Samory Touré as an ancestor and used the fact of Samory's resistance to the French and sense of widespread unity for political purposes in the mid-1950s.

TOURE, SIAKA. Born in Kankan (q.v) in 1935, he studied in Paris and Moscow. An army officer he also served as minister of transport. Placed in charge of Camp Boiro he was arrested in April 1984. He was executed in July 1985 in Kindia (q.v.).

TOWEL, YOURA. "King" of the Nalou (q.v) on the coast of Guinea in the second half of the nineteenth century. He died in 1887 and was succeeded by his nephew, Dinah Salifou (q.v.).

TRADE—EXTERNAL. Guinea's export earnings throughout the 1960s stagnated. Never recovering from the abrupt withdrawal of French price supports and technical expertise after independence, Guinean agriculture (q.v.) continued to perform poorly into the 1990s. Under Sékou Touré (q.v.) as much as one-third of the coffee (q.v.) crop, for example, was smuggled (q.v.) out since legal exportation required the surrender of international exchange in return for overvalued Guinean currency (q.v.), effectively reducing earnings by about three-fourths. Guinea still has a large international trade deficit and in spite of massive external capital infusions since independence, the balance of payments remains negative. Bauxite, alumina (qq.v.), gold, diamonds (q.v.), and potential iron ore exports continue to give Guinea some prospects of economic viability in the future.

TRADE—INTERNAL. Under the government of Sékou Touré (q.v.) critical shortages of food and other basic consumer products were ongoing realities. Illicit trade in soap, sugar, rice, and cooking oils, at three or four times the legal price, was rampant. Smuggling (q.v.) was widespread and many farmers produced only for family consumption rather than for a cash market. Domestic trade remained somewhat chaotic after the government's attempt to control all trade in 1960. Trade in perishable foodstuffs on a small scale continued between rural areas and the towns but never really grew. Since April 1984 a noticeable improvement in the availability of consumer goods has occurred and most goods are available for those who can pay.

TRADE UNIONS. Much of the African political activity in French Guinea from 1946 on was conducted within the framework of the French Confédération Générale du Travail (CGT [q.v.]). The iron and bauxite mines of Lower Guinea (q.v.) became fertile recruiting grounds for union organization by the early 1950s. After the 66-day strike in the fall of 1953, union membership in Guinea rose from 4,600 before the strike to 44,000 in 1955. Since Sékou Touré was the secretary-general of the CGT and most of its leaders, like him, were loyal members of the Parti Démocratique de Guinée (qq.v.), the politicization of the CGT in Guinea was almost total by January 1957, when Touré broke with this French Communist union and created the autonomous Union Générale des Travailleurs d'Afrique Noire (UGTAN; q.v.). By then the political base afforded by the union had helped Touré be elected to the French National Assembly and the union had outlived its political usefulness. See CONFEDERATION GENERALE DU TRAVAIL; UNION GENERALE DES TRAVAILLEURS D'AFRIQUE NOIRE.

TRANSHUMANCE (adj. TRANSHUMANT). Cyclical movement by herding peoples such as the Fulbé (q.v.) from rainy-season grazing lands to dry-season pastures. Each band generally has usage rights and rights of passage defined by customary law. Often pastoralists had seasonal symbiotic relations with farming communities, grazing their cattle, sheep and goats on stubble left after harvest, fertilizing the fields with manure, and exchanging milk for grain. In the last few decades of rapid population growth farmers have expanded into former herder drought refuges and become so land hungry that the old symbiosis is breaking down. Transhumance is being abandoned as herders are obliged to sedentarize along roads and around deep wells, taking up mixed farming.

TRANSPORTATION. Like most West African countries, Guinea suffers from an inadequate transportation infrastructure. The country has only about 30,000 kilometers (19,800 miles) of roads of any sort and less than 14,000 (9,200) of these are practical for ordinary vehicular traffic. Outside the capital, approximately 1,100 kilometers (700 miles) are hard-surfaced. The railroad from Conakry to Fria and the 135-kilometer (84-mile) heavy-gauge line from the Boké bauxite deposits to the new deep-water port at Kamsar are in good condition, but the antiquated narrow gauge line from Conakry to Kankan is hardly functioning beyond Kindia (qq.v.). The Guinean airline, Air Guinée (q.v.), functions at a loss on an irregular schedule while the port (q.v.) facilities at Conakry are badly in need for better managerial and technical direction.

TRAORE, DIARRA. A graduate of Fréjus, the French military training school, Traoré played a significant role in both the first and second Guinean republics. During the First Republic he was commander of the Koundara (q.v.) military garrison and, later, was appointed supervisor of the Futa Jalon (q.v.) military region. Perhaps perceived as a threat to the Touré regime he was removed from the army and appointed to civilian duties. He became regional governor and was regularly reposted to Koundara, Labé, Pita, Macenta, Boké, and Kindia (qq.v.). In the late 1970s he became a member of the PDG (q.v.) party's central committee.

Sékou Touré's (q.v.) death in 1984 placed him in a peculiar position. Caught between the army and the party in the struggle of succession, he publicly aligned himself with the army at the historic April 2nd meeting of the party central committee, the army leaders, and the provisional government. Following the military coup d'état (q.v.) the following day he became prime minister and Lansana Conté (q.v.), his senior in rank, became president. He was minister of education from December 1984 to July 3, 1985. He was arrested on July 4, 1985, as the leader of a plot, along with many Maninka (q.v.) officers, administrators, and business persons in a charged atmosphere of riots and looting apparently directed against persons of Upper Guinea (q.v.) origins in Conakry (q.v.). He was executed later in July.

TRAORE, JEAN. Born in the Forest Region (q.v.) Colonel Traoré received training as a military engineer in the Soviet Union and the United States. He was a founding member of the Comité Militaire de Redressement National (CMRN [q.v.]) and an important figure in the government of Lansana Conté (q.v.). He was minister of natural resources and geology, minister of foreign affairs from 1988–1992, and chair of the constitutional committee. He was chief of President Lansana Conté's (q.v.) cabinet in 1993.

TRAORE, MAMADOU. See RAY, AUTRA.

TSETSE FLIES. A dark-brown or yellow-brown fly of the genus *Glossina* about the size of a large housefly with a projecting proboscis which carries sleeping sickness to humans and domestic animals. Found more commonly in northeastern Guinea they are one reason for the relatively sparse population in some areas of Upper Guinea (q.v.).

TUBAB. Maninka (q.v.) word used throughout West Africa for strangers, especially people of European ancestry and, by extension, anyone who goes to non-Koranic school and/or dresses in a European manner.

TYAPI (or Tiapi). See LANDOMA.

- U -

UMAR, AL HAJJ. See TALL, AL HAJJ UMAR.

UNION DU MANDE. A voluntary association created in Conakry (q.v.) by Guinean civil servants of Maninka (q.v.) background in the 1940s. By 1946 the union had become a major ethnic-based political movement that dominated politics in Upper Guinea (q.v.). Sékou Touré (q.v.) was involved in its formulative years. The representatives of the Union du Mandeé played a prominent role in the Guinean territorial assembly but the organization disappeared in the early 1950s as a consequence of the emergence of territorial and transterritorial politics. The name was also used for a large voluntary association formed in the 1970s by Upper Guineans living in the Côte d'Ivoire and who opposed the regimes of both Sékou Touré and Lansana Conté (qq.v.).

UNION GENERALE DES TRAVAILLEURS D'AFRIQUE NOIRE (UGTAN). Interterritorial trade union founded in Cotonou, Benin (then Dahomey) in January 1957 in an attempt to create an autonomous African trade union movement free of French or other European trade union control. Headed by Sékou Touré (q.v.), UGTAN split at the 1959 Congress in Conakry (q.v.) and for all practical purposes ceased to function. The Confédération Nationale des Travailleurs de Guinée continued as a separate Guinean organization.

UNION GUINEENNE D'ASSURANCES ET DE RE-ASSURANCES (UGAR). UGAR is one of the two major insurance companies (see SOCIETE NOUVELLE D'ASSURANCE ET DE RE-ASSURANCE DE GUINEE) that have replaced the failing national company of Touré's era. UGAR is affiliated with a French company.

UNION INTERNATIONALE BANCAIRE DE GUINEE (UIBG). UIBG is a branch of a French bank established in Guinea after the April 1984 military coup.

UNION NATIONALE POUR LA PROSPERITE (UNP). See TOURE, COLONEL FACINET.

UNION POUR LA NOUVELLE REPUBLIQUE. See BA, MA-MADOU BOYE.

UNION POUR LE PROGRES DE LA GUINEE (UPG). One of the more moderate parties founded in the early 1990s to contest the December 1993 presidential elections. Jean-Marie Doré, the party's leader, received less than one percent of the votes in this election.

UNITED NATIONS (UN). Guinea became the eighty-second member of the United Nations in December 1958. Throughout the 1960s it played a leadership role among African and "Third World" nations at the UN. Guinea sent a 749-man battalion to the then Congo (Zaïre) as part of the UN peace-keeping force there in 1960. Guinea has ceased playing such an important role in the General Assembly in recent years, though the country still raises its voice occasionally over anti-colonial and African issues of immediate concern to its own interests. A member of most of the UN's specialized agencies, Guinea receives missions of the World Health Organization, UNESCO, and other agencies.

UPPER GUINEA (Haute Guinée). One of the four reasonably clearly marked topographical areas into which Guinea is divided. This eastern portion of the country is an extension of the Futa Jalon (q.v.) shading off into the basin of the Upper Niger in a classical orchard shrub and grassland savanna (q.v.). *Préfectures* included are the following: Dabola, Dinguiraye, Faranah, Kankan, Kérouané, Kouroussa (qq.v.), Mandiana, and Siguiri (q.v.).

URBANIZATION. With around 700,000 inhabitants, the capital of Guinea, Conakry (q.v.) is the country's only real urban center. The old city on Tumbo Island retains its colonial facade. To this is joined a Kaloum Peninsula community which has grown up in the past 20 years. From the tip of the peninsula to Sanoya 35 kilometers (23 miles) away is an industrial zone with a growing salaried urbanized population giving Greater Conakry a population in excess of 900,000.

The second largest town, Kankan, in Upper Guinea

(qq.v.), has perhaps 50,000 inhabitants, but it is more a large cluster of Maninka (q.v.) villages around an administrative and commercial core area than a truly urban area. Most other towns throughout Guinea with the possible exception of Labé (q.v.), follow basically the same pattern.

Boké and Fria (qq.v.) with their mining complexes are isolated outposts of what would seem to be transplanted towns deposited in Guinea from somewhere else. The high-rise apartments, tennis courts, swimming pools, and company commissaries for the European community connected with the bauxite works in these towns have little impact on the lives of most Guineans.

- V -

VICTOIRE DE 27 DECEMBRE. Refers to the election of December 27, 1974, in which President Touré (q.v.) was overwhelmingly reelected for the third time by popular election. (His first election has been by the National Assembly in 1958.) This election was made possible by a constitutional amendment which allowed unlimited reelection in place of the previous limit of two presidential terms in office.

VIEILLARD, GILBERT. A French colonel administrator who served in the Futa Jalon (q.v.) and became a student of Fulbé (q.v.) culture. The Amicale Gilbert Vieillard was a voluntary association very active among the French-educated Fulbé civil servants, including Yaciné Diallo (q.v.), during the 1940s.

VOILE DE LA MARIEE. A beautiful waterfall outside of Foulaya (Kindia [q.v.]). This is one of the many potential tourist attractions in Guinea.

VOIX DE LA REVOLUTION. This was the usual identification of Guinea's single government-owned radio station under Touré. It is now identified as Radiodiffusion Nationale or Radiodiffusion de la République de Guinée. Transmission is from Conakry (q.v.) in both short and medium wavelengths at between 10 and 100 kilowatts for 12 to 24 hours each day. Since the country has between 100,000 and 125,000 radio receivers, it is estimated that more than 50 percent of the population receive the broadcasts. These broadcasts consist of extensive coverage of governmental activities and speeches, various sporting events, news in both French and Guinean vernaculars, and African music and songs. There are 7,000 television sets in the country tuned to the partial day broadcasts for Radiodiffusion-Television Guinéenne (RTG). A rural radio broadcasting station with a wide audience and an additional television-broadcasting transmitter have been attempted in the Labé/Pita region and the Kankan (q.v.) area. Despite these efforts, Radio France Inter, Voice of America, and the Gabon Africa Number One remain the major sources of information for most Guineans.

- W -

WAHHABIYYA. The Muslim community or anti-brotherhood movement founded by Muhammed ibn Muhammed ibn abd al Wahhab in Arabia in the eighteenth century. Members of the Wahhabiyya strive to live simple lives, heeding what they see as the strict rule of the early followers of the Prophet Muhammed, and avoiding the changes and compromises of later Islamic teaching. Never very widespread in Guinea, the Wahhabiyya was represented in Guinea by a few reformist Maninka Muslim teachers in Kankan (qq.v.) in the 1950s. There are Wahhabi mosques in the Soguela area of Kankan and in Conakry (q.v.). Lansiné Kaba's (q.v.) Herskovitz Prize-winning *The Wahhabiyya: Islamic Reform and Politics in French West Africa* (1974) is a key source. See QADIRIYYA; TIJANIYYA.

WASSULU (Ouassoulou). A region of farming and herding in Upper Guinea (q.v.) along the borders of present-day Mali and Côte d'Ivoire, inhabited since the fifteenth century by people of Fulbé (q.v.) descent who are called "Wassulu-ka." Noticeable patronyms are Diakité, Sidibé, Diallo, and Sangaré. In the eighteenth and nineteenth centuries, different leaders of Wassulu waged war against the Muslim communities living in Kankan-Bateh (qq.v.). Samory Touré (q.v.) conquered Wassulu and practiced a policy of Islamization. The Wassulu-ka have become part of the larger Maninkakan group, their Fulbé patronyms notwithstanding. Since the 1960s Wassulu-ka persons have become a powerful force in trade and transportation in Kankan.

WATERWAYS. Few of Guinea's coastal rivers are navigable for more than a short distance inland. The Niger was navigable by river steamer from Kouroussa (qq.v.) to Bamako, Mali, in July and August until the steamer ceased functioning in 1948. Shallow-draft boats and barges still made the trip into the 1960s in certain years from July to November, depending on the quantity of rain received. The Milo, the Niger's largest southern tributary, also carried such traffic as far south as Kankan (qq.v.) until the decline in commercial traffic with Mali made these routes unnecessary.

WILLIAM PONTY SCHOOL. The principal secondary school established by the French in West Africa. This school was located at Saint-Louis, Senegal, from 1903 to 1913, on Gorée Island, Senegal, from 1913 to 1938 and at Sebilhotane (a suburb of Rufisque), Senegal, after that date. This school recruited the best of African students from the eight territories of French West Africa (AOF [q.v.]) and trained them in teaching, administration, law, and medicine for service to the colonial regime between 1918 and 1945. The vast majority of post-1945 African political activists throughout French West Africa were graduates of this school.

WOMEN. Within most traditional social systems of Guinea women were often placed in a subordinate position. To a large extent these roles have been changed since independence through the efforts of the PDG (q.v.) and its auxiliary, the Comité National des Femmes (q.v.). Traditional marriage practices have been changed greatly. Civil marriage is now compulsory and a minimum marriage age of 17 for women has been fixed. Bride wealth has been reduced to a symbolic sum payable to the woman herself in front of a civil authority. Polygamy has been outlawed in theory since 1968 though this law is not enforced. The percentage of girls in school has risen from four percent in 1958 to over 20 percent. Women's cooperatives in sewing, dyeing, embroidery, and other crafts have been given government support. Finally all professions are open to women and there are women in the army, militia, police, and administration. The ideal of total equality between men and women has been theoretically established in Guinea and in this predominantly Muslim society the changes in the years since independence have been quite remarkable.

WORLD WAR II. For the majority of Guineans the early years of the war represented a period of extreme hardship. The worst forms of racism and colonial oppression were openly practiced under the Vichy regime. Pressed into labor service on European plantations and government construction projects, forced to sell agricultural goods below market price, and subjected to shortages of basic commodities, Guineans suffered greatly. Not until well into 1943 did the Free French begin to govern throughout Guinea. Even then Guineans were forced to produce labor for a cause which was of very little importance to them. Production did rise and some small-scale industrialization was begun in Guinea during the war, but for the most part the Allied victory in 1945 was the occasion for little rejoicing among Guineans.

- Y -

YAM (*Dioscorea sativa, D. alata* and others). One of the important items in the Guinean diet. There are many varieties and subvarieties; most are planted in late November and December and may weigh up to 15 kilograms (33 pounds) when harvested three to five months later.

YIMBERING. A *sous-préfecture* in the Mali (q.v.) region which became well known in Guinea in the 1970s and 1980s for its high literacy rate. In large measure this was the result of the efforts of one man, Thierno Cherif (the ex-colonial canton chief), who had made school mandatory during his administration. The small area produced an exceptional number of eventual college graduates.

YANSANE, DR. AGUIBOU. A scholar born the Moreah region in Lower Guinea (q.v.), he received his doctorate from Stanford University in economic anthropology. He is on the faculty at the University of California, Berkeley, and an associate professor at San Francisco State University. He is the author of several studies on Guinean politics, education, and economic problems.

YANSANE, DR. KERFALA. A Guinean scholar and member of the University of Dakar law school, he was appointed governor of the Guinean central bank in 1989.

YEYE MUSIC. French-style popular music which was banned by the JRDA (q.v.) at its Sixth Congress held in 1971. This was part of a continuing effort by the PDG (q.v.) to return to African musical sources and part of the total cultural revolution attempted in all aspects of Guinean life under Touré (q.v.).

YOULA, NABI. Born about 1923 in the Moreah region of Lower Guinea, he as a school teacher and businessman. An active member of the Parti Démocratique de Guinée (q.v.) in the 1950s, he was an adviser to Sékou Touré (q.v.) and an influential member of the Guinean diplomatic service as Guinean ambassador to France. He lived in exile in various countries, most notably Zaïre, until 1980 after which he became a member of the private council of the presidency.

YOUMOU. A small *préfecture* created in the early 1970s located on the Liberian border south of Macenta and Nzérékoré (qq.v.). On the Liberian frontier this region is carefully watched as a smuggling outlet for the coffee grown in the Forest Region (qq.v.).

YOUNKOUNKOUN. Renamed Koundara (q.v.).

- Z -

ZIAMA FOREST. A reserve of primary forest in the Macenta (q.v.) region which has been reserved for exploitation by keeping out the local cultivators. In the late 1960s a concession of 1,000 square kilometers (390 square miles) in this forest was to ship timber to the sawmill at Nzérékoré (q.v.). The poorly maintained mountain roads made this 100-kilometer (62-mile) trip impractical and the forest has contributed little to Guinea forestry industries.

ZOUMANIGUI, KEKOUR. A major in the armed forces, Zoumanigui served Sékou Touré (q.v.) as director of housing attached to the presidency, as commanding officer of the gendarmerie, and a governor of Kérouané (q.v.). Arrested in 1971, he was executed in detention in Kindia (q.v.).

BIBLIOGRAPHY

INTRODUCTORY ESSAY

There are only a handful of really original books dealing with Guinea prior to the 1980s. Perhaps the best of the general works in Jean Suret-Canale's *La République de Guinée* (1970), strong on socioeconomic development but weak on political aspects of Guinea. Claude Rivière's *Guinea* (1977) is a more up-to-date source in English which supersedes his *Mutations Sociales en Guinée* (1971). 'Lapido Adamolekun's *Sékou Touré's Guinea* (1976) was the first comprehensive analysis in English of political, social, and economic developments in post-independence Guinea. Though somewhat naive in his analysis of Guinea's success in nation building, Adamolekun's work is still valuable. The *Area Handbook for Guinea* (1975) also provides relatively accurate data on the social, political, and economic aspects of Guinean society. This work was largely the result of research in secondary sources and lacks the insight which two study visits to Guinea in 1968 and 1970–71 give to Adamolekun's work.

Since Guinea never played as large a role as Senegal in the history of French West Africa, bibliographic citations from the pre-independence period are relatively infrequent. But Guinea was the second Black African nation to achieve its independence from European colonial rule in the twentieth century. When the people of Guinea rejected de Gaulle's proposed Franco-African community by an overwhelming *no* vote in the September 28, 1958 referendum, the country was suddenly thrust into the limelight of international affairs. For a time there was a large, if uneven, outpouring of literature on Guinea. A number of popular books appeared in the U.S. during this period. For example, William Attwood's *The Reds and the Blacks* (1967) and John H. Morrow's *First American Ambassador to Guinea* (1968), represent two such popular works with a sympathetic, though Amerocentric, view.

173

Guinea's first president, Sékou Touré, was much written about as an international figure. His outspoken anticolonial positions and his views on African socialism continued to attract the attention of the academic community throughout the 1960s in such works as Ruth Schachter Morgenthau's *Political Parties in French-Speaking West Africa* (1964), W. A. E. Skurnick's *African Political Thought* (1968), and Gwendolyn M. Carter's *African One-Party States* (1962).

With the Portuguese-backed commando raid on Guinea on November 21, 1970, the strain of extreme isolationism, which had always been present at time of internal political crisis, became dominant in Guinean affairs. Contemporary materials on Guinea suffer from the difficulties always present under totalitarian regimes. The foreign press and the more than two million Guineans living outside the country often presented a rather unflattering view of conditions within the country. The rise of Touré himself as the sole interpreter of national realities since 1970 (see Sékou Touré, *Le Chemin du Socialisme,* 1970) stifled most information emanating from Guinea. This bibliography does not list all of Touré's increasingly repetitious works of the late 1970s and 1980s. Guinea, to paraphrase the Eurocentric and racist viewpoints held about all Africa until recently, became, under Sékou Touré, part of the "Dark Continent." The 24-hour-a-day broadcasts by Radio Conakry, Voix de la Révolution, cast little light on affairs.

Since the coup d'état in 1984 several works have appeared in French, and until the elections of Fall 1993, little of a definitive nature was really possible. One could turn to Senen Andriamirado, *et al., Sékou Touré et la Guinée après Sékou Touré* (1984), Ardo Ousmane Ba, *Camp Boiro: sinistre geôle de Sékou Touré* (1986), Mahmoud Bah, *Construire la Guinée après Sékou Touré* (1990), Abdoulaye Conté, *République de Guinée: effets d'une carence patriotique* (1989), and Ibrahima B. Kake, *Sékou Touré: le héro et le tyran* (1987), as well as such sources as *Jeune Afrique* for relatively up-to-date materials. Lansiné Kaba's *Le "Non" de la Guinée à de Gaulle* (1989) and his *Kwame N'Krumah et le rêve de l'unité africaine* (1991) are important sources on early and Touré's international policy, respectively. Lansiné Kaba's forthcoming volume in the Profiles/Nations of Contemporary Africa series for Westview Press will be especially valuable.

ABBREVIATIONS IN THE BIBLIOGRAPHY

A.B.C.	Afrique Biblio-Club
A.G.	Annales de Géographie
A.U.F.S.	American Universities Staff
Bull. C.E.H.S.	Bulletin du Comité d'Etudes Historiques et Scientifiques de l'A.O.F.
Bull. I.F.A.N.	Bulletin de l'Institut Fondamental d'Afrique Noire
Bull. et Mém. Soc. Anthropologie	Bulletin et Mémoires Sociétés d'Anthropologie
Cahiers d'I.S.E.A.	Cahiers de l'Institut de Science Economique Appliquée
C.E.A.	Cahiers d'Etudes Africaines
C.O.M.	Cahiers d'Outre-Mer
C.R.A.S.	Comptes Rendus des Séances de l'Académie des Sciences
C.R.S.S.G.F.	Comptes Rendus des Séances de la Société Géologique de France
E.G.	Etudes Guinéennes
E.S.A.	Ecole Supérieure d'Administration
Fr.R.	French Review
G.P.O.	Government Printing Office
I.F.A.N.	Institut Fondamental d'Afrique Noire
I.N.R.D.G.	Imprimerie Nationale de République de Guinée
I.P.C.	Institut Polytechnique de Conakry
I.P.G.A.N.	Institut Polytechnique Gamal Abdel Nasser de Conakry
Hist. Africa	History in Africa
Int. J. Afric. Hist. Stud.	International Journal of African Historical Studies
J.A.H.	Journal of African History
J.A.T.B.A.	Journal d'Agronomie Tropicale et de Botanique Appliquée
J. Relig. Africa	Journal of Religion in Africa
J.S.A.	Journal de la Société des Africanistes
mech. dup.	mechanically duplicated
ms.	manuscript or typescript

n.d.	no date
n.s.	new series
O.R.S.T.O.M.	Office de la Recherche Scientifique et Technique Outre-Mer
P.A.	Présence Africaine
P.U.F.	Presses Universitaires de France
R.A.	Recherches Africaines
R.F.E.P.A.	Revue Française d'Etudes Politiques Africaines
R.F.H.O.M.	Revue Française d'Histoire d'Outre-Mer
R.G.D.	Revue de Géomorphologie Dynamique
R.J.P.U.F.	Revue Juridique et Politique de l'Union Française
trim.	trimestre

A NOTE ON THE SCOPE

The books and articles in the bibliography are mainly chosen from those available in English and French. A few Russian, German, and Portuguese language sources are also noted. All the citations are organized under the following broad subject headings, each of which is further divided into two or more of these four categories: books, articles, government documents, and dissertations.

BIBLIOGRAPHY CONTENTS

GENERAL WORKS

Books

Adamolekun, 'Lapido. *Sékou Touré's Guinea*. London: Methuen, 1976.

Afrique occidentale française. 2 vols. Paris: Encyclopédie Coloniale et Maritime, 1949.

Ajayi, J. F. Ade, and Crowder, Michael, eds. *History of West Africa*. vol. 1. London: Longman, 1971.

―――. *History of West Africa*. vol. 2. London: Longman, 1974.

Ameillon, B. *La Guinée: bilan d'une indépendance*. Paris: F. Maspero, 1964.

Autra, Ray (Traoré, Amadou). *Connaissance de la République de Guinée*. Dakar: A. Diop, 1960.

Charles, Bernard. *Guinée*. Lausanne: Editions Rencontre, 1963.

―――. *La République de Guinée*. Paris: Berger-Levrault, 1972.

Church, R. J. Harrison. *West Africa,* 6th ed. New York: John Wiley and Sons, 1968.

Cultural Policy in the Revolutionary People's Republic of Guinea. Paris: UNESCO, 1979.

Decouflé, A. *Sociologie des révolutions*. Paris: P.U.F., 1968.

Diagne, Pathé. *Pouvoir politique traditionnel en Afrique occidentale*. Paris: P.A., 1967.

Fage, J. D. *An Atlas of African History*. London: Edward Arnold, 1958.

————. *A History of West Africa: An Introductory Survey.* Cambridge, England: Cambridge University Press, 1969.

Gigon, Fernand. *Guinée, état-pilote.* Paris: Plon, 1959.

Hapgood, David. *Africa: From Independence to Tomorrow.* New York: Atheneum, 1965.

Hardy, George. *Histoire de la colonisation française.* Paris: Larose, 1943.

————. *Histoire de la colonisation française.* Paris: Larose, 1953.

————. *La Politique coloniale et le partage de la terre aux XIXe + XXe siècles.* Paris: Albin Michel, 1937.

Houis, M. *La Guinée française.* Editions maritimes et coloniales. Paris: 1953.

Legum, Colin, and Drysdale, John, eds. *African Contemporary Record: Annual Survey and Developments.* London: African Research, 1969; Exeter: African Research, 1970; London: Rex Collins, 1971; New York: Africana Publishing, thereafter.

Milcent, Ernest. *L'A.O.F. entre en scêne.* Paris: Editions Témoignage Chrétien, 1958.

Morgan, W. B., and Pugh, J. C. *West Africa.* London: Methuen, 1969.

Nelson, Harold C., *et al. Area Handbook for Guinea.* Washington, DC: U.S. Government Printing Office, 1975.

Paulme, Denise. *Les Civilisations africaines.* Paris: P.U.F., 1959.

Pedler, E. J. *Economic Geography of West Africa.* London: Longman Green, 1955.

Priestly, Herbert Inghram. *France Overseas: A Study of Modern Imperialism.* New York: Appleton-Century, 1938.

Richard-Molard, Jacques. *Afrique occidentale française.* Paris: Berger-Levrault, 1949.

Rivière, Claude. *Guinea: The Mobilization of a People.* Ithaca, NY: Cornell University Press, 1977.

Suret-Canale, Jean. *Afrique noire: occidentale et centrale.* vol. 1. Paris: Editions Sociales, 1964.

———. *Afrique noire: occidentale et centrale.* vol. 2. Paris: Editions Sociales, 1968.

———. *La République de Guinée.* Paris: Editions Sociales, 1970.

Suret-Canale, Jean, and Niane, Djibril Tamsir. *Histoire de l'Afrique occidentale.* Paris: P.A., 1961.

Thompson, Virginia, and Adloff, Richard. *French West Africa.* Stanford, CA: Stanford University Press, 1958.

Voss, Joachim. *Guinea.* Bonn: Schroeder, 1968.

Articles

Balandier, G. "Les Etudes guinéennes," *E.G.* 1 (1947), pp. 5–6.

Cowan, L. Gray. "Guinea," in *African One-Party States,* Gwendolen M. Carter, ed. Ithaca, NY: Cornell University Press, 1962, pp. 149–236.

"Dossier Guinée," *Remarques Africaines* 13, no. 388 (November 25, 1971), pp. 414–419.

"Guinea," *Africa South of the Sahara* (1993).

"Guinée," *Aujourd'hui, l'Afrique* #27 (1983), quarterly.

Henderson, Gregory. "Guinea," in *Public Diplomacy and Political Change: Four Case Studies,* Gregory Henderson, ed. New York: Praeger, 1973, pp. 317–339.

"Isolation of Guinea Makes Assessment of Nation Difficult," *Le Monde* (October 3, 1973), p. 1.

EARLY HISTORICAL AND EXPLORATION ACCOUNTS

Books

Alexander, James E. *Narrative of a Voyage of Observation Among the Colonies of Western Africa.* 2 vols. London: H. Colburn, 1837.

Astley, Thomas. *A New General Collection of Voyages and Travels.* 4 vols. London: 1745.

Barbot, Jean. *Description of the Coasts of North and South Guinea.* London: Henry Linto, 1732.

Binger, Capitaine Louis Gustave. *Du Niger au Golfe de Guinée par les pays de Kong et le Mossi.* Paris: Hachette, 1895.

Blagdon, Francis. *Modern Discoveries.* London: J. Ridgeway, 1803.

Ca Da Mosto, Alvise de. *Relation des voyages à la côte occidentale d'Afrique.* Paris: E. Leroux, 1895.

Fernandez, V. *Description de la côte occidentale d'Afrique (Sénégal au cap de Monte).* T. Monod, A. Teixeira da Mota, and R. Mauny, trans. Bissau: Centro des estudos da Guiné portuguesa, 1951.

Godinho, Victorino M. *L'économie de l'empire portugais aux 15e et 16e siècles.* Paris: S.E.V.P.E.N., 1969.

Gray, Major William, and Dochard, Staff Surgeon. *Travels in*

Western Africa in the Years 1819–1821 from the River Gambia, through Woolli, Bondoo, Galam, Kassan, Kaarta, and Foolidoo to the River Niger. London: Murray, 1825.

Labat, Jean Baptiste. *Nouvelle relation de l'Afrique occidentale.* 5 vols. Paris: Cavalier, 1782.

Laing, Gordon. *Voyage dans le Timanni, le Kouranko et le Soulimana.* Paris: Delaforest et Arthus-Bertrand, 1826.

Le Maire, Jacques-Joseph. *Voyage to the Canaries, Cape Verdo and the Coast of Africa under the Command of M. Dancourt, 1682.* Edmund Goldsmid, trans. Edinburgh, 1887 (private printing).

Madrolle, Claudius. *En Guinée.* Paris: Le 'Soudier, 1895.

Matthews, John. *A Voyage to the River Sierra Leone.* Bellart, trans. London: B. White and Son and T. Sewell, 1788.

Mollien, Gaspard. *Travels in the Interior of Africa to the Senegal and Gambia in the Year 1818.* T. E. Bowdich, ed. London: Phillips, 1820.

Noirot, E. *A travers le Fouta-Djalon et le Bambouk.* Paris: Dreyfus, 1885.

Pacheco Pereira, Duarte. *Esmeraldo de Situ Orbis.* Bissau: Centro de estudos da Guiné portuguesa, 1956.

Park, Mungo. *Travels in the Interior Districts of Africa.* 2 vols. London: Bulmer, 1816–1817.

———. *Travels in the Interior Districts of Africa.* London: Bulmer, 1799.

Rançon, A. *Dans la Haute-Gambia. Voyage d'exploration scientifique, 1891–1892.* Paris: Société d'Editions Scientifiques, 1894.

Sanderval, O. de. *La Conquête du Fouta-Djalon*. Paris: Challamel, 1899.

Smith, William. *A New Voyage to Guinea*. London: J. Nourse, 1744.

Walckenaer, Charles Athanase. *Nouvelle histoire générale des voyages; ou collection des relations de voyages par mer et par terre*. Paris: Chez Lefèvre, 1826.

Whitford, John. *Trading Life in Western and Central Africa*. London, 1877.

Zurara, Gomès Eanès de. *Chronique de Guinée*. Dakar: I.F.A.N., 1960.

Articles

Boriskovsky, P. I., and Soloviev, V. V. "New Data on the Stone Age of Guinée," *West African Journal of Archaeology* 8 (1978), pp. 51–74.

Debien, G., De LaFosse, M., and Tilmans, G. "Journal d'un voyage de traite en Guinée, à Cayenne et aux Antilles fait par Jean Barbot en 1678–1679," *Bull. I.F.A.N.* 40 (1978), pp. 235–395.

Girardin, Benoit. "Christianisme et territoire: Le cas des aumôniers de la Westindische Companie en Guinée au XVIIe et XVIIIe siècles," *Neue Zeitschrift für Missionswissenschaft* 38 (1981), pp. 19–29.

Gobel, Erik. "Danish Trade to the West Indies and Guinea, 1671–1754," *Scandinavian Economic History Review* 31 (1983), pp. 21–49.

Gouldsbury, Dr. "Englische Expedition unter Dr. Gouldsbury nach dem oberem Gambia und Futa-Djallon," *Petermann's Mitteilungen* 28 (1882), pp. 290–296.

Hair, P. E. H. "Some Minor Sources for Guinea, 1519–1559: Enciso and Alfonce Fonteneau," *Hist. Africa* 3 (1976), pp. 19–46.

Lambert, M. "Voyage dans le Fouta-Djalon," *Le Tour du monde* (1861), pp. 373–400.

Malowist, Marian. "Some Aspects of the Early Colonial Expansion as Presented by Zurara in the Chronicle of Guinea," *Africa Bulletin* no. 25 (1976), pp. 75–94.

Mouser, Bruce L. "Theophilus Conneau: The Saga of a Tale," *Hist. Africa* 6 (1979), pp. 97–107.

Vieillard, G. "Notes sur l'exode toucouleur," *C.E.A.* 1 (1960), pp. 193–197.

HISTORICAL STUDIES

Books

Amin, Samir. *L'Afrique de l'ouest bloquée: l'économie politique de la colonisation, 1880–1970.* Paris: Editions de Minuit, 1971.

Archinard, Louis. *Le Soudan français en 1888–1889.* Paris: Berger-Levrault, 1890.

Arcin, André. *Histoire de la Guinée française.* Paris: Challamel, 1907.

———. *Histoire de la Guinée française.* Paris: Challamel, 1910.

Aspe-Fleurimont. *La Guinée française.* Paris: Challamel, 1900.

Barry, Boubacar. *Bokar Biro, le dernier almamy du Fouta Djallon.* Paris: A.B.C., 1976.

Betts, Raymond F. *Assimilation and Association in French*

Colonial Theory, 1890–1914. New York: Columbia University Press, 1961.

Blanchet, André. *L'Itinéraire des partis africains depuis Bamako.* Paris: Plon, 1958.

Borella, F. *L'Evolution politique et juridique de L'Union Française depuis 1946.* Paris: R. Pichon & R. Durand-Auzias, 1958.

Chailley, Marcel. *Histoire de l'Afrique occidentale française.* Paris: Berger-Levrault, 1968.

Cohen, William B. *Rulers of Empire: The French Colonial Service in Africa.* Stanford, CA: Hoover Institution Press, Stanford University, 1971.

Corbett, Edward M. *The French Presence in Black Africa.* Washington, DC: Black Orpheus Press, 1972.

Cornevin, Robert. *Histoire de l'Afrique des origines à nos jours.* Paris: Payot, 1956.

———. *Histoire de peuples de l'Afrique noire.* Paris: Berger-Levrault, 1960.

Davidson, Basil. *A History of West Africa to the Nineteenth-Century.* Garden City, NY: Doubleday, 1966.

Davies, Oliver. *West Africa Before the Europeans: Archaeology and Prehistory.* London: Methuen, 1967.

Delafosse, Maurice. *Haut-Sénégal-Niger.* 3 vols. Paris: Larose, [1912] 1972.

Delavignett, Robert. *Freedom and Authority in French West Africa.* New York: Oxford University Press, 1957.

Deloncle, Pierre. *L'Afrique occidentale française: découverte, pacification, mise en valeur.* Paris: Editions Ernest Leroux, 1934.

Demougeot, A. *Notes sur l'organisation politique et administrative du Labé avant et depuis l'occupation française.* Paris: Larousse, 1944.

Deschamps, Hubert J. *Afrique noire pré-coloniale.* Paris: P.U.F., 1962.

———. *Les Méthodes et doctrines de colonisation de la France.* Paris: Armand Colin, 1953.

———. *Les Religions de l'Afrique noire.* Paris: P.U.F., 1960.

D'Horel, P. *Afrique occidentale: Sénégal, Guinée, Côte d'Ivoire, Dahomey.* Paris: 1905.

Diallo, Thierno. *Alfa Yaya: roi du Labé (Fouta Djalon).* Paris: A.B.C., 1976.

———. *Les Institutions politiques du Fouta Djalon.* Dakar: I.F.A.N., 1972.

Diane, Charles. *Les grandes heures de la F.E.A.N.F.* Paris: Chaka, 1990.

Du Bois, Victor D. *Guinea: The Years Before World War II* (A.U.F.S. Reports, West Africa Series, Guinea, vol. 5, no. 5). New York: A.U.F.S., 1962.

———. *The Guinean Vote for Independence: The Maneuvering Before the Referendum of September 28, 1958.* (A.U.F.S. Reports, West Africa Series, Guinea, vol. 5, no. 7). New York: A.U.F.S., 1962.

———. *Guinea's Prelude to Independence: Political Activity, 1945–1958.* (A.U.F.S. Reports, West Africa Series, Guinea, vol. 5, no. 6). New York: A.U.F.S., 1962.

Duchène, Albert. *La Politique coloniale de la France.* Paris: Payot, 1928.

Famechan, M. *Notice sur la Guinée française.* Paris: Alcan-Lévy, 1900.

Galéma, Guilavogui. *La Résistance à la pénétration française dans la région de Macenta.* Conakry: I.P.C., 1968.

Gifford, Prosser, and Louis, William Roger, eds. *France and Britain in Africa: Imperial Rivalry and Colonial Rule.* New Haven, CT: Yale University Press, 1971.

Gorges, E. H. *The Great War in West Africa.* London: Hutchinson, 1927.

Hargreaves, John D. *Prelude to the Partition of West Africa.* New York: St. Martin's Press, 1966.

———. *West Africa: The Former French States.* Englewood Cliffs, NJ: Prentice-Hall, 1967.

Harmand, Jules. *Domination et colonisation.* Paris: Payot, 1940.

Histoire et épopée des troupes coloniales. Paris: Presse Moderne, 1956.

Holt, P. M., Lambton, Ann K. S., and Lewis, Bernard, eds. *The Cambridge History of Islam:* vol. 2, *The Further Islamic Lands, Islamic Society and Civilization.* Cambridge, England: Cambridge University Press, 1970.

Ingold, Commandant François. *Les Troupes noires au combat.* Paris: Berger-Levrault, 1940.

Joseph-Noel-Behanzin, Yolande. *Deux exemples de l'exploitation économique dans la Guinée coloniale: les concessions et l'exploitation de l'or.* Conakry: Ministère de l'Enseignement Supérieur et de la Recherche Scientifique, 1980.

———. *La contribution forcée du peuple du Guinée à la Première Guerre mondiale.* Conakry: Ministre du Domaine de l'Education et de la Culture, 1975.

———. *La "Résistance" et la "Dissidence" dans la Guinée sous domination coloniale pendant la Deuxième Guerre Mondiale.* Conakry: Ministère de l'Education et de la Culture, 1978.

———. *Une illustration de l'économie marchande coloniale: le commerce du caoutchouc dans la Guinée coloniale.* Conakry: I.P.G.A.N., 1977.

———. *Quelques aspects de la participation contrainte de la Guinée, sous domination coloniale française, à la Deuxième Guerre mondiale, 1939–1945.* Conakry: Institut Polytechnique Gamal Abdel Nasser, 1980.

Kaba, Lansiné. *Sonni Ali-Ber: fondateur de l'empire Songhay.* Paris: A.B.C., 1977.

Kobélé-Keita, Aboubakar Sidiki. *L'illustration future d'un leader (1945–1947).* Conakry: I.N.R.D.G., 1975.

———. *Les sources coloniales de l'histoire de la Guinée jusqu'en 1939.* Conakry: I.P.C., 1970.

Levtzion, Nehemia. *Ancient Ghana and Mali.* Studies in African History, no. 7. London: Methuen, 1973.

Machet, J. *Guinée française: les rivières du sud et le Fouta-Djalon.* Paris: Challamel, 1906.

Martin, Gaston. *Histoire de l'esclavage dans les colonies françaises.* Paris: P.U.F., 1948.

Morrow, John H. *First American Ambassador to Guinea.* New Brunswick, NJ: Rutgers University Press, 1968.

Mortimer, Edward. *France and the Africans, 1944–1960: A Political History.* New York: Walker, 1969.

Neres, Philip. *French-Speaking West Africa: From Colonial Status to Independence.* London: Oxford University Press, 1962.

Niane, Djibril Tamsir. *Histoire des Mandingues de l'Ouest.* Paris: Karthala, 1989.

———. *Recherches sur l'Empire du Mali au Moyen Age,* no. 2. Conakry: Institut National de Recherches et de Documentation, 1962.

———. *Soundiata ou l'épopée mandingue.* Paris: P.A., 1960.

Niane, Djibril Tamsir, and Suret-Canale, Jean. *Histoire de l'Afrique occidentale,* Ministère de l'Education nationale. Conakry: I.N.R.D.G., 1960.

Oliver, Roland, and Fage, J.D. *A Short History of Africa.* Baltimore, MD: Penguin Books, 1962.

Panikkar, Kavalan Madhusudan. *Revolution in Africa.* Bombay: Asia Publishing House, 1961.

Peroz, Etienne. *Au Niger: Récits de campagnes 1891–1892.* Paris: Calmann-Levy, 1895.

Person, Yves. *Samori. Une révolution dyula.* 3 vols. Nîmes: Barnier, 1968.

Pré, Roland. *L'Avenir de la Guinée française.* Conakry: Editions guinéennes, 1951.

Robert, André P. *L'Evolution des coutumes de l'ouest africain et la législation française.* Paris: Encyclopédie d'Outre-mer, 1955.

Roberts, Stephen H. *History of French Colonial Policy (1870–1925).* vol. 1. London: P. S. King, 1929; reprinted London: Frank Cass, 1963.

Rouget, F. *La Guinée.* Corbeil: Crété, 1906.

Santos, Anani. *L'Option des indigènes en faveur de l'application de la loi française en A.O.F. et au Togo.* Paris: Maurice Lavergne, 1943.

Saurrat, Albert. *La Mise en valeur des colonies françaises.* Paris: Payot, 1923.

Schnapper, Bernard. *La Politique et le commerce française dans le golfe de Guinée de 1838 à 1871.* Paris: Mouton, 1961.

Stride, G. T., and Ifeka, Caroline. *Peoples and Empires in West Africa: West Africa in History, 1–1800.* New York: Africana Publishing, 1971.

Suret-Canale, Jean. *L'Ere coloniale.* Paris: Editions Sociales, 1964.

————. *French Colonialism in Tropical Africa, 1900–1945.* Till Gottheiner, trans. New York: Pica Press, 1971.

Teixeira da Mota, A. *Inquérito etnográfico.* Bissau: 1947.

Webster, J. B., and Boahen, A.A. *History of West Africa: The Revolutionary Years--1815 to Independence.* New York: Praeger, 1970.

Weygand, Général Maxime. *Histoire de l'armée française.* Paris: Flammarian, 1953.

Yansané, Aguibou Y. *Decolonization in West African States with French Colonial Legacy: Comparison and Contrast: Development in Guinea, the Ivory Coast, and Senegal, 1945–1980.* Cambridge, MA: Schenkman Pub. Co., 1984.

Articles

Allainment, Y. "Note sur l'identification des tombes de Campbell et Peddie à Boké (Guinée)," *Bull. I.F.A.N.* 3 (1941), pp. 74–78.

Arlabosse, Générale. "Une Phase de la lutte contre Samory 1890–1892," *Revue de l'histoire des colonies françaises* 25 (1932), pp. 385–432, 465–514.

Attwood, William, and Loeb, James I. "Africa and Acts of Dissent," *Washington Post* (December 12, 1971), p. 21.

Autra, Ray (Mamadou Traoré). "La République de Guinée . . . en bref," R.A. (1959), pp. 7–17.

Bah-Lalya, Ibrahima. "Des Archives Nationales," *Recherches guinéennes* 3 (1975), pp. 49–61.

————. "Bokar Biro et la Bataille de Porédaka," *Recherches guinéennes* 5 (1975), pp. 6–20.

————. "Niany, Capitale de l'Empire des Mansa du Mali," *Miriya* I.P.G.A.N. (Oct. 1975).

Bah-Lalya, Ibrahima, Sanoussi, Zainou, and Diallo, Oury. "Les Relations entre le NGabou et le Foutah Djallon selon les traditions du Labé et du Kansala." Paper presented at the International Colloquium on Ngabou, Dakar, Senegal, May 19–24, 1980. ms.

Baillaud, E. "Observations and Reflections on European Agriculture in Guinea," *Journal of the African Society* 6 (1907), pp. 267–280.

Boubakar, Barry. "Crise politique et importance des révoltes populaires au Futa Djalon au XIXe siècle," *Afrika Zamani* (Dec. 1978), pp. 51–61.

Brière, D. "Souvenirs guinéennes. Les Débuts du Cercle de Télimélé," *E.G.* 8 (1952), pp. 3–12.

Chaleur, O. "La Guinée après trois ans d'independence," *Etudes* (November, 1961), pp. 202–215.

Cissoko, Sekene Mody. "A Fulgurant Victory for the Almamy Samory," *Afrique Histoire U. S.* no. 1 (1982), pp. 17–22.

Colombier, Th. du. "Une Expédition franco-belge en Guinée,"

Bulletin Société belge d'études coloniales (May–June, 1920), pp. 43ff.

Crespin, M. "Alpha Yaya et M. Frézouls," *Revue indigène* no. 2 (1906), pp. 45–46.

Cruise O'Brien, Donal. "Guinea, Recent History," *Africa South of the Sahara* 1974 (1974), pp. 377–378.

Davidson, Basil. "Guinea: Past and Present," *History Today* 9, no. 6 (June, 1959), pp. 392–398.

Demougeot, A. "Histoire du Núñez," *Bull. C.E.H.S.* 21 (1938), pp. 177–289.

Diallo, Ousmane. "Connaissance historique de la Guinée," *P.A.* 29 (December, 1959-January, 1960), pp. 45–52.

———. "Evolution sociales chez les Peuls du Fouta-Djalon," *R.A.* (October–December, 1961), pp. 73–94.

Fillot, Henri. "Alpha Yaya et M. Frézouls," *Revue indigène* no. 4 (1906), pp. 85–88.

Fisher, G. "Quelques Aspects de la doctrine politique guinéenne," *Civilisations* 9 (1959), pp. 457–476.

Gaillard, M. "Niani, ancienne capitale de l'empire mandingue," *Bull. C.E.H.S.* no. 4 (1923), pp. 620–636.

Georg, Odile. "La destruction d'un réseau d'échange précolonial: L'exemple de la Guinée," *J.A.H.* 21 (1980), pp. 467–484.

Halle, C. "Notes sur Koly Tenguella, Olivier de Sanderval et les ruines de Gueme-Sangan," *R.A.* 1 (1960).

Harris, Joseph E. "Protest and Resistance to the French in Fouta Diallon," *Genève-Afrique* 8 (1969), pp. 3–18.

Hughes, John. "Communist Focus on Guinea," *New Leader* 42 (July 6, 1959), pp. 3–4.

Humblot, P. "Kankan, métropole de la Haute-Guinée," *Afrique française, renseignements coloniaux* no. 6 (1921), pp. 129–141 and no. 7, pp. 153–163.

———. "Origine et légende de Kankan et du Baté," *La Guinée française* (June 15, 1950).

Hunwick, John O. "Salih al-Fullani of Futa Jallon: An Eighteenth-Century Scholar and Majaddid," *Bull. I.F.A.N.* 40 (1978), pp. 879–885.

"In memoriam: Monseigneur Lerouge, premier évêque de Guinée, n'est plus," *E.G.* 4 (1950), p. 81.

"Independent Guinea," *P.A.* Special No. (1960).

Jessula, David. "Un projet d'établissement d'israelites en 1939 en Guinée française," *Notes africaines* (Oct. 1977), pp. 97–100.

Kaba, Lansiné. "Archers, Musketeers, and Mosquitos. The Moroccan Invasion of the Sudan and the Songhay Resistance (1591–1612)," *J.A.H.* 22 (1981), pp. 457–475.

———. "Islam, State and Politics in Pre-Colonial Baté, Guinea," *Bull. I.F.A.N.* 35, B.2 (1973), pp. 323–344.

———. "The Pen, the Sword, and the Crown. Islam and Revolution in Songhay Reconsidered, 1464–1493," *J.A.H.* 25 (1984), pp. 241–256.

Keita, Sidiki Kabele. "Les realités coloniales en Guinée (1945–1958)," *Banda* (1977), pp. 14–23.

Maguet, E. "La Condition juridique des terres en Guinée française," *Afrique française, renseignements coloniaux* no. 3 (1926), pp. 121–126.

Maigret, J. "A la recherche du temps perdu," *E.G.* 1 (1947), pp. 7–8.

Mangolte, Jacques. "Le Chemin de fer de Konakry au Niger (1890–1914)," *Revue française d'histoire d'outremer* 55 (1968), pp. 37–105.

Maupoil, B. "Notes concernant l'histoire des Coniagui-Bassari et en particulier l'occupation de leur pays par les Français," *Bull. I.F.A.N.* 16B (1954), pp. 378–389.

McGowan, Winston. "Fula Resistance to French Expansion into Futa Jallon, 1889–1896," *J.A.H.* 22 (1981), pp. 245–262.

Monod, T. "Introduction [sur *Richard-Molard*]," *R.A.* 4 (1961), pp. 6–7.

Mouser, Bruce L. "Landlords-Strangers: A Process of Accommodation and Assimilation," *Int. J. Afric. Hist. Stud.* 8 (1975), pp. 425–440.

Muhmammad, Akbar. "The Samorian Occupation of Bondoukou: An Indigenous View," *Int. J. Afric. Hist. Stud.* 10 (1977), pp. 242–258.

Ndiaye, Moustapha. "Rapports entre Qâdirites and Tijânites au Fouta Toro aux XIXe et XXe siècles à travers 'Al-Haqq al-mubin' de Cheikh Moussa Kamara," *Bull. I.F.A.N.* 41 (January, 1979), pp. 190–207.

Newbury, C. W. "The Formation of the Government General of French West Africa," *J.A.H.* 1 (1960), pp. 11–128.

Niane, Djibril Tamsir. "A propose de Koli Tenguella," *R.A.* 4 (1960), pp. 33–36.

———. "Soundjata ou l'épopée mandingue," *P.A.* (1960).

Ousmane, D. "Connaissance historiques de la Guinée," *P.A.* 29 (1959–1960), pp. 45–52.

Person, Yves. "Cartes historique de l'Afrique Manding, fin du 19e siècle: Samori, une révolution dyula," *Centre des recherches africaines* (1990).

———. "La Jeunesse de Samori," *R.F.H.O.M.* 49 (1962), pp. 151–180.

Portères, Roland. "Vieilles Agricultures de l'Afrique intertropicale," *Agronomie tropicale* nos. 9–10 (1950), pp. 489–507.

Poujade, J. "La Guinée est-elle le dernier jalon d'un ancien empire? Nos méthods de travail," *E.G.* 2 (1947), pp. 3–7.

Quinquaud, J. "La Pacification du Fouta-Djalon," *Revue d'histoire des colonies* 4e trim. (1938), pp. 49–134.

Richard-Molard, J. "Découverte de la Guinée. Extraits d'un carnet de route," *R.A.* 4 (1961), pp. 8–23.

Rivière, Claude. "La Fin de la Chefferie en Guinée," *J.A.H.* 7 (1966), p. 3.

———. "Le Long des côtes de Guinée avant la phase coloniale," *Bull. I.F.A.N.* 30B, 2 (1968), pp. 727–750.

———. "Les partis politiques guinéens avant l'indépendance," *R.F.E.P.A.* 9 (1974), pp. 61–82.

Robinson, Kenneth. "Constitutional Reform in French Tropical Africa," *Political Studies* 6 (February, 1958), pp. 45–69.

———. "The Public Law of Overseas France Since the War," *The Journal of Comparative Legislation* 32 (1950).

Rudin, Harry R. "Guinea Outside the French Community," *Current History* 37 (July, 1959), pp. 13–16.

Sanneh, Lamin. "Futa Jallon and the Jakhanké Clerical Tradition. Part I: The Historical Setting," *J. Relig. Africa* 12 (1981), pp. 38–64.

————. "Futa Jallon and the Jakhanké Clerical Tradition. Part II: Karamokho Ba of Touba in Guinea," *J. Relig. Africa* 12 (1981), pp. 105–126.

Soubbotine, V. A. "Du régime foncier au Fouta-Djalon avant la colonisation," *Congrès international des sciences anthropologiques et ethnologiques* VIIe (August, 1964).

Summers, Anne, and Johnson, R. W. "World War I Conscription and Social Change in Guinea," *J.A.H.* 19 (1978), pp. 25–38.

Suret-Canale, J. "A propose du Ovali de Goumba," *R.A.* (1964), pp. 160–164.

————. "L'Almamy Samory Touré," *R.A.* 1–4 (1959), pp. 18–22.

————. "La Fin de la chefferie en Guinée," *J.A.H.* 7 (1966), pp. 459–493.

————. "La Guinée dans le système colonial," *P.A.* 29 (December, 1959-January, 1960), pp. 9–44.

————. "Le Siège de Boussèdou (février-avril 1907)," *R.A.* (1964), pp. 165–166.

Teixeira da Mota, A. "Nota sobre a historia dos Fulas. Coli Tenguéla e a chegada dos primeiros Fulas aô Futa-Jalom," *Conférence internationale des Africanistes de l'ouest* 5 (1950), pp. 53–70.

"Traités conclus entre le gouvernement français et des chefs des Rivières du Sud de 1884 à 1885," *R.A.* (1962), pp. 23–37.

Trentadue, Michel. "Mouvements commerciaux et évolution économique de la Guinée française de 1928 à 1938: l'essor de la specialisation bananière," *R.F.H.O.M.* 63 (1976), pp. 575–589.

————. "La Société guinéenne dans la crise de 1930: fiscalité et pouvoir d'achat," *R.F.H.O.M.* 63 (1976), pp. 628–639.

Vignes, K. "Etude sur la rivalité d'influence entre les puissances européenes en Afrique équatoriale et occidentale depuis l'acte générale de Berlin jusqu'au seuil du XXe siècle," *R.F.H.O.M.* 48 (1961), pp. 5–95.

"Voyage au pays des Bagas et du Rio Núñez," *Le Tour du monde* 51, 1er sem. (1886), pp. 273–304.

"Le Vrai Visage de Sanderval," *R.A.* 3 (1960), pp. 3–14.

Wallerstein, Immanuel M. "How Seven States Were Born in Former French Africa," *Africa Report* 6, no. 3 (March, 1961), pp. 3, 4, 7, 12, 15.

Weeks, George. "The Armies of Africa," *Africa Report* 4 (January, 1964), p. 11.

Yansané, Aguibou. "Political Economy of Decolonization and Dependency of African States of French Colonial Legacy, 1945–75," in *Decolonization and Dependency: Problems of Development of African Societies,* Aguibou Yansané, ed. Westport, CT: Greenwood Press, 1979, pp. 113–144.

Government Documents

Dequecker, M. *La Guinée de la loi-cadre à l'indépendence.* Paris: Centre Militaire d'Information et de Spécialisation pour l'Outre-mer, 1960. mech. dup.

Dissertations

Bah-Lalya, Ibrahima. "L'Implantation Coloniale à Travers ses Vestige Matériels - Le Rio Núñez (1850–1890)." Diplôme des études supérieures thesis, Institut Polytechnique de Conakry, 1970.

Camara, L. P. "Les Structures de l'administration de la Guinée sous la colonisation française (1890–1958), Etude analytique et critique." Mémoire de fin d'études supérieures (Institut Polytechnique Gamal Abdel Nasser de Conakry, Ecole Supérieure d'Administration), 1967–1968.

DuBois, Victor D. "The Independence Movement in Guinea; a study in African nationalism." Ph.D. dissertation, Princeton University, 1962.

Kaba, Lansiné. "Evolution of Islam in West Africa: The Wahhabi Movement and Its Contribution to Political Development 1945–1958." Ph.D. dissertation, Northwestern University, 1972.

Keita, S. K. "L'Etat de domination française en Guinée de 1945 à 1968." Cours de l'Institut Polytechnique Gamal Abdel Nasser (Conakry), October, 1970. mech. dup.

ANTHROPOLOGY, ETHNOLOGY AND SOCIOLOGY

Books

Attwood, William. *The Reds and the Blacks.* New York: Harper and Row, 1967.

Barbé, Raymond. *Les Classes sociales en Afrique noire.* Paris: Editions Sociales, 1964.

Baumann, Hermann, and Westermann, Diedrich. *Les Peuples et les civilisations de l'Afrique.* Paris: Payot, 1957.

Binet, Jacques. *Les Soussous de Guinée.* Paris: O.R.S.T.O.M., 1960. ms.

Brasseur, G., and Savonnet, G. *Cartes ethno-démographiques de l'Afrique occidentale,* feuille 2. Dakar: I.F.A.N., 1960.

Bunot, Raoul. *Forêts du sud, Brindilles de la forêt toma.* Mayenne: Collet, 1950.

Camara, Sory. *Gens de la parole: essai sur la condition et le rôle des griots dans la société malinké.* Paris and The Hague: Mouton, 1976.

Comité d'Etudes Historiques et Scientifiques de l'Afrique Occidentale Française. *Coutumiers juridiques de l'Afrique occidentale française III. Mauritanie, Niger, Côte d'Ivoire, Dahomey, Guinée française,* Serie A. Paris: Larose, 1939.

Condé, I. *Groupements et rapports sociaux dans un comité de Haute-Guinée: Komonida.* Conakry: I.P.C., 1966.

Decker, Henry de. *Nation et développement communautaire en Guinée et au Sénégal.* Paris: Mouton, 1967.

Delafosse, Maurice. *Enquête coloniale dans l'Afrique française occidentale et équatorial sur l'organisation de la famille indigène.* Paris: Société d'Editions Géographqiues, Maritimes et Coloniales, 1930.

Derman, William. *Serfs, Peasants and Socialists: A Former Serf Village in the Republic of Guinea.* Berkeley, CA: University of California Press, 1973.

Dupire, Marguerite. *Organisation sociale des Peul.* Paris: Plon, 1970.

Fréchou, Hubert. *Le Régime foncier dans les Timbis et dans la région du Moyen-Konkouré.* Paris: O.R.S.T.O.M., 1961. ms.

Froelich, Jean Claude. *Animismes.* Paris: Orante, 1964.

Gaisseau, P. *Forêt sacrée; magie et rites secrets des Tomas (Guinée française).* Paris: Albin-Michel, 1953.

Germain, Jacques. *Peuples de la forêt de Guinée.* Paris: Académie des Sciences d'Outre-mer, 1984.

Guillabert, Lieutenant. *Les Religions en Haute-Guinée.* Paris: Centre de Haute Etudes Administratives sur l'Afrique et l'Asie Modernes, 1951. ms.

Hachten, William A. *Muffled Drums: The News Media in Africa.* Ames, IA: Iowa State University Press, 1971.

Hanry, Pierre. *Erotisme Africain.* vol. 1. Paris: Payot, 1970.

Hodge, Carleton T., ed. *Papers on the Manding.* Bloomington, IN: Indiana University Press, 1971.

Holas, Bohumil. *Le Culte de Zié. Eléments de la religion Kono.* Dakar: I.F.A.N., 1954.

————. *Les masques Kono (Haute-Guinée française).* Paris: Geuthner, 1952.

Labouret, H. *Les Manding et leur langue.* Paris: Larose, 1934.

Lee, J. M. *African Armies and Civil Order.* New York: Praeger, 1969.

Lelong, M. H. *Ces Hommes qu'on appelle anthropophages.* Paris: Alsatia, 1946.

Leroi-Gourhan, André, and Poirer, Jean. *Ethnologie de l'Union Française (Territoires Extérieures).* vol. 1, *Afrique.* Paris: P.U.F., 1953.

Lestrange, Monique de. *Les Coniagui et les Bassari.* Paris: P.U.F., 1955.

Lévi-Strauss, Claude. *Le Totémisme aujourd'hui.* Paris: P.U.F., 1962.

Mauny, Raymond. *Glossaire des expressions et terms locaux employés dans l'Ouest africain.* Dakar: I.F.A.N., 1954.

Moreira, José Mendes. *Fulas do Gabu,* Memorias no. 6. Bissau: Centro de estudos da Guiné portuguesa, 1948.

Morrison, Donald G., *et al. Black Africa: A Comparative Handbook.* New York: Free Press, 1972.

Murdock, G. P. *Africa: Its Peoples and Their Cultural History.* New York: McGraw-Hill, 1959.

N'Diaye, Bokar. *Groupes ethniques au Mali.* Bamako: Editions Populaires, 1970.

Niane, Djibril Tamsir. *Expédition archéologique à Niani.* Conakry: I.N.R.D.G., 1965. ms.

Ottenberg, Simon, and Ottenberg, Phoebe. *Cultures and Societies of Africa.* New York: Random House, 1960.

Paulme, Denise. *Femmes d'Afrique noire.* Paris: Mouton, 1960.

———. *Les Gens du riz.* Paris: Plon, 1954.

Rencontres internationales de Bouaké. *Tradition et modernisme en Afrique noire.* Paris: Seuil, 1965.

Richard-Molard, J. *Problèmes humains en Afrique occidentale.* Paris: P.A., 1946.

Rivière, Claude. *Ethno-sociologie de la Basse-Guinée.* Conakry: I.P.C., 1968. mech. dup.

———. *Mutations sociales en Guinée.* Paris: Rivière, 1971.

Savineau, M. *Rapport sur la condition sociales de la femme indigène en Guinée française.* Dakar: I.F.A.N., 1938. ms.

Les Sorciers-panthères. Conakry: Archives de l'I.N.R.D.G., n.d. ms.

Tagliaferri, Aldo. *Fabulous ancestors: stone carvings from Sierra Leone and Guinea.* Milan: Il Polifilo, 1974.

Tagliaferri, Aldo, and Hammacher, Arno. *Fabulous Ancestors: Stone Carvings from Sierra Leone and Guinea.* New York: Africana Publishing, 1974.

Tauxier, Louis. *Moeurs et histoire des Peuls.* Paris: Payot, 1937.

Touré, Moussa. *Contribution à l'étude de "l'investissement humain" en Afrique noire.* Paris: Pensée universelle, 1976.

Vieillard, Gilbert. *Notes sur les coutumes des Peuls au Fouta-Djalon.* Paris: Larose, 1939.

Zolberg, Aristide R. *Creating Political Order; The Party-States of West Africa.* Chicago: Rand McNally, 1966.

Articles

Ala, Jean-Paul. "Problèmes culturels guinéens depuis l'indépendence," *Comptes Rendus Trimestre Séances d'Academie des Sciences d'Outre-Mer* (1976), pp. 585–600.

André-Marie, Frère. "De quelques coutumes barbares chez les Kissiens," *La voix de Notre-Dame* (October 1926).

Appia, B. "Les Forgerons du Fouta-Djalon," *J.S.A.* 35 (1965), pp. 317–352.

———. "Masques de Guinée française et de Casamance," *Journal Ouest Africain* 13 (1943), pp. 155–182.

Autra, M. T. R., and Sampil, M. "Notes ethnographiques recueillies en pays kissien," *R.A.* 3 (1960), pp. 58–67; 1 (1961), pp. 50–58.

Autra, Ray (Mamadou Traoré). "Les unités de mesure dans

l'ancienne société mandingue de Guinée," *Notes africaines* (1979), pp.63–65.

———. "Quelques aspects de la vie communautaire au sein des collectivités guinéennes," *Notes africaines* (1977), pp. 94–96.

Balandier, G. "Ethnologie et psychologie," *E.G.* 1 (1947), pp. 47–54.

———. "Toponymie des Iles de Kabak et Kakoussa," *E.G.* 8 (1952), pp. 49–54.

Balanghien, Etienne. "Voix des ancêtres chez les Malinké," *Vivant Univers* no. 267 (1970), pp. 22–31.

Balde, Chaikhou. "Les Associations d'âge chez les Foulbé du Fouta-Djalon," *Bull. I.F.A.N.* no. 1(1939), pp. 89–109.

Balde, Chaikhou, Camara, Nene-Khaly, and Suret-Canale, J. "Les Sites archéologiques de Guémé-Sangan et Pété-Bonôdji," *R.A.* 3 (1962), pp. 51–68.

Bernus, Edmond. "Kobané, un village malinké du Haut-Niger," *C.O.M.* no. 35 (1956), pp. 239–262.

Binet, Jacques. "Budgets familiaux africains," *Cahiers de l'I.S.E.A.* série "Humanités" 5 (November, 1962), pp. 62–83.

———. "Foires et marchés en pays soussou," *C.E.A.* 3 (1962), pp. 104–114.

———. "Groupes socio-professionnels en Guinée," *Le Monde non chrétien* no. 74 (April–June, 1965), pp. 67–93.

———. "Marchés africains," *Cahiers de l'I.S.E.A.* série "Humanités" 1 (November, 1959), pp. 67–85.

Boubakar, D. T. "Le Divorce chez les Peuls au Fouta-Djallon," *R.J.P.U.F.* 11 (1957), pp. 333–355.

Boutillier, J. L. "Les Rapports du système foncier Toucouler et de l'organisation sociale et économique traditionnelle: Leur évolution actuelle," *African Agrarian Systems* (1963), pp. 116–136.

Brass, William. "The Demography of French-Speaking Territories," in *The Demography of Tropical Africa*, W. Brass, ed. Princeton, NJ: Princeton University Press, 1968, pp. 342–439.

C., J. "L'Alcoolisme en Guinée française," *Zaire* 8 (1954), pp. 857.

Cantrelle, Pierre, and Dupire, Marguerite. "L'Endogamie des Peuls du Fouta-Djalon," *Population* no. 3 (1964), pp. 529–558.

Charles, Bernard. "Cadres politiques et administratifs dans la construction nationale en Guinée," *Revue de l'Institut de Sociologie* 4, nos. 2–3 (1967), pp. 345–353.

Cheron, G. "La Circoncision et l'excision chez les Malinké," *J.S.A.* 3 (1933), pp. 297–303.

Clavier, J. L. "Coutumier Coniagui," *Bull. I.F.A.N.* 19 (1952), pp. 321–336.

Conde, Julien. "La situation démographique en République de Guinée (émigration)," *R.F.E.P.A.* (March, 1976), pp. 102–125.

Corre, A. "Les Peuples du Rio Núñez," *Revue d'anthropologie* (1881), pp. 42–73.

Cournanel, Alain. "Situation de la classe ouvière en République de Guinée," *Partisans* 61 (September–October, 1971), pp. 119–136.

Coutouly, F. De. "Les Populations de l'ancien cercle de Touba-Kadé," *E.G.* no. 8 (1952), pp. 40–48.

————. "Toucouleurs et Dialonké de Dinguiray," *Bulletin de la Société de Géographie commerciale de Paris* (1913), pp. 588–597.

"Coutumier soussou," *Coutumier de l'A.O.F.* (1939), pp. 575–610.

Crespin, M. "La Question du Coniagui," *Revue indigène* no. 4 (1906), pp. 88–93.

Dabla, Sewanou. "De l'Enfance à l'age adulte: L'Initiation," *Notre Librairie* (1983), pp. 43–48.

Davies, O. "The Distribution of Old Stone-Age Material in Guinea," *Bull. I.F.A.N.* 21 (1959), pp. 102–108.

Delacour, A. "La Propriété et ses modes de transmission chez les Coniagui et les Bassari," *E.G.* no. 2 (1947), pp. 53–56.

————. "Sociétés secrètes chez les Tenda," *E.G.* no. 2 (1947), pp. 37–52.

————. "Les Tenda (Koniagui, Bassari, Badyaranké) de la Guinée française," *Revue d'ethnographie et de sociologie* (1912), pp. 287–299, 370–381; (1913), pp. 31–52, 105–153.

"Les Densités de population au Fouta Djalon," *P.A.* 15 (1953), pp. 95–106.

Diallo, Ousmane. "Evolution sociale chez les Peuls du Fouta-Djalon," *R.A.* no. 4 (1961), pp. 73–94.

Dobert, Margarita. "Guinea, the Role of Women," *Africa Report* 14, no. 7 (October, 1970), pp. 26–28.

————. "Who Invaded Guinea?" *Africa Report* 16, no. 3 (March, 1971), pp. 16–18.

Duffner. "Croyances et coutumes religieuses chez les Guerzé et les Manon de la Guinée française," *Bull. C.E.H.S.* no. 4 (1934), pp. 525–563.

"En Guinée française: le grenier de Conakry," *Zaire* 6 (1952), pp. 975–976.

"Essai sur la vie paysanne au Fouta-Djalon," *P.A.* 15 (1953), pp. 155–251.

Filipowiak, W. "L'Expédition archéologique polono-guinéenne à Niani," *Africana Bulletin* 4 (1966), pp. 116–130.

Fode, P. "La Révolution pacifique en marche: la nouvelle législation sociale de la République de Guinée," *R.A.* 3 (1961), pp. 38–59.

Foucault, Bertrande F. de. "Vers un réaménagement des relations entre les riverains du fleuve Sénégal," *Revue de Défense Nationale* 28, no. 2 (February, 1971), pp. 244–257.

Fréchou, Hubert. "Le régime foncier chez les Soussous du Moyen Konkouré," *Cahiers de l'I.S.E.A.,* série "Humanités," no. 4 (1962), pp. 109–198.

————. "Le Régime foncier des Timbi (Fouta-Djalon)," *Etudes de droit africain et malgache.* Etudes malgaches, no. 16 (1965), pp. 407–502.

Gamory-Dubourdeau, P. M. "Notice sur les coutumes des Toma," *Bull. C.E.H.S..* no. 2 (1926), pp. 288–350.

Gavinet, M. "Quelques Superstitions chez les Soussou de Basse-Guinée," *E.G.* 2 (1947), p. 67.

Germain, J. "L'Au-Delà chez les Guerzé," *E.G.* 2 (1947), pp. 27–35.

————. "Extrait d'une monographie des habitants du Cercle de N'Zérékoré (Guerzé, Kono, Manon)," *E.G.* no. 13 (1955), pp. 3–54.

Gessain, Monique. "Apropos de l'évolution actuelle des femmes Coniagui et Bassari," *J.S.A.* 34, no. 11 (1964), pp. 258–276.

————. "Etude socio-démographique du mariage chez les Coniagui et Bassari," *Bull. et Mém. Soc. Anthropologie* 5, 11e série (1963), pp. 5–85.

————. "Note sur les Badiaranké," *J.S.A.* 27, no. 1–2 (1963), pp. 43–89.

Gibbs, J. L. "Poro Values and Courtroom Procedures in a Kpelle Chiefdom," *Sociologus* 18 (1962), pp. 341–350.

Guebhard, P. "Les Peuls du Fouta-Djalon," *Revue d'étude ethnographique et sociologique* 2, 16–18 (April–June, 1909), pp. 85–105.

Guery, André. "Les Classes sociales en Guinée," *Remarques Africains* 21, no. 365 (November 5, 1970), pp. 390–397.

"Guinée: aujourd'hui la révolution culturelle," *Jeune Afrique* no. 405 (October 7, 1968), pp. 37–38.

Holas, B. "Danses masquées de la Basse-Côte," *E.G.* 1 (1947), pp. 61–67.

————. "Décès d'une femme Guerzé (cercle de Nzérékoré, Guinée française)," *Africa* 23 (1953), pp. 145–155; English summary, pp. 154–155.

————. "Denkongo, dieu de la foudre des Kissiens," *Notes africaines* no. 36 (n.d.), p. 12.

————. "Echantillons du folklore Kono (Haute-Guinée française)," *E.G.* 9 (1952), pp. 3–90.

————. "Note complémentaire sur l'abri sous roche Blandé (fouilles de 1951)," *Bull. I.F.A.N.* 14 (1952), pp. 1341–1352.

————. "Notes préliminaires sur les fouilles de la grotte de Blandé," *Bull. I.F.A.N.* 12 (1950), pp. 999–1006.

————. "Pratiques divinatoires Kissi (Guinée française)," *Bull. I.F.A.N.* 14 (1952), pp. 272–308.

————. "Quelques remarques complémentaires autour de la circoncison kissi," *E.G.* 13 (1955), pp. 60–67.

Holas, B., and Mauny, R. "Nouvelles Fouilles à l'abri sous roche de Blandé (Guinée)," *Bull. I.F.A.N.* 15 (1953), pp. 1605–1618.

Houis, Maurice. "Les Minorités ethniques de la Guinée côtière," *E.G.* 4 (1950), pp. 25–48.

————. "Que sont les Soso?" *E.G.* 6 (1950), pp. 77–79.

————. "Toponymie et sociologie," *Bull. I.F.A.N.* 22 (1960), pp. 443–445.

I.F.A.N. "Autour d'un casse-tête africain," *Bull. I.F.A.N.* 14 (1952), pp. 358–362.

Keita, Fodéba. "Chansons du Dioliba," *P.A.* 4 (1948), pp. 595–598.

Keita, Mamadou Madeira. "La Famille et le mariage chez les Tyapi," *E.G.* 2 (1947), pp. 63–66.

————. "Le Noir et le secret," *E.G.* 1 (1947), pp. 69–78.

Kourouma, Koly. "Le Revenu annuel d'une famille guerzé," *E.G.* 1 (1947), pp. 55–59.

Lambin, R. "Notes sur les cérémonies et les épreuves rituelles d'émancipation et d'initiation chez les Kissiens," *Bull. I.F.A.N.* 8 (1946), pp. 64–70.

Lassort, R. R., and Leong, P. P. "Chez les Kpélé du Liberia et les Guerzé de la Guinée française," *E.G.* 8 (1952), pp. 9–20.

Leriches, A. "Anthroponymie toucouleur," *Bull. I.F.A.N.* 18 (1956), pp. 169–188.

Lerouge, R. P. "Le Pays Coniagui," *Les missions catholiques* (May-June, 1918).

Lestrange, M. De. "Contes et légends des Fulakunda du Badyar avec une introduction et des notes sur leurs croyances et coutumes," *E.G.* (1951), pp. 3–66.

———. "Génies de l'eau et de la brousse en Guinée française," *E.G.* 4 (1956), pp. 3–24.

———. "La Population de la région de Younkounkoun en Guinée française," *E.G.* 7 (1951), pp. 67–69.

———. "Pour une méthode socio-démographique (Etude du mariage chez les Coniagui et les Bassari)," *J.S.A.* 21 (1951), pp. 97–109.

———. "Les Sarankolé de Badyar (technique de teinturiers)," *E.G.* 6 (1950), pp. 17–27.

———. "Sociétés secrètes, circoncision et excision en Afrique noire," *Le Concours Médical* (November, 1953), pp. 3815–3818.

Letnev, Artem. "Problème de l'évolution des rapports familiaux en Afrique occidentale," *Revue internationale des sciences sociales* no. 1 (1964), pp. 434–445.

Lhote, H. "L'Extraordinaire aventure des Peuls," *P.A.* n.s. 22 (1958), pp. 48–57.

Lombard, Jacques. "Tribalism et intégration nationale en Afrique Noire," *Homme et Société* 12 (April–June, 1969), pp. 69–86.

Ly, Madina. "La femme dans la société traditionnelle mandingue (d'après une enquête sur le terrain)," *P.A.* (1979), pp. 101–111.

Madeira-Keita, M. "Aperçu sommaire sur les raisons de la polygamie chez les Malinké," *E.G.* 4 (1950), pp. 49–55.

Meillassoux, Claude. "Essai d'interprétation du phénomène économique dans les sociétés traditionnelles d'autosubsistance," *C.E.A.* 1 (1960), p. 4.

———. "Histoire et institution du *bafo* de Bamako d'après la tradition des Niaré," *C.E.A.* 4 (1963), pp. 186–207.

Mengrelis, Thanos. "Esquisse sur l'habitat Guerzé," *Africa* 33, no. 1 (January, 1963), pp. 45–53.

———. "Fête de la sortie d'excision en pays guerzé," *Notes africaines* 50 (1951), pp. 11–13.

———. "Le Sens des masques dans l'initiation chez les Guerzé de la Guinée Française," *Africa* 22 (1952), pp. 257–262.

———. "La Sortie des Jeune filles excisées en pays Mano [n]," *E.G.* 8 (1952), pp. 55–58.

Moety, M. "Notes sur les Mani (Guinée française)," *Bull. I.F.A.N.* 19B, 1–2 (1957), pp. 302–307.

Neel, H. "Notes sur deux peuplades de la frontière libérienne, les Kissi et les Toma," *L'Anthropologie* 24 (1913), pp. 445–475.

Niane, Djibril Tamsir. "Mise en place des population de la Haute-Guinée," *R.A.* 2 (1960), pp. 40–53.

"Notes démographiques sur la région de Labé," *P.A.* 15 (1953), pp. 83–94.

"Organization, Motivating Forces of Society Discussed," *Révolution Africaine* (October 22–28, 1971), pp. 28–34, 37–38.

Paroisse, G. "Notes sur les Peuplades autochtones de la Guinée française (Rivières du Sud)," *L'Anthropologie* 7 (1896), pp. 428–442.

Paulme, Denise. "Des riziculteurs africains, les Baga," *C.O.M.* (1957), pp. 257–278.

———. "Les Kissi—'gens du riz'," *P.A.* 6 (1949), pp. 226–248.

———. "Un Mouvement féminin en pays kissi," *Notes africaines* 46 (April, 1950), p. 55.

———. "La Notion de sorcier chez les Baga," *Bull. I.F.A.N.* 20B, nos. 1–2 (January–April, 1958), pp. 406–416.

———. "L'Initiation des jeunes filles en pays kissi," *Conferencia internacional dos africanistas* (1952).

———. "La Société Kissi: son organisation politique," *C.E.A.* 1, no. 1 (January, 1960), pp. 75–85.

———. "Structures sociales en pays Baga," *Bull. I.F.A.N.* 18B, nos. 1–2 (January–April, 1956), pp. 98–116.

Person, Yves. "Les Kissi et leurs statuette de pierre dans le cadre de l'historie ouest-africaine," *Bull. I.F.A.N.* 23B, 1–2 (1961), pp. 1–59.

———. "Soixante Ans d'évolution en pays Kissi," *C.E.A.* 1, 1 (1960), pp. 86–114.

Poreko, D. O. "Evolution sociales chez les Peuls du Fouta-Djallon," *R.A.* 4 (1961), pp. 73–94.

Portères, R. "La Monnaie de fer dans l'Ouest africain au XXe siècle," *J.A.T.B.A.* 7, nos. 1–3 (1960).

———. "Un Problème d'ethnobotanique: relations entre le riz flottant du Rio Núñez et l'origine médi-nigérienne des Baga de Guinée française," *J.A.T.B.A.* nos. 10–11 (October–November, 1955), pp. 538–543.

"Rapport de la Commission des Programmes," *Horoya* no. 1893 (May 5, 1972), pp. 3–4.

Richard-Molard, Jacques. "A propos de deux contres sous-sous," *Notes africaines* 112 (October, 1966), pp. 129–130.

————. "Découverte de la Guinée," *R.A.* no. 4 (1961), pp. 8–23.

————. "Démographie et structure des sociétés négropeul, parmi les hommes libres et les 'serfs' du Fouta-Djalon (région de Labé, Guinée française)," *Revue de géographie humaine et d'ethnologie* no.4 (October, 1948-October, 1949), pp. 45–51.

————. "Essai sur la vie paysanne au Fouta-Djalon," *Revue de géographie alpine* 32, 2 (1944), pp. 135–240.

Rivière, Claude. "Bourgeoisies du tracteur," *R.F.E.P.A.* (March, 1977), pp. 74–101.

————. "Dixinn-Port, enquête sur un quartier de Conakry," *Bull. I.F.A.N.* 19, nos. 1–2 (January–April, 1967), pp. 425–452.

————. "Dynamique de la stratification sociale chez les Peuls de Guinée," *Anthropos* 69 (1974), pp. 361–400.

————. "Dynamique des systèmes fonciers et inégalités sociales: le cas Guinéen," *Cahiers Internationaux de Sociologie* no. 20 (1973), pp. 61–94.

————. "Fétischisme et démystification: l'exemple Guinéen," *Afrique Documents* nos. 102 and 103 (1969), pp. 131–168.

————. "Guinée: la difficile émergence d'un artisanat caste," *C.E.A.* 11, no. 38 (1969), pp. 600–625.

————. "Les Incidents sociologiques du développement," *Développement et Civilisations* no. 30 (June, 1967), pp. 55–69.

————. "Les Libanais en Guinée," *Kroniek afrika* 6 (1975), pp. 266–282.

————. "La Mobilisation politique de la jeunesse Guinéenne," *R.F.E.P.A.* no. 42 (June, 1969), pp. 67–89.

————. "Les Résultats d'un enseignement révolutionnaire en Guinée," *R.F.E.P.A.* no. 52 (April, 1970), pp. 35–36.

————. "Les Travailleurs de Wassa-Wassa: enquête sur l'Entreprise Nationale de Tabacs et Allumettes," *Canadian Journal of African Studies* 2, no. 1 (Spring, 1968), pp. 81–96.

Roberty, M. "Quelques Règles de droit coutumier malinké en Haute-Guinée," *Bull. C.E.H.S.* 1–2 (1930), pp. 212–223.

Rutz, Werner. "Etnographische-geographische Beobachtungen im Stammesbereich der Nalu," *Petermann's Mitteilungen* 103 (1959), pp. 273–276.

Saïdou, Baldé. "La Femme foulah et l'évolution," *L'Education africaine* 98 (1937), pp. 214–219.

Saint-Père. "Création du royaume du Fouta-Djalon," *Bull. C.E.H.S.* (1929), pp. 484–555.

————. "Petit Historique des Sossoe du Rio Pongo," *Bull. C.E.H.S.* (1930), pp. 26–47.

Sampli, M. "Une Société secrète en pays nalou: Le Simo," *R.A.* 1 (1961), pp. 46–49.

Schaeffner, A. "Musiques rituelles Baga," *Congress of the International Society of Anthropology and Ethnology* 6, no. 2 (1960), pp. 123–125.

————. "Les Rites de circoncision en pays Kissi (Haute Guinée française)," *E.G.* 12 (1953), pp. 3–56.

Schnell, Roland. "La Fête rituelle excisées en pays baga," *Notes africaines* no. 43 (1949), pp. 84–86.

————. "Vestiges archéologiques et agriculture ancienne dans le Nord du Fouta-Djalon," *Bull. I.F.A.N.* 19B, 1–2 (1957), pp. 295–301.

Silva, A. A. Da. "Arte Nalú," *Boletin culturel da Guiné portuguesa* 11, no. 44 (1956), pp. 27–47.

Stainer, M. "Notice sur les Coniagui," *E.G.* 2 (1947), pp. 57–61.

Suret-Canale, J. "Les Fondements sociaux de la vie politique africaine contemporaine," *Recherches internationales* no. 22, 11–12 (1960) pp. 6–56.

———. "Les Noms de famille toma," *R.A.* (August–September, 1963), pp. 34–35.

Suzzoni, Jean. "Monographie de l'île de Kaback," *La Guinée française* (August 5–25, 1948).

Szumowski, G. "Fouilles de l'Abri sous roche de Kourouunkorokalé (Soudan français)," *Bull. I.F.A.N.* 18 (1956), pp. 462–508.

Techer, H. "Coutumes des Tendas," *Bull. C.E.H.S.* no. 4 (1933), pp. 630–666.

Telli, Diallo. "Le Divorce chez les Peuls," *P.A.* n.s. 22 (October–November, 1958), pp. 29–47.

Teullière, G. "Alpha Yaya et la politique indigène," *Revue indigène* (1911), pp. 615–620.

Thomas, Louis-Vincent. "L'Africain et le sacré," *Bull. I.F.A.N.* 29B, 3–4 (1967), pp. 620–623.

———. "Philosophie de la religion négro-africaine traditionnelle," *Afrique-Documents* 79 (1965).

"Les Traits d'ensemble du Fouta-Djalon," *P.A.* 15 (1953), pp. 141–154.

Verdat, M. Le Ouali de Goumba," *E.G.* no. 3 (1949), pp. 3–81.

Vieillard, Gilbert. "Notes sur les Peuls du Fouta-Djalon," *Bull. I.F.A.N.* 2 (1940), pp. 87–210.

Wane, Y. "Etat actuel de la documentation au sujet des Toucouleurs," *Bull. I.F.A.N.* 25 (1963), pp. 457–477.

Government Documents

Guinea. Ministère de la Santé et les Affaires Sociales. "Développement des services sanitaires et sociaux," Conakry: 1966. mech. dup.

Yugoslavia. Institut d'Urbanisme. *Plan d'urbanism de Conakry.* Zagreb: 1963.

Dissertations

Charles, Bernard. "Cadres guinéens et appartenances ethniques." Thèse de doctorat, 3e cycle, Sorbonne, 1968.

Diallo, Thierno. "Les Institutions politiques du Fouta-Djalon." Thèse de doctorat, 3e cycle, Sorbonne, 1968.

Dobert, Margarita. "Civic and Political Participation of Women in French Speaking West Africa." Ph.D. dissertation, George Washington University, 1970.

Fofana, Mamadou Lamire. "Le Divorce en droit guinéen." Dissertation, I.P.C., 1968. mech. dup.

Rivière, Claude. "Dynamique de la stratification sociale en Guinée." Thesis, Université Lille III, 1975.

POSTCOLONIAL POLITICS

Books

L'Agression portugaise contre la République de Guinée. Conakry: I.N.R.D.G., 1971.

Ainslie, Rosalynde. *The Press in Africa*. New York: Walker, 1967.

Alata, Jean-Paul. *Prison d'Afrique: cinq ans dans les geôles de Guinée*. Paris: Le Seuil, 1976.

Amnesty International. *Guinée: emprisonnement, "disparitions" et assassinats politiques en République populaire et révolutionnaire de Guinée*. Paris: Ed. francophone d'Amnesty International, 1982.

Andriamirado, Senen, *et al. Sékou Touré et la Guinée après Sékou Touré*. Paris: P.U.F., 1984.

Ansprenger, Franz. *Politik in Schwarzen Afrika*. Cologne: Westdeutscher Verlag, 1961.

Ba, Ardo Ousmane. *Camp Boiro: sinistre geôle de Sékou Touré*. Paris: L'Harmattan, 1986.

Bah, Mahmoud. *Construire la Guinée après Sékou Touré*. Paris: L'Harmattan, 1990.

Bell, M. J. V. *Army and Nation in Sub-Saharan Africa* (Adelphi Papers, no. 21). London: International Institute for Strategic Studies, 1970.

————. *Military Assistance to Independent African States* (Adelphi Papers, no. 15). London: International Institute for Strategic Studies, 1970.

Bénot, Yves. *Idéologies des indépendances africaines*. Paris: F. Maspero, 1969.

Camara, Sylvain Soriba. *La Guinée sans la France*. Paris: Presses de la Fondation nationale des sciences politiques, 1976.

Carter, Gwendolen M., ed. *African One-Party States*. Ithaca, NY: Cornell University Press, 1962.

Chaffard, G. *Les Carnets secrets de la décolonisation.* Paris: Calman Levy, 1967.

Condé, Alpha. *Guinée: Albanie d'Afrique ou néo-colonie américaine.* Paris: Editions Gît-le Coeur, 1972.

Conté, Abdoulaye. *République de Guinée: effets d'une carence patriotique.* Paris: Editions La Bruyère, 1989.

De Gaulle, Charles. *Mémoires d'espoir.* vol. 1. Paris: Plon, 1970.

Diakité, Claude A. *Guinée enchaînéeou le livre noir de Sékou Touré.* Paris: Diané, 1972.

———. *Lettre Ouverte au Président Mitterand* (pamphlet). Paris: Le groupe d'action des Guinéens Libres et la Ligue Guinéenne des Droits de l'Homme, 1982.

Diallo, Abdoulay. *La Verité du ministre: dix ans dans les geôles de Sékou Touré.* Paris: Calman Levy, 1985.

Diawara, A. *Guinée, la marche du peuple.* Dakar: Edition Cerda, 1968.

Du Bois, Victor D. *The Decline of the Guinean Revolution, Part I: The Beginnings of Disillusionment* (A.U.F.S. Reports, West Africa Series, 8, no. 7). New York: A.U.F.S., November, 1965.

———. *The Decline of the Guinean Revolution, Part II: Economic Development and Political Expediency* (A.U.F.S. Reports, West Africa Series, 8, no. 8). New York: A.U.F.S., November, 1965.

———. *The Decline of the Guinean Revolution, Part III: The Erosion of Public Morality.* (A.U.F.S. Reports, West Africa Series, 8, no. 8). New York: A.U.F.S., November, 1965.

———. *The Guinean Vote for Independence: The Maneuvering*

Before the Referendum of September 28, 1958. (A.U.F.S. Reports, West Africa Series, 5, no. 7). New York: A.U.F.S., 1962.

————. *The Problems of Independence: The Decolonization of Guinea.* (A.U.F.S. Reports, West Africa Series, 5, no. 8). New York: A.U.F.S., November, 1962.

————. *The Rise of an Opposition to Sékou Touré, Part I: Reform and Repression by the Parti Démocratique de Guinée.* (A.U.F.S. Reports, West Africa Series, 9, no. 1). New York: A.U.F.S., March, 1966.

————. *The Rise of an Opposition to Sékou Touré, Part II; The Estrangement Between the Leaders and the People of Guinea.* (A.U.F.S. Reports, West Africa Series, 9, no. 2). New York: A.U.F.S., March, 1966.

————. *The Rise of an Opposition to Sékou Touré, Part III: The Plot Against the Government and the Accusations Against the Council of the Entente and France.* (A.U.F.S. Reports, West Africa Series, 9, no. 3). New York: A.U.F.S., March, 1966.

————. *The Rise of an Opposition to Sékou Touré, Part IV: The Entente's Reactions to the Guinean Accusations.* (A.U.F.S. Reports, West Africa Series, 9, no. 4). New York: A.U.F.S., April, 1966.

————. *The Rise of an Opposition to Sékou Touré, Part V: The Formation of a Common Front Against Guinea by the Ivory Coast and Ghana.* (A.U.F.S. Reports, West Africa Series, 9, no. 5). New York: A.U.F.S., April, 1966.

————. *The Rise of an Opposition to Sékou Touré, Part VI: The Activation of the Guinean Exiles: The Front de Libération Nationale de Guinée (F.L.A.G.).* (A.U.F.S. Reports, West Africa Series, 9, no. 6). New York: A.U.F.S., July, 1966.

————. *Thaw in the Tropics: France and Guinea Move Toward a*

Rapprochement. (A.U.F.S. Reports, West Africa Series, 6, no. 2). New York: A.U.F.S., 1963.

Egyptian Society of International Law. *Constitutions of the New African States.* Cairo: The Society, 1962.

Gavrilov, N. *La République de Guinée".* Moscow: Editions de Littérature Orientale, 1961.

Gigon, Fernand. *Guinée; Etat pilote.* Paris: Plon, 1959.

Guinée, Présidence de la République. *Evolution des rapports franco-guinéens.* Conakry: Impr. Nationale Patrice Lumumba, 1982.

Hamon, Hervé. *L'affaire Alata.* Paris: Editions du Seuil, 1977.

Hodgkin, Thomas. *African Political Parties.* London: Penguin, 1961.

International Institute for Strategic Studies. *The Military Balance 1973–1974.* London: The Institute, 1974.

Jalloh, A. A. *Political Integration in French-Speaking Africa.* Berkeley, CA: Institute of International Studies, University of California, 1973.

Kaba, Lansiné. *Kwame N'Krumah et le rêve de l'unité africaine.* Paris: Editions Chaka, 1991.

Kaba, Lansiné. *Le "Non" de la Guinée à de Gaulle.* Paris: Editions Chaka, 1989.

Kaké, Ibrahima B. *Sékou Touré: le héro et le tyran.* Paris: Jeune Afrique Livres, 1987.

Kobélé-Keita, Aboubakar Sidiki. *Ahmed Sékou Touré, l'homme du 28 septembre 1958.* Conakry: I.N.R.D.G. Bibliothèque nationale, 1977.

————. *Le PDG, artisan de l'indépendance, nationale en Guinée, 1947–1958.* Conakry: I.N.R.D.G., 1978.

Kondé, Sako. *Guinée, le temps des fripouilles.* Paris: La Pensée universelle, 1974.

Krueger, Heinz, and Umann, Joachim. *Blende auf für Guinea.* Leipzig: F.A. Brockhaus Verlag, 1961.

Legvold, Robert. *Soviet Policy in West Africa.* Cambridge, MA: Harvard University Press, 1970.

Lewin, André. *La Guinée,* Collection Que Sais-Je? Paris: P.U.F., 1984.

————. *Le Tragic destin d'un grand homme.* Paris: Jeune Afrique Plus, 1990.

Lewin, André, Andriamirado, Senen, and Diallo, Sifadou. *Sékou Touré.* Paris: Editions Jeune Afrique, Collection Plas, 1985.

Lusignan, Guy. *French-Speaking Africa Since Independence.* New York: Praeger, 1969.

Mabileau, A., and Meyriat, I., eds. *Décolonisation et régimes politiques en Afrique noire.* Paris: Fondation Nationale des Science Politiques, 1967.

Melady, Thomas Patrick. *An Evaluation of the United States Position in: the Republic of Guinea—implications for American foreign policy; Liberia—an old friend gets a new deal; the Republic of Ghana—a reappraisal after three years.* Pittsburgh, PA: Duquesne University Press, 1960.

Morgenthau, Ruth Schachter. *Political Parties in French-Speaking West Africa.* Oxford, England: Oxford University Press, 1964.

Morrow, J. H. *First American Ambassador to Guinea.* New Brunswick, NJ: Rutgers University Press, 1968.

Partie démocratique de Guinée. *50e et 51e sessions du Conseil national de la Révolution (resolutions).* Conakry: Impr. Nationale Patrice Lumumba, 1982.

Peter J. *Annuaire des états d'Afrique noire—gouvernement et cabinets ministériels des républiques d'expression française.* Paris: Ediafric, 1961.

Peyrega, Catherine. *Sékou Touré, est-il marxiste?* Pessac: Association des cercle d'études du développement économique et social, 1977.

Salacuse, Jeswald W. *An Introduction to Law in French-Speaking Africa,* vol. 1: *French-Speaking Africa South of the Sahara.* Charlottesville, VA: Michie, 1969.

Segal, Ronald. *Political Africa: A Who's Who of Personalities and Parties.* New York: Praeger, 1961.

Skogan, Wesley. *Bibliography on Party Politics in Guinea, 1950–1962.* Evanston, IL: Northwestern University, International Comparative Political Parties Project, 1967.

Skurnik, W. A. E., ed. *African Political Thought: Lumumba, Nkrumah, Touré.* Denver: University of Denver, 1968.

Sy, S. *Recherches sur l'exercice du pouvoir politique en Afrique-Côte d'Ivoire, Guinée, Mali.* Paris: Editions A. Pedonne, 1964.

Tanine, S. *L'Edification de l'Etat de la République de Guinée.* Moscow: Editions d'Etat de Littérature Juridique, 1960. (In Russian.)

Tanoh (pseud.). *Causes, Effects of Guineans' Exodus Discussed.* Washington DC: US Department of Commerce no. 1107,

January, 1972. (Translated from French: *Remarques Africaines* November 5, 1971).

Thomas, L. V. *Le Socialisme et l'Afrique.* Paris: Le livre africain, 1966.

Touré, Ahmed Sékou. *L'Action politique du Parti démocratique de Guinée.* 18 vols. Conakry: I.N.R.N.G., 1958–1972.

———. *Le Chemin du Socialisme.* Conakry: I.N.R.N.G., 1970.

———. *IIe Congrès nationale de la J.R.D.A* (Conakry, les 14, 15 et 16 septembre 1961). Conakry: I.N.R.N.G., 1961.

———. *Discours commémoratif de la proclamation de la République de Guinée* (IIe anniversaire de l'indépendance nationale), 2 octobre 1961. Conakry: I.N.R.N.G., 1961.

———. *Des Etats-Unis d'Afrique.* Conakry: Bureau de presse de la Presidence de la République, 1980.

———. *Expérience guinéene et unité africaine.* Conakry: I.N.R.D.G., 1959.

———. *8 Novembre 1964.* Conakry: I.N.R.N.G., 1964.

———. *La Lutte du Parti démocratique de Guinée pour l'emancipation africaine.* vol. 6. Conakry: I.N.R.N.G., 1961.

———. *Poèmes militants.* Conakry: I.N.R.N.G., 1964.

———. *Le Pouvoir populaire.* vol. 16. Conakry: I.N.R.N.G., 1968.

———. *Rapport de doctrine et de politique générale* (Ve Congrès national du P.D.G.-R.D.A. tenu à Conakry les 14, 15, 16, et 17 septembre 1959). Conakry: I.N.R.N.G., 1958.

———. *Rapport de doctrine et d'orientation* (Conférence nationale de Conakry des 14, 15, 16, et 17 août 1961). Conakry: I.N.R.N.G., 1961.

—————. *Rapport d'orientation et de doctrine présenté au Congrès générale de l'U.G.T.A.N.*, tenu à Conakry du 15 au 18 Janvier 1959. Conakry: I.N.R.N.G., 1959.

—————. *La révolution culturelle.* Conakry: I.N.R.D.G., 1972.

—————. *La révolution guinéenne et le progrès social.* Conakry: I.N.R.D.G., 1962.

—————. *La Technique de la Révolution.* vol. 18. Conakry: I.N.R.D.G., 1972.

—————. *Texte des interviews accordés aux représentants de la presse.* Conakry: I.N.R.D.G., 1959.

Touré, Kindo. *Guinée: unique survivant du "Complot Kaman-Fodéba".* Paris: L'Harmattan, 1989.

United Nations. *Foreign Trade Statistics of Africa. Series A. Direction of Trade.* New York: Economic Commission for Africa, 1962.

Veit, Winfried. *Natonale Emanzipation: Entwicklungsstrategie u. Aussenpolitik in Tropisch-Afrika, d. Beispiele Elfenbeinkuste u. Guinea.* Munich: Weltforum-Verlag, 1978.

Voss, Joachim. *Der Progressistische Entwicklungstaat: Das Beispiel der Republik Guinea* (vol. 81 of the papers of the Friedrich Ebert Foundation). Hannover: Verlag für Literatur und Zeitgeschehen, 1971.

Articles

"Action conjointe dans le Fouta-Djalon (Mamou, République de Guinée, 2–7 mai 1960)," *R.A.* 3 (1960), pp. 15–57.

Adamolekun, 'Lapido. "L'agression du 22 novembre 1970: Faits et commentaires," *R.F.E.P.A.* (June, 1975), pp. 79–114.

——. "Politics and Administration in West Africa: The Guinean Model," *Journal of Administration Overseas* 8, no. 4 (October, 1969), pp. 235–242.

——. "Some Reflections on Sékou Touré's Guinea," *West Africa* (London) no. 2950 (March 19 and 26, April 2 and 9, 1973).

Adrian, Charles, F. "Political Thought of Sékou Touré," *African Political Thought,* W.A.E. Skurnik, ed. Denver: University of Denver, 1968, pp. 101–135.

Africa Research Bulletin. London (monthly).

African Development. London (monthly).

Agbobli, Atsutse Kokouvi. "Guinée: La Démocratie au Ralenti; Un pas en avant, deux pas en arrière," *Jeune Afrique* 1561 (November 28-December 4, 1990).

"Agence guinéenne de presse," *Guinée actualités* (1967—irregular).

"Airmen Going to USSR for Training Courses," *Journal Officiel de la République de Guinée* (February 15, 1972), pp. 26–27.

Alata, Jean-Paul. "Prisons d'Afrique," *Esprit* 44 (September, 1976), pp. 835–846.

Ameillon, B. "Vérités sur la Guinée ou contre-vérités sur la décolonisation," *Partisans* no. 19 (February-March, 1965), pp. 37–43.

Andrain, C. "Guinea and Senegal: contrasting types of African socialism," *African Socialism* (1964), pp. 160–174.

Aribisala, Femi. "Sékou Touré and the Failure of Balkanized

African Radicalism," *Nigerian Forum* 4 (1984), pp. 145–151.

Beaujeu-Garnier, J. "Essai de géographie électorale guinéenne," *C.O.M.* no. 44 (1958), pp. 309–333.

———. "Guinée indépendante," *Revue politique et parlementaire* no. 684 (November, 1958), pp. 353–361.

Benot, Yves. "L'Afrique en mouvement: La Guinée à l'heure de plan," *La Pensée* no. 94 (November–December, 1960), pp. 3–36.

———. "Sékou Touré: Essayer de Comprendre," *Politique Africaine* (June, 1984), pp. 121–141.

Berg, Eliot J. "The Economic Basis of Political Choice in French West Africa," *American Political Science Review* 54, 2 (June, 1960), pp. 391–405.

———. "Socialism and Economic Development in Tropical Africa," *Quarterly Journal of Economics* 78 (1964), pp. 549–573.

Bornstein, R. "Organization of Senegal River States," *Journal of Modern African Studies* 10, no. 2 (July, 1972), pp. 267–283.

Buchmaus, Jean. "Régimes politiques d'Afrique noire," *Zaire, Revue Congolaise* (1960), pp. 283–306.

Camara, Sikhé. "Les mécanismes juridiques de protection des droits de la personne en République populaire révolutionnaire de Guinée," *R.J.P.U.F.* 36 (January–March, 1982), pp. 147–158.

"Causes, Effects of Guineans' Exodus Discussed," *Remarques Africaines* (November 25, 1971).

Césaire, Aimé. "La Pensée politique de Sékou Touré," *P.A.* 29 (December, 1959–January, 1960), pp. 65–74.

Chamers, Albert. "Un Diplomate Déjoue un Complot Contre la Guinée," *Afrique Hist.* 10 (1984), pp. 62–65.

Charles, Bernard. "Cadres politiques et administratifs dans la construction nationale en Guinée," *Revue de l'Institut de Sociologie* 4, nos. 2–3 (1967), pp. 345–353.

―――. "Un Parti politique africain: Le Parti démocratique de Guinée," *Revue française des sciences politiques* 12, no. 2 (June, 1962).

Chauleur, Pierre. "La Guinée de M. Sékou Touré," *Etudes* 347 (November, 1977), pp. 437–454.

"Communique Describes 2nd Session of PDG Central Committee," *Horoya* (May 27, 1972), pp. 2, 4.

Cournanel, Alain. "Situation de la classe ouvrière en République de Guinée," *Partisans,* no. 61 (September–October, 1971), pp. 119–136.

Deboste, Michel. "Radio Kankan: Média parallèle, pouvoir d'analyse ou fait accompli?" *Mois en Afrique* 16 (February–March, 1981), pp. 95–116.

Decraene, Philippe. " 'Le Dialogue avec Conakry se poursuit' déclare Président Houphouët-Boigny," *Le Monde* (July 28, 1972), p. 1.

―――. "Retour de Guinée ou Conakry à l'heure de l'OUA," *L'Afrique et l'Asie moderne* 139 (Winter, 1983–84), pp. 17–34.

"Decree Establishes Police Services Bureau," *Journal Officiel de la République de Guinée* (July 1, 1974), p. 161.

Diallo, Alpha Abdoulaye. "Introduction à l'étude de la Constitution guinéenne," *R.A.* no. 2 (1960) pp. 52–58.

Diallo, S. "Guinée: une démocratie en trompe l'oeil," *Jeune Afrique* (October 2, 1990), p. 1552.

———. "Guinée: à la recherche de la regle du jeu," *Jeune Afrique* (October 23, 1990), p. 1555.

———. "Les Jours Comptés de Lansana," *Jeune Afrique* (June 4, 1991), p. 1587.

Diawara, Mamadi. "La coopération entre les Etats en vue de la prévention et de la répression de la criminalité de caractère internationale en Guinée," *R.J.P.U.F.* 37 (1983), pp. 174–183.

Dubois, Jacques. "Guinée, An I," *Horizons* 9, no. 104 (January, 1960), pp. 58–67.

Du Bois, Victor D. "The Role of the Army in Guinea," *Africa Report* 8, no. 1 (January, 1963), pp. 3–5.

Dumbuya, A. R. "Emergence and Development of the PDG and the SLPP: A Comparative Study of the Differential Development of Political Parties in Guinea and Sierra Leone," *Journal of the Historical Society of Sierra Leone* 1 (January, 1977), pp. 16–34.

"Eighth District Officials Purged," *Horoya* (August 31–September 7, 1971), pp. 38–39.

Elections présidentales du 9 mai 1982 et 35ème anniversaire du PDG. Conakry: Presses de la Présidence de la République populaire révolutionnaire du Guinée, 1982.

Europe-Outremer. Paris (monthly).

Everett, Richard. "Guinea: A Tough Road Ahead," *Africa Report* 30 (July-August, 1985), pp. 19–24.

"La Femme guinéenne, militante du P.D.G.," *Cahier du militant* 21 (n.d.), p. 13.

Fischer, Georges. "Quelques Aspects de la doctrine politique guinéenne," *Civilisation* 9, no. 4 (1959), pp. 457–478.

————. "La Signification de l'indépendance de la Guinée," *Cahiers internationaux* no. 100 (November, 1958), pp. 1–14.

Gastaud, Maurice. "Naissance et évolution du parti démocratique de Guinée," *Cahiers du Centre d'études et de recherches marxistes* no. 55 (n.d.).

Gaulme, François. "Vingt-cinq ans après l'indépendance: la Guinée de l'ouverture," *Marchés tropicaux et meditérranéens* 39 (1983), pp. 2963–2973.

Goblot, L. "Bantoustans à Gogos: La Torture pour l'Espérance," *Peuples noirs, Peuples Africaines* 7 (May–June, 1984), pp. 75–87.

Guilavogui, Galema. "Cultural Policy in the Revolutionary People's Republic of Guinea," *Prospects* 12, no. 4 (1982), pp. 477–483.

"Guinée: Décès d'Ahmed Sékou Touré et coup d'état militaire," *Afrique contemporaine* (July–September, 1984), pp. 54–55.

"Guinée, prélude à l'indépendance," *P.A.* (1958).

"Guinée: vingt-cinq années d'indépendance," *Aujourd'hui l'Afrique* 27 (1983), pp. 2–80 (special number).

Hamon, Léo. "Le Parti démocratique de Guinée, d'avant l'indépendance à 1960," *R.J.P.U.F.* 15, no. 3 (1961), pp. 354–368.

Harshe, Rajen. "Non-Alignment and Francophone Africa: The Case of Guinea," *Non-Aligned World* 1 (July–September, 1983), pp. 371–385.

Hodgkin, Thomas, and Schachter, Ruth. "French-Speaking West

Africa in Transition," *International Conciliation* no. 528 (May, 1960), pp. 375–436.

Hutschenreuter, Klaus, and Schmidt, Ulf. "Volk, Partei und Staat in der politischen Ideologie Ahmed Sékou Touré," *Asien, Afrika, Latein Amerika* 5 (1976), pp. 739–750.

Industries et Travaux d'Outre-Mer. Paris (monthly).

Johnson, R. W. "The PDG and the Mamou Deviation," *African Perspectives* (1970), pp. 347–369.

————. "Sékou Touré and the Guinean Revolution," *African Affairs* 69 (October, 1970), pp. 350–365.

Journal officiel de la Guinée française. Conakry (weekly 1899–1958).

Journal officiel de la République de Guinée. Conakry (fortnightly, 1958-).

Julit, A. "Conférence sur la Guinée, bilan d'une indépendance," *Partisan* no. 19 (February–March, 1965), pp. 33–37.

"Justice in Guinea," *Review of the International Commission of Jurists* no. 7 (December, 1971), pp. 4–8.

Kaba, Lansiné. "Change in Guinea-Conakry: Myth and Reality," *Africa Report* 26 (May–June, 1981), pp. 53–57.

————. "From Colonialism to Autocracy: Guinea Under Sékou Touré, 1957–1984," in *Decolonization and African Independence, The Transfers of Power, 1960–1980,* Prosser Gifford and William Roger Louis, eds. New Haven, CT: Yale University Press, 1988, pp. 225–244.

————. "Guinea: Rhetoric and Reality in Conakry," *African Report* 23 (May-June, 1978), pp. 43–47.

————. "Guinean Politics: A Critical Historical Overview,"

Journal of Modern African Studies 15 (March 1977), pp. 344–345.

————. "A New Era in Guinea," *Current History* 84 (April 1985), pp. 174–178, 187.

————. "The Politics of Quranic Education among Muslim Traders in the Western Sudan: The Subbanu Experience," *Canadian Journal of African Studies* 10 (1976), pp. 409–421.

"Kissidougou Federal Bureau Purged and Reorganised," *Horoya* (June 13, 1974), pp. 1–2.

Lewin, André. "Les relations franco-guinéennes: la normalisation des relations entre la France et la Guinée depuis 1974," *Mondes Culturels* 40 (1980), pp. 161–169.

Malinga, Phineas. "Ahmed Sékou Touré—An African Tragedy," *African Communist* (1985), pp. 56–65.

Marcum, John A. "Report from Guinea," *New Leader* 41, no. 44 (December 1, 1958), pp. 3–7.

Marton, I., Cesaire, Aimé, and Mars, Jean Price. "La pensée politique du président Ahmed Sékou Touré," *Revue du Parti/Etat de Guinée* 90 (1975), pp. 9–176.

Mendy, Justin. "Sékou Touré's Ouverture," *Africa Report* 29 (March–April, 1984), pp. 43–46.

Miandre, J. "L'Expérience guinéenne," *Espirit* 10 (October, 1963), pp. 514–531.

"Military Men to USSR," *Journal Officiel de la République de Guinée* (October 1, 1972), pp. 167–168.

"Military-Paramilitary Committees' Duties Defined," *Horoya* (August 10–17, 1974), pp. 43–44.

Le Mois en Afrique: Revue Française d'Etudes Politiques Afri-caines. Dakar and Paris (monthly).

Otayek, René. "Guinée, 1979," *Annuaire de legislation française et étrangère T. 28: année 1979–1980* (1983), pp. 447–499.

Otero, Luis Marinas. "Guinea-Conakry Finaliza su Aislamiento y se Reincorpora al Sistema Afrolatino," *Revue de Politique Internationale* (January–February, 1979), pp. 49–62.

Pachter, Elise Forbes. "Contra-Coup: Civilian Control of the Military in Guinea, Tanzania, and Mozambique," *Journal of Modern African Studies* 20 (1982), pp. 595–612.

Perroux, François. "Une Nation en voie de se faire: la République de Guinée," *Revue de l'action populaire* no. 129 (June, 1959), pp. 683–705.

Poli, F. "La Guinée, un an après l'aggression," *Jeune Afrique* 570 (December 11, 1971).

"President Describes Army's Social and Economic Role," *Horoya* (February 19, 1974), pp. 1–2.

"President Touré Reviews Information Organs, Suggests Im-provements," *Horoya-Hebdo* (February 26–March 3, 1972), pp. 3–27.

"Les P.R.L.," *Horoya-Hebdo* (July 13–20, 1974), pp. 34–41.

Quarterly Review of Labour Problems in Africa. Brazzaville (quarterly).

"Quelques Aspects du problème des cadres en République de Guinée," *R.A.* 4 (October–December, 1960), pp. 40–47.

Rabemananjara, J. "Variations sur le thème guinéen," *P.A.* 29 (1959–1960), pp. 75–88.

"Réorganisation de la Justice," *Horoya* (August 25, 1973), pp. 4–7.

Rivière, Claude. "Les Mécanismes de constitution d'une bourgeoisie commerçante en République de Guinée," *C.E.A.* 11, 43 (1971), pp. 378–399.

———. "La Politique étrangère de la Guinée," *R.F.E.P.A.* no. 68 (August, 1971), pp. 37–68.

———. "Purges et complots au sein du PDG," *R.F.E.P.A.* no. 95 (November, 1973), pp. 31–45.

———. "Théorie de la dynamique conflictuelle dans les nouveaux états. Réflexions à propos du cas guinéen," *Cultures et développement* 2, 3–4 (1969–1970), pp. 657–678.

Sainville, Léonard. "La Presse française et la Guinée," *P.A.* 29 (December, 1959–January, 1960), pp. 109–116.

Schneider-Barthold, Wolfgang. "La grande ouverture de Guinée: aussenpolitische Neuordung und Wirtschaftsreform oder Rückkehr zum Stand der fruhen sechziger Jahre?" *Afrika Spectrum* 14 (1979), pp. 177–202.

Smouts, Marie Claude. "La normalisation des rapports franco-guinéens: analyse d'une médiation," *Revue française de science politique* 31 (June, 1981), pp. 563–580.

Soriba-Camara, Sylvain. "La Guinée et la coopération économique en Afrique de l'Ouest," *Cultures et développement* 8 (1976), pp. 517–532.

———. "Les origines du conflit franco-guinéen," *R.F.E.P.A.* (June, 1975), pp. 31–47.

"Les Statuts du Parti Démocratique de Guinée," *R.A.* 4 (1963), pp. 34–47.

Suret-Canale, Jean. "L'Afrique à l'heure de l'indépendance et la communauté rénovée," *Cahiers du Communism* 36e année, no. 11 (November, 1960) pp. 1735–1761.

———. "La Guinée face à son avenir," *Nouvelle revue internationale* (Prague) no. 90 (June, 1966), pp. 58–75.

———. "Les Relations internationales de la République de Guinée," *Foreign Relations of African States* (1974), pp. 259–276.

———. "République de Guinée, un an d'indépendance," *La Nouvelle Critique,* no. 109 (September–October, 1959), pp. 33–67.

———. "Théorie et pratique du "Parti-Etat" en République populaire et révolutionnaire de Guinée (Conakry)," *R.F.H.O.M.* 68 (1981), pp. 296–310.

———. "Vérités sur la Guinée," *Cahiers du communisme* (réponse à B. Ameillon) (October, 1964), pp. 56–67.

Sy, Madiou, and Soto Diallo, Boubacar. "Influences Philosophiques et Idéologiques de L'Islam sur le Droit Moderne Guinéen," *R.J.P.U.F.* 38 (April–June, 1984), pp. 133–142.

Touré, S. "The Republic of Guinea," *International Affairs* 36 (1960), pp. 168–173.

"Touré Discusses Militia Organization," *Horoya* (March 31, 1974), pp. 3–4.

Vernay, A. "La Guinée dans le sillage de Sékou Touré," *Les Echos* (July 10, 1961).

"Vers la normalisation des rapports Franco-Guinéenns," *Marchés Tropicaux et Méditerrannéens* (January 31, 1975), pp. 249–250.

Vinet, Jean-Maurice. "La Guinée vingt ans après l'indépendance:

situation intérieure," *Afrique contemporaine* (January–February, 1979), pp. 10–12.

"Violement mis en cause par M. Sékou Touré: Sénégal et Côte d'Ivoire," *Le Monde* (September 30, 1973), pp. 1–8.

Wallerstein, I. "The Political Ideology of the PDG," *P.A.* 40, no. 1 (1962), pp. 30–41.

Warburg, G. "Guinea in the Grip of U.S. Aid," *New Africa* 6, no. 7 (1964), pp. 11–12.

West Africa. London (weekly).

Whiteman, Kaye. "Guinea in West African Politics," *The World Today* 27, no. 8 (August, 1971), pp. 350–358.

World Agricultural Economics and Rural Sociology Abstracts. Oxford, England (monthly).

Yahmed, Ben Bechir. "Le cas Guinéen," *Jeune Afrique* 570 (December 11, 1971), p. 15.

Yansané, Aguibou Y. "Guinea: The Significance of the Coup of April 1984 and Economic Issues," *World Development* 18 (September, 1990), pp. 1231–1246.

Government Documents

Guinea. *Le Guinée Nouvelle,* Conakry (irregular).

———. *Statut du PDG,* Edition 1969 Permanence nationale. Conakry: I.N.R.D.G., 1969.

———. *Statut particulier des divers cadres uniques.* Conakry: I.N.R.D.G., n.d.

———. *Textes des interviews accordées par le Président Sékou Touré.* Conakry: April, 1959. mech. dup.

————. Ministère de la Fonction Publique et du Travail. *Etat des fonctionnaires guinéens en service avant l'indépendance.* Conakry: August, 1964. mech. dup.

————. Ministère de l'Intérieur [Territoire de la Guinée]. *Nouvelle Structure Administrative.* Conakry: Imprimerie du Gouvernement, 1958.

————. ————. *La Verité sur les événements de la Guinée.* Conakry: May 6, 1958. mech. dup.

————. Parti Démocratique de Guinée-RDA. *Bulletin d'information du BPN (formerly Bulletin du compte-rendu des activités du BPN),* Conakry (irregular, 1962-).

————. *Huitième congrès du parti démocratique de Guinée (RDA), tenu à Conakry du 25 septembre au 20 octobre 1967,* Conakry: I.N.R.D.G., n.d.

Dissertations

Adamolekun, O. O. "Central Government Administration in Guinea and Senegal Since Independence: A Comparative Study." D. Phil. thesis, University of Oxford, 1972.

Bah, T. O. "Etude au système des budgets locaux et d'arrondissements appliquée aux régions administratives de Conakry et Forécariah." Dissertation, I.P.C. (E.S.A.), 1969–70.

Camara, Sikhe. "La Guinée vers le socialisme." Thesis, Université de Guinée, Conakry, 1973.

Charles, B. "Cadres guinéens et appartenance ethnique." Ph.D. dissertation, Fondation Nationale de Science Politique, 1968.

Cournanel, A. "Planification et investissements privés en République de Guinée." Doctorat du troisième cycle dissertation, University of Paris, 1980.

Diallo, A. L. "L'Evolution des institutions administratives de la République de Guinée de 1958 à 1968." Dissertation, I.P.C. (E.S.A.), 1967–68.

Dioubaté, M. L. "Les Institutions politiques de la République de Guinée." Dissertation, I.P.C. (E.S.A.), 1966–67.

Douno, M. "Le Rapport du parti avec l'Etat guinéen." Dissertation, I.P.C. (E.S.A.), 1969–70.

Kourouma, K. R. "L'Evolution des institutions judiciaires en Guinée." Dissertation, I.P.C. (E.S.A.), 1967–68.

Yansané, Aguibou Y. "OERS as a Step Toward Political, Economic and Technical Cooperation in West Africa." Ph.D. Dissertation, Stanford University, 1971.

ECONOMICS

Books

Amin, Samir. *Le Mali, La Guinée et le Ghana: Trois expériences africaines de développement.* Paris: P.U.F., 1965.

Banque Internationale pour la Reconstruction et le Développement. *The Economy of Guinea.* Washington, DC: World Bank, 1966. mech. dup.

Bettelheim, Charles. *Directives générales à suivre par les régions et les villages dans l'élaboration du plan triennal guinéen.* Conakry: I.N.R.D.G., 1959. mech. dup.

Bureau de Développement pour la Production Agricole. *Texts relatifs au développement rural.* Paris: Caisse Centrale de Coopération Economique, 1962. mech. dup.

Campbell, Bonnie K. *Les enjeux de la bauxite: La Guinée face aux multinationales de l'aluminum.* Montreal: Presses de l'Université de Montréal, 1983.

Decker, Henry de. *Le Développement communautaire, une stratégie d'édification de la nation, analyse des modèles de développement communautaire en Guinée et au Sénégal.* Paris: Mouton, 1968.

————. *Nation et développement en Guinée et au Sénégal.* The Hague: Mouton, 1967.

La Dépêche Coloniale. *Comment se pose le problème agricole en A.O.F. et plus particulièrement en Guinée.* Paris: 1924.

Doré, Ansoumane. *Economie et société en Guinée, 1958–84.* Paris: Editions Bayardère, 1986.

Dumont, René. *Afrique noire: développement agricole: réconversion de l'économie agricole: Guinée, Côte d'Ivoire, Mali.* Paris: P.U.F., 1962.

————. *Etude provisoire des actions d'urgence agricoles en quelques points de Guinée.* 1959. mech. dup.

Fabre, M. *Note sur l'industrialisation de la Guinée française.* 1956. mech. dup.

Firsov, A. A. *Les Problèmes économiques de la République de Guinée.* Moscow: Editions "Science," 1965. (In Russian.)

Goldman, Marshall I. *Soviet Foreign Aid.* New York: Praeger, 1967.

Harbison, Frederick, and Myers, Charles A., eds. *Manpower and Education: Country Studies in Economic Development.* New York: McGraw-Hill, 1965.

Haut commissariat de l'A.O.F. *Etude sur les échanges routiers en Guinée française.* Dakar: Haut commissariat de l'A.O.F., 1957.

I.F.A.N. *Etudes agricoles et économiques de quatre villages de Guinée française.* Dakar: I.F.A.N., 1956.

International Labour office. *African Labour Survey* (Studies and Reports, New Series, no. 48). Geneva: International Labour Organization, 1958.

Johnson, H., ed. *Economic Nationalism in Old and New States.* Chicago: University of Chicago Press, 1967.

Laynaud, Emile. *Contribution à l'étude des structures sociales et de la modernisation rurale dans la haute vallée du Niger.* 3 vols. Paris: Bureau de Développement pour la Production Agricole, 1964. mech. dup.

Maynaud, J., and Salah-Bey, A. *Le Syndicalisme africain.* Paris: Payot, 1963.

November, A. *L'Evolution du mouvement syndical en Afrique occidentale.* Paris: Mouton, 1965.

Organisation for Economic Cooperation and Development. *Development Cooperation: 1972 Review; 1973 Review.* Paris: O.E.C.D., 1972, 1973.

————. *Geographical Distribution of Financial Flows to Less-Developed Countries.* Paris: O.E.C.D., 1965.

Reconversion de l'economie agricole: Guinée, Côte d'Ivoire, Mali. Paris: P.U.F., 1961.

Stokke, Baard Richard. *Soviet and Eastern European Trade and Aid in Africa.* New York: Praeger, 1967.

Touré, Ismaël. *Le Développement économique de la République de Guinée.* Conakry: I.N.R.D.G., 1964. mech. dup.

Yansané, Aguibou Y., ed. *Decolonization and Dependency: Problems of Development of African Societies.* Westport, CT: Greenwood Press, 1980.

Yansané, Hamy Mouké Layah. *L'Industrialisation de la République de Guinée.* Paris: 1962. ms.

Articles

Africa: An International Business, Economic and Political Monthly. London (monthly).

Alata, Jean-Paul. "L'Economie guinéenne," *Afrique contemporaine* (May–June, 1976), pp. 1–8.

Alpha, D. "Perspectives sur l'élevage en République de Guinée," *R.A.* 1–4 (1959), pp. 47–62.

Amir, Samin. "Guinea: Economy," *Africa South of the Sahara, 1973* (1973), pp. 397–404.

Badouin, R. "A la recherche d'un système économique en Guinée," *Droit social* (January, 1963), pp.11–21.

Balandier, G. "L'Or de la Guinée française," *P.A.* 4 (1948), pp. 539–548.

Balde, S. "L'Elevage au Fouta-Djallon (régions de Timbo et Labé)," *Bull. I.F.A.N.* 1 (1939), pp. 630–644.

Barthe, M. "Le Labour attelé en Guinée française," *Agronomie tropicale* nos. 1–2 (January–February, 1951), pp. 73–76.

"La Bauxite et le fer dans l'économie guinéenne," *Industries et travaux d'outre mer* no. 106 (September, 1961), pp. 701–705.

Beaujeu-Garnier, J. "L'agriculture guinéenne," *L'Information géographique* (November–December, 1960), pp. 3–36.

Berg, Eliot J. "French West Africa," *Labor and Economic Development* (1959), pp. 186–259.

Binet, J. "Marchés en pays Soussou," *C.E.A.* 3 (1962), pp. 104–114.

Bodin, F. "Où en sont les projets industriels de Guinée?" *Indus-*

tries et travaux d'outre-mer no. 66 (May, 1959), pp. 262–266.

C., J. "Combinat industriel en Guinée française," *Zaire* 8 (1954), p. 642.

Charles, Bernard. "La Guinée," *Décolonisation et régimes politiques en Afrique noire* (1967), pp. 159–204.

———. "Un Parti politique africain, le parti démocratique de Guinée," *Revue française de science politique* 12, 2 (June, 1962), pp. 312–359.

Charrière, Jacques. "Une Expérience de planification, la Guinée," *Cahiers internationaux* no. 117 (March–April, 1961), pp. 65–88.

Clapp, Jennifer A. "Interpreting Agricultural Performance in Guinea under Structural Adjustment," *Canadian Journal of African Studies* (1993), pp. 173–195.

Cournanel, Alain. "Idéologie et Développement en Guinée," *Africa Development* 2 (February, 1977), pp. 63–88.

———. "Le capitalism d'Etat en Afrique: le cas guinéen," *R.F.E.P.A.* (March, 1976), pp. 18–51.

———. "Le F. M. I. en Guinée: un Programme Très Contestable," *Mois Afrique* (June–July, 1985), pp. 69–76.

Denis, Paul-Yves. "Réalisations recentes et perspectives de développement en Guinée," *C.O.M.* 29 (October–December, 1976), pp. 321–347.

Diallo, Alpha. "Perspectives sur l'élevage en République de Guinée," *R.A.* (1959), pp. 47–62.

Dresch, Jean. "La Riziculture en Afrique occidentale," *A.G.* (1949), pp. 295–312.

Edwards, John. "Bauxite Supplies Concern," *Financial Times* (September 24, 1974), p. 18.

"Entreprise minière en Guinée française," *Zaire* 7 (1953), pp. 75–76.

Friedland, William H. "Paradoxes of African Trade Unionism," *Africa Report* (June, 1965), pp. 6–13.

Georg, Odile. "Les entreprises guinéennes de commerce: destruction ou adaptation (fin XIXe siècle-1913)," in *Enterprises et entrepreneurs en Afrique XIXe et XXe siècles,* Association française des historiens économistes, ed. vol. 1. Paris: L'Harmattan, 1983, pp. 165–179.

Grisoni, A. "La Main-d'oeuvre guinéenne," *Industries et travaux d'outre-mer* no. 46 (September, 1957), pp. 635–637.

Hauser, A. "Les Industries extractives en Guinée," *E.G.* no. 13 (1955), pp. 55–59.

Hazard, John N. "Guinea's Non-Capitalist Way," *Columbia Journal of Transnational Law* 5, no. 2 (1966), pp. 231–262.

Hirschfield, André. "Le Rôle du mouvement coopératif dans la commercialisation de la banane en République de Guinée," *Revue des études coopératives* no. 143 (1966), pp. 33–44.

―――. "Sur quelques expériences coopératives ou précoopératives en Afrique noire," *Revue des études coopératives* no. 139, 1er trim. (1965), pp. 39–60.

Hodgkinson, Edith. "Guinea: Economy," *Africa South of the Sahara, 1974* (1974), pp. 378–384 and *Africa South of the Sahara, 1984* (1984), pp. 440–445.

"L'Industrie et les exportations . . . ," *Europe-France-outre-mer* no. 417 (October, 1964), pp. 15–18.

"Les Industries alimentaires en Guinée," *Revue du développement économique* no. 4 (November, 1964), pp. 17–20.

Kourouma, K. "Le Revenu annuel d'une famille guerzé," *E.G.* 1 (1947), pp. 55–59.

Laminé, T. M. "Les Ports de Guinée," *R.A.* 1–4 (1959), pp. 63–69.

Latremolière, Jacques. "La Guinée, pays minier. Realités et perspectives," *Afrique Contemporaine* 14 (September–October, 1975), pp. 9–12.

Leduc, G. "L'Application de la notion de 'pôle de développement' aux ensembles industriels de l'Afrique subsaharienne," *Marchés Tropicaux* no. 615 (August 24, 1957), pp. 2029–2032.

Leunda, Xavier. "La Réforme de l'enseignement et son incidence sur l'évolution rurale en Guinée," *Civilisations* 22, no.2 (1972), pp. 232–262.

Litvak, I. A. "The Impact of the International Bauxite Agreement: 1974–1979," *Canadian Journal of Development Studies* 3 (1982), pp. 321–340.

McCord, William. "A Wager in West Africa: Third World Report—II," *New Leader* 67 (1984), pp. 6–11.

Noumouke, D. "Le Service de l'élevage et des industries animales en Guinée," *R.A.* 1 (1962), pp. 5–10.

O'Connor, Michael. "Guinea and the Ivory Coast: Contrast in Economic Development," *Journal of Modern African Studies* 10, no. 3 (October, 1972), pp. 409–426.

Plazanet, Claude. "L'Aide étrangère à la Guinée se chiffre théoriquement à 180 millions de dollars," *Europe-France-outre-mer* no. 399 (April, 1963), pp. 14–17.

"Les Recherches minières de Guinée: le Diamant," *Revue du*

développement économique no. 4 (November, 1964), pp. 11–13.

"La Réglementation domaniale depuis 1958 et les conséquences du nouveau régime," *Revue du développement économique* no. 4 (1964), pp. 9–10.

Revue des marchés Tropicaux et Méditerranéens. Paris (weekly).

"Richesses minières et agricoles de la Guinée," *A.O.F. Magazine* no. 3 (November, 1953), p. 76.

Rivière, Claude. "Les Conséquences de la réorganisation des circuits commerciaux en Guinée," *R.F.E.P.A.* no. 66 (June, 1971), pp. 74–96.

———. "L'Economie guinéenne," *R.F.E.P.A.* (June, 1975), pp. 48–78.

———. "Les Coopératives agricoles en Guinée," *R.F.E.P.A.* no. 59 (November, 1970), pp. 55–64.

Salvadori, R. "Esplorazione pratica della Guinea francese," *Africa* 10 (1955), pp. 115–119.

———. "Oromuoviamo in Africa la collaborazione del lavoro," *Africa* 10 (1955), pp. 147–148.

Soriba-Camara, Sylvain. "La Guinée et la coopération économique en Afrique de l'Ouest," *Cultures et développement* 8 (1976), pp. 517–532.

———. "Le parti démocratique de Guinée et la politique des investissement privés étrangers," *R.F.E.P.A.* (March, 1976), pp. 52–53.

Suret-Canale, Jean. "Fria, établissement industriel guinéen," *R.A.* nos. 2–3 (1963), pp. 3–27.

————. "Fria, un exemple d'industrialisation africaine," *A.G.* 73 (1964), pp. 172–188.

————. "Notes sur l'économie guinéenne," *Economie et politique* no. 123 (October, 1964), pp. 74–96.

————. "Quelques Données statistiques sur la Guinée," *R.A.* 2 (1960), pp. 74–80.

Swindell, Kenneth. "Industrialization in Guinea," *Geography* 54, no. 245 (November, 1969), pp. 456–458.

————. "Iron ore mining in West Africa: some recent developments in Guinea, Sierra Leone and Liberia," *Economic Geography* 43, 4 (October, 1967), pp. 333–346.

Touré, Ahmed Sékou. "Guinea: What Role for U.S. Capital?" *Africa Report* 27 (September–October, 1982), pp. 18–22.

Touré, Ismaël. "L'Avenir économique de la Guinée," *Revue du développement économique* no. 3 (November 1963), pp. 2–3.

Touré, M. Laminé. "Les Ports de Guinée," *R.A.* (1959), pp. 63–69.

————. "Les Ressources hydro-électriques de la République de Guinée," *R.A.* no. 1 (1968), pp. 42–50.

Vidaihet, J. "La Future Industrie de l'aluminum en Guinée," *Revue économique française* 70, 2 (May, 1967), pp. 23–25.

————. "Some Problems of Monetary Dependency in French-speaking West African States," *Journal of African Studies* 5, no. 4 (Winter, 1978), pp. 444–470.

Government Documents

France. Institut National de la Statistique et des Etudes Economiques. *Compendium des Statistiques du Commerce Extérieur des Pays Africains et Malgache.* Paris: annual, 1957.

———. Secrétariat d'Etat aux Relations avec les Etats de la Communauté. *Aspects économiques et financiers du projet de Fria.* Paris: French Government, 1961. mech. dup.

Guinea. [République de Guinée.] *Huitième Congrès du parti démocratique de Guinée (RDA), tenu à Conakry du 25 septembre au 20 octobre 1967.* Conakry: I.N.R.D.G, n.d.

———. *Plan comptable national et textes d'application.* Conakry: I.N.R.D.G., 1965.

———. Banque Nationale de Développement Agricole. "Rapport sur le fonctionnement et l'activité de banque nationale de développement agricole," Exercice, 1965–1966.

———. Ministère du Développement Economique. *Huit années de développement économique.* Conakry: 1967.

———. Bibliography. Ministère du Domaine Economique. *Revue du développement économique.* Conakry: 1964–.

———. Ministre de la Fonction Publique et du Travail. Assemblée Nationale. *Exposée fait le 25 octobre 1963 par le Ministre de la Fonction Publique et du Travail.* Conakry: n.d. mech. dup.

United States. Agency of International Development. Statistics and Development Division. *Africa: Economic Growth Trends.* Washington, DC: annual, 1969.

———. Arms Control and Disarmament Agency. *World Military Expenditures, 1971.* Washington, DC: G.P.O., July, 1972.

———. *World Military Expenditure and Arms Trade, 1963–1973.* Washington, DC: G.P.O., 1975.

———. Department of Commerce. Office of International Marketing. *Market Profiles for Africa* (Overseas Business Reports, OBR 72–074). Washington, DC: G.P.O., December, 1972.

————. Department of Health, Education, and Welfare. *Social Security Programs Throughout the World.* Washington, DC: G.P.O., 1973.

————. Department of State. Bureau of Intelligence and Research. *Communist States and Developing Countries: Aid and Trade in 1973* (Research Studies no. INR RS-20). Washington, DC: October 10, 1974.

Dissertations

Baldé, O. D. "La Portée de la loi cadre du 8 novembre 1964 dans le développement économique de la Guinée." Dissertation, I.P.C. (E.S.A.), 1966–67.

Barry, M. A. S. "Contribution à l'étude des techniques et des méthodes de planification de l'économie guinéenne." Dissertation, I.P.C., 1969–70.

Bokoum, B. "Importance des entreprises d'Etat dans l'économie guinéenne." Dissertation, I.P.C. (E.S.A.), 1969–70.

Diallo, Tierno Nabica. "Bilan et perspectives de la Coopération dans le développement de l'agriculture guinéenne." Dissertation, I.P.C. (E.S.A.), 1967. mech. dup.

Olémou, M. P. "Organisation et évolution des institutions du travail, République de Guinée." Dissertation, I.P.C. (E.S.A.), 1967–68.

EDUCATION

Books

Bah, Alpha Mamadou. *Géographie, la République de Guinée.* Conakry: Ministère de l'enseignement supérieur et de téléenseignement, 1974.

Bolibaugh, Jerry B. *Educational Development in Guinea, Mali, Senegal, and Ivory Coast.* Washington, DC: U.S. Department of Health, Education and Welfare, 1972.

Fass, Simon *et al. The Political Economy of Education in the Sahel: Efficiency Indicators Activity.* Tallahassee, FL: Florida State University, 1991.

Grange, Christiane. *Géologie.* Conakry: Ministère de l'Education Nationale, 1962.

Kitchen, Helen, ed. *The Educated Africa.* New York: Praeger, 1962.

United Nations. *Statistical Yearbook.* New York: UN Department of Economic and Social Affairs, Statistical Office, annual, 1973+.

Articles

Adamolekun, 'Lapido. "Administrative Training in the Republic of Guinea, 1957–1970," *Journal of Administration Overseas* 11, no. 4 (October, 1972), pp. 233–252.

Adams, Milton, Bah-Lalya, Ibrahima, and Mukweso, Mwenene. "Higher Education in Francophone West Africa," in *International Encyclopedia of Comparative Higher Education,* Philip G. Altbach, ed. New York: Garland Publishing, 1991, pp. 349–371.

Benot, Yves. "La Réforme de l'enseignement," *Europe* no. 378 (October, 1960), pp. 116–127.

Camara, Djigui. "A la veille des examens de fin de cycle dans nos CER," *Horoya* 2124 (June 20, 1974), p. 4.

Conté, Sendou. "Discours d'ouverture du séminaire des enseignants organisé à l'Institut polytechnique de Conakry," *Revue R.D.A.* 10 (1966), p. 6.

"Decret No. 0047 PRG du 8 Mars 1974," *Journal Officiel de la República de Guinée* 16th year, no. 5 (March 1, 1974), pp. 64–66.

Diallo, A. "Mass Education in the R.P.R. of Guinea," *Eduafrica* (June, 1981), pp. 77–83.

Diallo, Alpha Amadou. "Die Gründung eines Institutes für traditionelle Heilkunde," *Afrika Heute* no. 14 (July 15, 1967), pp. 105–108.

Diop, David Mandessi. "Autour de la réforme de l'enseignement en Guinée," *P.A.* 29 (December, 1959–January, 1960), pp. 105–108.

Doré, Michel Blecko. "Institut Polytechnique de Kankan," *Horoya* (December 20, 1973), p. 3.

Du Bois, Victor D. "Guinea Educates a New Generation," *Africa Report* 6, no. 7 (July, 1961), pp. 3–4, 8.

Fofana, Amara. "Education et Travail Productif en Guinée," *Perspectives* 12 (1982), pp. 515–521.

Ggebnonvi, Roger. "Alphabétisation: éviter une nouvelle désillusion?" *Binndi e jande* 7 (1982), pp. 11–26.

Guilavogui, Galema. "Les Fondements de la réforme de l'enseignement en République de Guinée," *Recherches Pédagogie Culturel* (May–August, 1976), pp. 8–15.

LaCroix, B. "L'Enseignement en République de Guinée," *Etudes africaines du C.R.I.S.T.* 116–117 (November, 1970), pp. 2–37.

Leunda, Xavier. "La Réforme de l'enseignement et son incidence sur l'évolution rurale en Guinée," *Civilizations* 22, no. 2 (1972), pp. 233–262.

Pretty, Margaret. "L'Education en Guinée, 1878–1962," *West*

African Journal of Education 12, no. 2 (June, 1968), pp. 134–136.

"Recommendations du Conseil Supérieur de L'Education," *Horoya* no. 1993 (April 28, 1973), pp. 2–3.

"Révolution culturelle en Guinée: Création de Centre d'Enseignement Révolutionnaire," *Afrique Nouvelle* no. 1097 (August 15–21, 1968), p. 4.

Rivière, Claude. "Les Investissement éducatifs en République de Guinée," *C.E.A.* no. 20 (1965), pp. 618–634.

———. "Les Résultats d'un enseignement révolutionnaire en Guinée," *R.F.E.P.A.* 52 (1970), pp. 35–36.

Stern, T. Noel. "Political Aspects of Guinean Education," *Comparative Education Review* 8, no. 1 (June, 1964), pp. 98–103.

"Les Travaux du CNR: Rapport de la Commission de la Culture et de l'Education," *Horoya* nos. 1925 and 1926 (August 18–21, 1972).

Weinstein, Brian. "Guinea's School of Public Administration," *Journal of Local Administration Overseas* 4, no. 4 (October, 1968), pp. 239–243.

Government Documents

Guinea. Secrétariat d'Etat à l'Idéologie, au Télé-Enseignement et à l'Alphabétisation. *Les Budgets. Séminaires de formation professionnelle.* Conakry: Centre de diffusion Télé-Enseignement, 1er trimestre, 1970. mech. dup.

———. ———. *Gestion de l'entreprise. Responsibilité du comptable.* Conakry: Centre de diffusion Télé-Enseignement, 2ème trimestre, 1970. mech. dup.

————. *Le Phénomène de l'échange.* Conakry: Centre de diffusion Télé-Enseignement, 2ème trimestre, 1970. mech. dup.

————. *Problèmes monétaires et cours des compte.* Conakry: Centre de diffusion Télé-Enseignement, 1er trimestre, 1970. mech. dup.

Dissertations

Bah-Lalya, Ibrahima. "An Analysis of Education Reforms in Post-Independence Guinea: 1958–1985." Ph.D. dissertation, Florida State University, 1991.

Fofana, Amara. "La Réforme de l'enseignement en République de Guinée, 1958–1984." Doctorat du troisième cycle dissertation, University of Paris, 1988.

SCIENTIFIC STUDIES

Books

Adam, Jacques-Georges. *Flore descriptive des monts Nimba (Côte d'Ivoire, Guinée, Libéria).* vol. 6. Paris: Centre National des Recherches Scientifiques, 1983.

Bertrand, J. M. *et al. Afrique de l'Ouest: introduction géologique et terms stratigraphiques/West Africa: geological introduction and stratigraphic terms.* Oxford, England: J. Fabre, New York: Pergamon, 1983.

Bonnet, P., Vidal, P., and Vérot, P. *Premiers Résultats des parcelles expérimentales d'études de l'érosion de Sérédou en Guinée forestière.* Dakar: n.d.

Christoffer, Erich. *Aménagement du bassin du fleuve Sénégal. Les barrages et leurs incidence et aménagements hydro-électriques.* Genève: Publications des Nations Unies, 1963. ms.

Daget, J. *Les Poissons du Fouta Dialon et la Basse Guinée.* (Mémoires de I.F.A.N., no. 65). Dakar: I.F.A.N., 1962.

Dollfus, O. *Essai morphologique sur la presqu'îledu Kaloum et les îlesde Los.* Paris: Bibliothèque de l'Institut de géographie de Paris, n.d. ms.

Frohlich, Gerd. *Guinea nach der Regenzeit.* Leipzig: Brockhaus, 1961.

Grebaut, S., and Brengues, Jacques. *Rapport de la mission Commission de Coopération Technique en Afrique sur la trypanosomiase dans les territoires Kissis et dans les régions frontières limitrophes en Guinée, Sierra Leone et Libéria, April–June.* Bobo-Dioulasso: O.R.S.T.O.M. Mission entomologique auprès de l'Organisation de Coopération contre les Grandes Endémies, 1964. mech. dup.

Hance, William A. *The Geography of Modern Africa.* New York: Columbia University Press, 1964.

Houis, M. *La Guinée française.* Paris: Editions géographiques, maritimes et coloniales, 1953.

Jamme, Gabriel. *Mission d'étude de l'aménagement hydraulique de la zone côtière de la Guinée française,* Rapport du chef de mission. Paris: Bulletin du Comité d'études d'outre mer, 1952. mech. dup.

Le Barbier, L. *La Vallée du Moyen-Niger et la Haute Guinée.* Paris: Dujarric, 1904.

Leclerc, J.-C., Richard-Molard, J., Lamotte, M., Rougerie, G., and Portères, R. *La Chaîne du Nimba, essai géographique,* Mémoire I.F.A.N., no. 43 (La réserve naturelle intégrale du mont Nimba, vol. 3). Dakar: I.F.A.N., 1955.

Le Cochec, F. *Rapport de Tournée dans le Samoh, à Kaback, et à Kakossa.* Koba: Centre Rizicole du Koba, 1956. mech. dup.

Maignien, Roger. *Le Cuirassement des sols en Guinée, mémoires du service de la carte géologique d'Alsace et de Lorraine,* no. 16. Strasbourg: 1958.

Rocher, Marcel, and Chartier, Roger. *Rapport préliminaire aux études hydrologiques. Bassine expérimentaux des Timbis.* Paris: O.R.S.T.O.M., 1963. mech. dup.

Rouard de Card. *Traités de délimitation concernant l'Afrique française.* Paris: Pédone, 1900 (suppl., Paris: Pédone, 1913).

—————. *Les Traités de protectorat conclus par la France en Afrique (1870–1895).* Paris: Pédone, 1897.

Schnell, R. *La Forêt dense.* Paris: Lechavalier, 1950.

United Nations.. *Demographic Yearbook, 1959.* New York: UN Department of Economic and Social Affairs, Statistical Office, periodical.

—————. *Production Yearbook, 1972.* Rome: United Nations Food and Agriculture Organization, annual.

—————. *Survey on the Scientific and Technical Potential of the Countries of Africa.* Paris: U.N.E.S.C.O., 1970.

Articles

Abbayes, H. des. "Liches récoltés en Guinée française et en Côte d'Ivoire. III. Physciacées," *Bull. I.F.A.N.* 13 (1951), pp. 749–761.

—————. —————. "IV. Parméliacées," *Bull. I.F.A.N.* 13 (1951), pp. 965–977.

—————. —————. "V. Genres: Roccella, Coenogonium, Sticta, Caldonia, Ramalina," *Bull. I.F.A.N.* 14 (1952), pp. 19–27.

————. ————. "VI. Collémancées, Heppiacées, Pannariacées," *Bull. I.F.A.N.* 14 (1952), pp. 450–456.

————. ————. "VII. Pyrénulacées, Trypéthéliacées, Astrothéli-acées, Cyphéliacées," *Bull. I.F.A.N.* 15 (1953), pp. 48–58.

Abbayes, H. des, Alston, A. H. G., and Tardieu-Blot, M. L. "Contribution à la flore des Ptéridophytes d'A.O.F. (Guinée et Côte d'Ivoire)," *Bull. I.F.A.N.* 13 (1951), pp. 79–86; 15 (1953), pp. 1384–1386.

Abbayes, H. des, and Motyka, J. "Lichens récoltés en Guinée française et en Côte d'Ivoire," *Bull. I.F.A.N.* 12 (1950), pp. 601–610.

Adam, J. "La Végétation de la source du Niger," *A.G.* (July–September, 1947), pp. 192–200.

Arnould, Michel, Aymé, J.-M., and Guillaume, R. "Nouvelle Stratigraphie des séries primaires du Nord du Fouta Djalon (Guinée-Sénégal)," *C.R.S.S.G.F.* fasc. 7 (1959), pp. 160–167.

Balachowsky, A. S. "Deux *Pseudaonidia* Ckll. (Hom. *Coccoidea-Diaspidinae*) nouveaux du massif du Béna (Moyenne Guinée) A.O.F.," *Bull. I.F.A.N.* 15 (1953), pp. 1512–1522.

Balandier, G. "L'Or de la Guinée française," *P.A.,* no. 4, 1ère série (1948), pp. 539–548.

————. "Toponymie des îles de Kabak et Kakoussa," *E.G.,* no. 8 (1952), pp. 45–54.

Barry, Sory. "La Chasse en Guinée, *R.A.,* no. 1 (1960), pp. 51–57.

————. "Le Problème de la conservation des sols en Guinée," *R.A.* (1959), pp. 70–75.

"La Bauxite et l'industries de l'Aluminum," *Industries et travaux d'outre-mer,* no. 87 (February, 1961), pp. 123–129.

Bonnet, P., and Vidal, Prosper. "Les Premiers Travaux du secteur pilote de conservation et d'utilisation des sols du Milo (Guinée forestière)," *IIIe Conférence inter-africaine des sols* 2 (1959), pp. 659–670.

———. "Protection contre l'érosion hydrologique assurée par diverse cultures en Guinée forestière," *Journal d'agronomie tropicale et de botanique appliquée* no. 10 (1958), pp. 627–637.

Champion, J., Dugain, F., Maignien, R., and Domergues, U. "Les Sols de bananeraies et leur amélioration en Guinée," *Fruits* 13, nos. 9–10 (1958), pp. 415–462.

Chételat, E. de. "Le Modelé latéritique de l'Ouest de la Guinée française," *Revue de géographie physique et de géologie dynamique* (1938).

Chevalier, Auguste. "Les Hauts Plateaux du Fouta-Djalon," *A.G.* (1909), pp. 253–261.

Colemansky, V. "Faune muscicole de Guinée forestière (Rhizopodes testacés)," *R.A.* 4 (1962), pp. 33–60.

"Contribution du service météorologique national au développement économique de la Guinée," *Revue de développement économique* no. 4 (November, 1964), pp. 16.

Corfec, J. le. "Notes sur la Canton Tanda-Kade (Cercle de Gaoual)," *E.G.* 8(1952), pp. 13–39.

Cousturier, Lucie. "La Forêt du Haut-Niger," *Cahiers d'aujourd'hui* no. 12 (1923).

Cuille, J. "Contribution à l'étude de l'ethologie de Cosmopolites sordidus Germ," *E.G.* 1 (1947), pp. 9–22.

Daget, J. "Caractéristiques des cours d'eau du Fouta-Djalon," doc. no. 7, *IVe Colloque sur l'hydrobiologie et les pêches en eau douce.* Fort Lamy, Commission de Coopération Technique en Afrique—Conseil Scientific pour l'Afrique au Sud du Sahara (May 4–10, 1961). mech. dup.

Dars, René, Sougy, Jean, and Vogt, Jean. "Observations nouvelles sur le 'Cambro-ordovicien' du plateau mandingue occidental," *C.R.S.S.G.F.* 7 (1959), p. 65.

Daveau, S. "Principaux Types de paysages morphologiques des plaines et plateau soudanais," *Information géographique* no. 2 (1962), pp. 61–72.

———. "Ruissellement et soutirage dans la haute vallée du Denkalé (Monts Loma), Sierra Leone," *Bulletin de l'Association des géographes français* nos. 330–331 (1965), pp. 20–27.

"Décret No. 145 PRG du 2 Juillet 1973" [concerning the result of the December 1972 general population census] *Journal Officiel de la République de Guinée* 15th year, no. 18 (September 1, 1973), p. 187.

"Décret No. 246 PRG du 20 Septembre 1972" [concerning the taking of a general population census], *Journal Officiel de la République de Guinée* 14th year, no. 21 (November 1, 1972), p. 182.

Dekeyser, P. L. "Présence de *Thos adustus* en Guinée Française," *Bull. I.F.A.N.* 13 (1951), pp. 371–375.

Diallo, Noumouké. "Le Service de l'élevage et des industries animales en Guinée," *R.A.* no. 1 (January–March, 1962), pp. 5–10.

Dollfus, O. "Conakry en 1951–1952, étude humaine et économique," *E.G.* nos. 10–11 (1952), pp. 3–111.

Dresch, Jean. "Dépôts de couverture et relief en Afrique occidentale française," *Congrès international de géographie* (1952), pp. 323–326.

————. "Pénéplaines africaines," *A.G.* (April–June, 1947), pp. 125–137.

————. "Pénéplaines en Afrique noire française" (rapport de la commission pour la cartographie des surfaces d'aplanissement) *Congrès international de géographie* (1949), pp. 140–148.

————. "Plaines soudanaises," *R.G.D.* (1953), pp. 39–44.

Ducos, Pierre. "L'Elevage en Guinée et la structure génétique de la race N'Dama," *Bull. I.F.A.N.* série A no. 3 (July, 1961), pp. 886–903.

Dugain, François, and Fauck, Roger. "Mesures d'érosion et de ruissellement en Moyenne-Guinée. Relations avec certaines cultures," *Comptes Rendus IIIe Conférence interafricaine des sols* vol. 2 (1959), pp. 597–600.

Eichenberger, J. Y. "L'Exploitation de la bauxite en Guinée française," *Industries et Travaux d'outre-mer* no. 4 (March, 1954), pp. 156–160.

Fauck, R. "Matière organique et azote des sols de la Moyenne-Guinée et relations avec les rendements des cultures," *Comptes rendus de l'Académie d'agriculture française* 46 (1960), pp. 152–155.

Gallais, Jean. "La Riziculture de plaine en Haute Guinée," *A.G.* no. 367 (1959), pp. 207–223.

Gaspard, G. "La guinea e l'elefante," *Nigrizia* 94 (September, 1976), pp. 29–38.

Gautier, E. F. "Climatic and physiographic notes on French Guinea," *The Geographical Review* 23 (1933), pp. 248–258.

Godfriaux, I., Lamotte, M., and Rougerie, G. "La série stratigraphique du Simandou (Guinée française)," *C.R.A.S.* 245 (1957), pp. 2343–2346.

Golemansky, V. "Etudes sur la faune des rhizopodes de Guinée forestière," *R.A.* 3 (1962), pp. 3–24.

Hain, Werner von. "Die Landwirtschaft der Republik Guinea," *Geographische Berichte* 9, no. 3 (1964), pp. 179–193.

Henry, L. "Données sur la population de la Guinée," *Population* 11, 3 (1956), pp. 554–562.

Hiernaux, C.-R., and Villiers, A. "Spelcologica africana. Etude préliminaire de six cavernes de Guinée," *Bull. I.F.A.N.* 17A, no. 3 (1955), pp. 926–946.

Jaeger, Paul. "Contribution à l'étude du modelé de la dorsale guinéenne. Les Monts Loma (Sierra Leone)," *R.G.D.* 4 (1953), pp. 105–113.

Jaeger, Paul, and Adam, J.-G. "Aperçu sommaire sur la végétations de la région occidentale de la dorsale Loma-Man. La galerie forestière de la source du Niger," *Bulletin de la Société de botanique de France* 94, nos. 7–8 (1947), pp. 323–334.

Jeremine, E. "Etude des statuettes Kissiennes au point de vue mineralogique et pétrographique," *J.S.A.* 15 (1945), pp. 3–14.

Karst, J. "L'Achèvement du projet de Boké," *Industrie et Travaux d'Outre-Mer* 20, no. 242 (January, 1974), pp. 38–43.

Kayser, B. "La Démographie de l'Afrique occidentale et centrale," *C.O.M.* (1965), pp. 73–85.

Killian, C. "Contribution à l'étude de la biologie de quelques *Utricularia* tropicaux," *Bull. I.F.A.N.* 13 (1951), pp. 1029–1036.

———. "Mesures écologiques sur des végétaux types du Fouta-Djallon (Guinée Française) et sur leur milieu, en saison sèche," *Bull. I.F.A.N.* 13 (1951), pp. 601–681.

―――――. "Observations biologiques sur un Ascomycète, parasite du *Cyathea dregeri*," *Bull. I.F.A.N.* 13 (1951), pp. 1037–1050.

―――――. "Observations sur l'écologie et les bescins édaphiques du Quinquina," *Bull. I.F.A.N.* 15 (1953), pp. 901–971.

Lacroix, Alfred. "La Constitution minéralogique de l'archipel de Los (Guinée)," *C.R.A.S.* 141 (1905), p. 948; 142 (1906), p. 681; 146 (1908), p. 213; 156 (1913), p. 653.

Lamotte, M., and Rougerie G. "Les Apports autochtones dans la genèse des cuirasses ferrugineuses," *R.G.D.* nos. 10–12 (1962), pp. 145–160.

―――――. "Coexistence de trois types de modelé dans les chaînes quartzitiques du Nimba et du Simandou (Haute-guinéenne)," *A.G.* (1952), pp. 432–442.

―――――. "Les Niveaux d'érosion intérieurs dans l'Ouest africain," *R.A.* no. 4 (1961), pp. 51–70.

Lamotte, M., Rougerie, G., and Godfriaux, I. "Les Accumulations de quartzite à mineral de fer dans la Chaîne du Simandou (guinéenne française)," *C.R.A.S.* 247, no. 3 (1958), pp. 315–318.

Lamotte, M., and Roy, R. "Les Principaux Traits du peuplement animal de la prairie montagneuse du mont Nimba (Guinée)," *R.A.* no. 1 (1962), pp. 11–30.

Lamotte, M., and Zuber-Vogeli, M. "Contribution à l'étude des Batraciens de l'Ouest africain. Le développement larvaire de *Rana oxyrhynchus gribinguiensis Angel*," *Bull. I.F.A.N.* 15 (1953), pp. 178–184.

Lavau, G. de. "Boké, Guinée française," *Annales Africaines* (1958), pp. 245–258.

Leclerc, J.-C., Lamotte, M., and Richard-Molard, J. "Nivaux et cycles d'érosion dans le massif du Nimba (Guinée française)," *C.R.A.S.* 228 (1949), pp. 1510–1512.

Legoux, Pierre. "Les Péridotites de Conakry et du Kaloum (République de Guinée) et leur serpentinisation," *C.R.S.S.G.F.* 3 (1960), p. 51.

Legoux, Pierre, and Percival, F.-G. "Sur la structure des cuirasses latéritiques ferugineuses de Conakry," *C.R.A.S.* 248 (1959), pp. 2226–2228.

Lestrange, Monique de. "La Population de la région de Youn-kounkoun en Guinée française," *Population* (October–December, 1950), pp. 643–668.

Maignien, R. "Le Fouta-Djalon dans l'ouest Africain," *R.A.* 3 (1960), pp. 25–38.

————. "Les Sols du Fouta-Djalon," Comptes Rendus Colloque Commission de Coopération Technique en Afrique—Conseil Scientifique pour l'Afrique au Sud du Sahara sur la conservation des sols (April 30–May 7, 1960).

Marshall, G. A. K. "New Curculionidae (Col.) from French West Africa," *Bull. I.F.A.N.* 13 (1951), pp. 319–325.

Mathis, Dr. Maurice. "Le Problème du miel, de la cire et des abeilles en Guinée française," *Agronomie tropicale* nos. 11–12 (November–December, 1949), pp. 605–613.

Mécanisation de la riziculture autochtone en Haute-Guinée," *Riz et riziculture* 1er trim. (1959), pp. 15–29.

Michel, P. "L'Evolution géomorphologique des bassins du Sénégal et de la Haute-Gambie," *R.G.D.* nos. 5–12 (May–December, 1959), pp. 117–143.

Millot, Georges, and Dars, René. "L'Archipel des îles de Los," *C.R.S.S.G.F.* (1959), p. 8.

Monod, R. "Sur une Podestémonacée nouvelle pour l'A.O.F.," *Bull. I.F.A.N.* 7 (1945), pp. 156–159.

Pelissier, P., and Rougerie, G. " Problèmes morphologiques dans le bassin de Siguiri (Haut-Niger)," *Bull. I.F.A.N.* 15 (1953), pp. 1–47.

"Les Petits Aménagements d'hydraulique agricole du Haut-Niger (Guinée)," *Agronomie tropicale* nos. 7–8 (July–August, 1949), pp. 420–423.

Picot, J. "N'Zérékoré, Guinée française," *Annales Africaines* (1958), pp. 273–286.

Picq, J.-J. "Onchocercose de savane et de forêt en Afrique de l'Ouest et complexe pathogène et l'onchocercose," in *De l'épidémiologie à la géographie humaine.* Paris: Agence de Coopération Culturelle et Technique, 1983.

Pitot, A. "Sur l'anatomie de *Psiolotum triquetrum* Sw.," *Bull. I.F.A.N.* 12 (1950), pp. 315–334.

Portères, M. R. "Le Problème de la restauration du Fouta-Djalon," *R.A.* 3 (1960), pp. 49–57.

Portères, Roland. "Observations sur les possibilités de culture du soja en Guinée française," *Bulletin agronomique* no. 1 (November, 1946), p. 62.

Poujade, J. "Technologie," *E.G.* 2 (1947), pp. 85–89.

Pouquet, J. "Altération de dolérites de la presqu'île du Cap-Vert (Sénégal) et du plateau de Labé (Guinée française)," *Bulletin de l'Association des géographes français* nos. 245–246 (1954), pp. 173–182.

———. "Aspects morphologiques du Fouta-Djalon," *Revue de géographie alpine* 43 (1955), pp. 231–245.

"Quelques Données statistiques sur la Guinée," *R.A.* 2 (1961), pp. 74–80.

"Rapport sur la protection des sols au Fouta-Djalon," *R.A.* 3 (1960), pp. 38–47.

"La Réserve naturelle intégrale et la station scientifique nationale des Monts Nimba," *R.A.* 2 (1960), pp. 69–71.

Richard-Molard, J. "Les Densités de population au Fouta-Djalon et dans les régions environnantes," *Congrès international de géographie* 2 (1952), pp. 192–204.

Ristorcelli, M. "Le traitement indigène de la trypanosomiase chez les Peuls du Fouta-Djallon (Guinée française)," *J.S.A.* 9 (1930), pp. 1–2.

Rivière, Claude. "La Toponymie de Conakry et du Kaloum," *Bull. I.F.A.N.* 28B, 3–4 (1966).

Rouanet, R. "Le Problème de la conservation des sols en Guinée," *E.G.* 8 (1952), pp. 59–65.

Rougerie, Gabriel. "Modelés et dynamique de savane en Guinée orientale," *R.A.* no. 4 (1961), pp. 24–50.

Rougerie, Gabriel, and Lamotte, M. "Le mont Nimba," *Bulletin de l'Association des géographes français* nos. 226–228 (1952), pp. 113–120.

Sautter, G. "Le Fouta-Djalon," *Bulletin de la Société languedocienne de géographie,* Montpellier, 2e série 15, 1 (1944), pp. 3–76.

Schnell, R. "Contribution préliminaire à l'étude botanique de la Basse-Guinée française," *E.G.* no. 6 (1950), pp. 29–72.

———. "Esquisse de la végétation côtière de la Basse-Guinée français," *IIe Conférence internationale des Africanistes de l'Ouest (1947)* 2, 1 (1950), pp. 201–214.

———. "Etudes préliminaires sur la végétations et la flore des hauts plateaux de Mali (Fouta-Djallon)," *Bull. I.F.A.N.* 12 (1950), pp. 905–926.

———. "Les Forêts primitives de la Basse-Guinée française," *Comptes rendus sommaire des séances de la Société de biogéographie* no. 248 (1952), pp. 12–16.

———. "Noms vernaculaires et usages indigènes de plantes d'Afrique Occidentale," *E.G.* 4 (1950), pp. 57–80.

———. "Note sur les îlots forestiers reliques de la Basse-Guinée française," *C.R.A.S.* 225 (1947), pp. 254–255.

———. "Plante nouvelles ou peu connues d'Afrique occidentale française (Guinée et Côte d'Ivoire)," *Bull. I.F.A.N.* 15 (1953), pp. 93–97.

Serand, J.-M. "Les Iles de Los (Guinée française)," *La Géographie* 47 (1927), pp. 1–28.

Silverstov. "Eléments de géomorphologie de la Guinée et ses principaux problèmes," *R.A.* no. 4 (1963), pp. 51–67.

Sory, B. "Le Problème de la conservation des sols en Guinée," *R.A.* 1–4 (1959), pp. 70–75.

"Statistics: Vital Rates," *Population Index* 40, no. 3 (July, 1974), pp. 596–608.

T., J. "Conditions des études statistiques en Guinée," *E.G.* 12 (1953), pp. 60–63.

Touré, L. "Les Ressources hydro-électriques de la République de Guinée," *R.A.* 1 (1960), pp. 42–50.

Tuzet, O. *et al.* "Trichophytes et ciliés parasites intestinaux de *Pachybolus* sp., *Scaphiostreptus obesus* Attems et *Termatodiscus nimbus* Attems (Myriapodes Diplopodes)," *Bull. I.F.A.N.* 15 (1953), pp. 133–142.

United Nations. "Population and Vital Statistics: Data Available as of 1 October 1974," *Population and Vital Statistics Report* 26, no. 4 (1974), pp. 6–7.

Vigneron, B. "Kindia, Guinée française," *Annales africaines* (1958), pp. 259–272.

Vogt, J. "Aspects de l'évolution géomorphologique récente de l'Ouest africain," *A.G.* (1959), pp. 193–206.

Government Documents

France. *Rapport de mission sur le Moyen-Konkouré,* by Fritsch, Pierre. Dakar: Gouvernement Général de l'A.O.F., Service de l'Hydraulique, 1956. mech. dup.

———. "Observations nouvelle sur les alluvions inactuelle de Côte d'Ivoire et de Haute-Guinée," *Actes du LXXXIVe Congrès national des Sociétés savantes,* section de géographie. Dijon: Ministère de l'Education Nationale, Comité des Travaux Historiques et Scientifiques, 1959, pp. 205–210.

———. *Documents et Statistiques, L'Enquête Démographique de Guinée, 1954–1955: Résultats Provisoires.* Paris: Ministère de la France d'Outre-Mer, n.d.

———. *Etude Démographique par Sondage en Guinée, 1954–1955: Résultats Définitifs.* 2 vols. Paris: Service des statistiques Chargé des Relations et de la Coopération avec les Pays d'Outre-Mer, 1956.

Germany. *Länderberichte: Guinea,* Statistisches Bundesamt, Series Allgemeine Statistik des Auslandes. Stuttgart: Kohlhammer, 1967.

Dissertations

Bah, Alpha Amadou. "Les Transport en Guinée." Dissertation, I.P.C. (E.S.A.), 1967.

Chautard. "Etude sur la géographie physiques et la géologie du Fouta-Djalon." Dissertation, Sorbonne, 1905.

RELIGION

Books

Arnaud, R. *L'Islam et la politique musulmane en A.O.F.* Paris: Publications du Comité l'Afrique Française, 1912.

Begries, Gouverneur. *L'Islam en Guinée française.* Paris: Centre de Hautes Etudes Administratives sur l'Afrique et l'Asie Modernes, 1954.

Cardaire, M. *L'Islam et le territoire africain.* Bamako: I.F.A.N., 1954.

Deschamps, H. *Les Religions d'Afrique noire.* Paris: P.U.F., 1960.

Diané, El Hadj Kabiné. *Recueil des cinq piliers de l'Islam,* 3rd ed. Conakry: I.N.R.D.G., 1964.

Feral, G. *Notes sur l'Islam en Guinée française.* Paris: Centre de Hautes Etudes Administratives sur l'Afrique et l'Asie Modernes, 1948.

Froelich, J. C. *Les Musulmans d'Afrique noire.* Paris: Orante, 1962.

Gouilly, A. *L'Islam dans l'Afrique occidentale française.* Paris: Larose, 1952.

Kaba, Lansiné. *The Wahhabiya: Islamic Reform and Politics in French West Africa.* Evanston, IL: Northwestern University Press, 1974.

Lelong, M.-H. *N'Zérékoré: L'evangile dans la forêt.* Paris: Librairie Missionaire, 1949.

Lewis, I. M., ed. *Islam in Tropical Africa.* London: Oxford University Press, 1966.

Marty, Paul. *L'Islam en Guinée. Fouta-Djalon.* Paris: Leroux, 1921.

Monteil, Vincent. *L'Islam noir.* Paris: Seuil, 1964.

Tchidimbo, Raymond-Marie. *Mon père et ma mère.* Paris: Fayard, 1985.

Trimingham, J. Spencer. *A History of Islam in West Africa.* London: Oxford University Press, 1962.

Articles

"Cinquantenaire de la mission de Boffa," *La Voix de Notre-Dame,* Bulletin diocesain (July, 1927).

"Islam ou colonisation au Fouta-Djalon," *P.A.* 15 (1953), pp. 357–364.

Le Grip, R. "Aspects actuels de l'Islam en A.O.F.," *L'Afrique et l'Asie* 28 (1954), pp. 43–61.

Maka, Léon. "Le P.D.G. et les religions," *Horoya* no. 1238 (June 30, 1967).

Rivière, Claude. "Bilan de l'Islamisation," *Afrique Document* no. 5–6 (1960), pp. 319–359.

———. "Une Eglise étouffée par l'Etat," *Cultures et Développement* 8, no. 2 (1976), pp. 219–241.

"Situation de l'Eglise en Guinée," *Telema* 3 (January–March, 1977), pp. 13–14.

Suret-Canale, Jean. "Touba in Guinea: Holy Place of Islam," *African Perspectives* (1970), pp. 53–81.

Tchidimbo, Mgr. R.-M. "L'Homme noire dans l'Eglise," *P.A.* (1963), pp. 89–90.

Thomas, L. V. "L'Eglise chrétienne d'Afrique noire," *Tam-Tam* (December 1, 1963), p. 10.

Vilar, J. B. "Isabel II y la expedición misional española a Guinea de 1856," *Scriptorum Victoriense* 25 (1978), pp. 296–320.

LITERATURE AND POETRY

Books

Brench, Anthony C. *The Novelists' Inheritance in French Africa.* London: Oxford University Press, 1967.

—————. *Writing in French from Senegal to Cameroon.* London: Oxford University Press, 1967.

Cissé, Ahmed-Tidjani. *Au nom du peuple.* Paris: Nubia, 1990.

—————. *Maudit soit Cham!* Paris: Nubia, 1982.

—————. *Le tana de Soumangourou.* Paris: Nubia, 1988.

Diare, Ibrahima Khalil. *Les dits de nul et de tous: contes et légendes de Guinée.* no place: I. K. Diare, 197?.

—————. *Liane des générations: recueil de récits folkloriques.* no place: I. K. Diare, 197?.

Herdeck, Donald E. *African Authors: A Companion to Black African Writing, 1300–1973.* Washington, DC: Black Orpheus Press, 1973.

Jahn, Janheinz. *Who's Who in African Literature.* Tübingen: Horst Erdmann Verlag, 1972.

Keita, Fodéba. *Aube africaine.* Paris: P. Seghers, 1965.

Niane, Djibril Tamsir. *Sikasso: ou la dernière citadelle: suivi de Chaka.* Honfleur: P.J. Oswald, 1971.

Sacko, Biram. *Dalanda: ou, La fin d'un amour.* Dakar: Nouvelles Editions Africaines, 1975.

Sassine, William. *Le jeune homme de sable.* Paris: P. A., 1979.

———. *Saint Monsieur Baly.* Paris: P. A., 1973.

———. *Wirriyamu.* Paris: P. A., 1976.

———. *Le Zeheros n'est pas n'importe qui.* Paris: P. A., 1985.

Thiam, Djibi. *My Sister, The Panther.* Mercer Cook, trans. New York: Dodd, Mead, 1980.

Zell, Hans, and Silver, Helene, eds. *A Reader's Guide to African Literature.* New York: Africana Publishing Company, 1971.

Articles

Appia, B. "Quelques Proverbes guinéens," *Bull. I.F.A.N.* 2 (1940), pp. 396–415.

B., A. "L'Enfant noir," *P.A.* 16 (1954), pp. 419–420.

Balogun, F. Odun. "Mythopoetic Quest for the Racial Bridge: *The Radiance of the King* and *Henderson the Rain King,*" *Journal of Ethnic Studies* 12 (Winter, 1985), pp. 19–35.

Bernard, Paul R. "Camara Laye: A Bio-Bibliography," *Africana Journal* 9 (1978), pp. 307–322.

Brodeur, Leo A. "Une critique de la perception occidentale de l'Afrique noire, selon le modèle layen de Clarence dans *Le Regard du Roi,*" *L'Afrique Littéraire* 58 (1981), pp. 126–134.

Burness, Donald. "The Radiance of Camara Laye," *Journal of Black Studies* 11 (June, 1981), pp. 499–501.

"Camara Laye: le maître de la parole," *Actuel Développement* (May–June, 1981), pp. 45–48.

Cesaire, A. "Salut à la Guinée," *P.A.* n.s. 26 (1959), p. 89.

Cessain, M. "La Littérature orales des Coniagui (République de Guinée)," *R.A.* 3 (1961), pp. 24–37; 3 (1962), pp. 25–50.

"Chants révolutionnaires guinéens," *P.A.* n.s. 29 (1959–1960), pp. 89–103.

Chemain, Roger, and Chemain, Arlette. "Pour une Lecture Politique de 'Le Regard du Roi' de Camara Laye," *P.A.* 3 (1984), pp. 155–168.

Chitour, M.-F. "Les Intellectuels dans 'Les Crapauds-Brousse'," *Peuples Noirs, Peuples Afriques* (July–August, 1984), pp. 41–50.

Donner, Regime. "Promenade avec Camara Laye dans le Temple Africain," *Ngam* 6 (1981), pp. 108–118.

Etonde-Ekoto, Grace. "Le Regard du Roi," *Ngam* 6 (1981), pp. 32–55.

Green, Robert. "'L'Enfant Noir' and the Art of Auto-Archaeology," *English Studies in Africa* 27 (1984), pp. 61–72.

Hale, Thomas A. "From Written Literature to the Oral Tradition and Back: Camara Laye, Babou Condé and *Le maîtrede la parole: Kouma Lafolo Kouma*," *Fr. R.* 55 (1982), pp. 790–797.

Harrow, Kenneth. "The Mystic and the Poet: Two Literary Visions of Islam in Africa (Camara Laye and Ahmed Sefroui)," *Africana Journal* 13 (1982), pp. 152–171.

Henebelle, Guy. "Côte d'Ivoire, Sénégal, Guinée: six cinéastes Africains parlent," *L'Afrique Littéraire et Artistique* 8 (December, 1969), pp. 58–70.

Herbstein, Denis. "Camara Laye—Involuntary Exile," *Index on Censorship* 9 (June, 1980), pp. 5–8.

Houis, M. "Caractères et possibilités de la langue Soso," *R.A.* 1 (1962), pp. 3–4.

———. "Contes Baga," *E.G.* 6 (1950), pp. 3–15.

———. "Notes lexicologiques sur les rapports du soso avec les langues mandé-sud du groupe mana-busa," *Bull. I.F.A.N.* 16 (1954), pp. 391–401.

———. "Le Rapport d'annexion en baga," *Bull. I.F.A.N.* 15 (1953), pp. 848–854.

———. "Le Système pronominal et les classes dans les dialectes baga," *Bull. I.F.A.N.* 15 (1953), pp. 381–404.

Joffre, J. "Sur un nouvel alphabet ouest-africain le Toma (frontière franco-libérienne)," *Bull. I.F.A.N.* 7 (1945), pp. 160–173.

Johnson, Lemuel A. "Safaris in the Bush of Ghosts: Camara Laye, Saul Bellow, and Ayi Kwei Armah," *Issue* 13 (1984), pp. 45–54.

Julien, Eileen. "A Narrative Model for Camara Laye's *Le regard du roi*," *Fr. R.* 55 (1982), pp. 798–803.

Kapolo, Kampoyi. "Idéologies du développement et développement des idéologies dans Dramouss de Camara Laye," *Afrique Littéraire et Artistique* 51 (1979), pp. 19–26.

Keita, Cherif Cheick M. "Le regard du roi de Camara Laye et Noces Sacrées de Seydou Badian: l'assimilation du colonisateur," *Proceedings of the French Colonial Historical Society* 6–7 (1982), pp. 102–108.

Lafontant, Julien J. "Self-identification and Assimilation in *The Dark Child*," *Ngam* 6 (1981), pp. 5–13.

Lassort. "La Langue Kpèlè," *E.G.* 2 (1947), pp. 21–25.

Laye, Camara. "The Eyes of the Statue," *Black Orpheus* 5 (1959), pp. 19–27.

Magel, Emil A. "Levels of Thematic Interpretation of Camara Laye's *Le Regard du Roi*," *Ngam* 6 (1981), pp. 56–72.

Mamadou, S. "Contes et légendes d'Afrique," *R. A.* 2 (1961), pp. 30–44.

"Un mariage chez les Mandegnis," *P.A.* 4 (1948), pp. 637–640.

Mengrelis, T. "Contes de la forêt," *E.G.* 5 (1950), pp. 3–6.

———. "Curiosités linguistiques," *Africa* 21 (1951), p. 138.

———. "Deux Contes toma," *E.G.* 1 (1947), pp. 27–45.

Modum, E. P. "Politics and Polemics in Camara Laye's *Dramouss*," *Okikie* 23 (1983), pp. 57–66.

Moukako, Gobina. "Camara Laye et la Tentation de l'Occident," *Ngam* 6 (1981), pp. 86–107.

Obumselu, Ben. "The French Moslem Backgrounds of the Radiance of the King," *Research in African Literatures* 11 (1980), pp. 1–25.

Ojo-ade, F. "Une lecture contemporaine de Camara Laye," *Peuples Noirs, Peuples Afriques* 4 (January-February, 1981), pp. 60–94.

Okeh, Peter Igbonekwu. "Aliénation, Conflit et Authenticité dans *L'Enfant Noir* de Camara Laye," *Ngam* 6 (1981), pp. 14–31.

Poreko, D. O. "A propos des phonèmes spéciaux de la langue Peule," *R.A.* 4 (1960) pp. 37–39.

Portères, P. "Notes de toponymie rurale au Fouta-Djallon," *R.A.* 1–4 (1964), pp. 151–159.

Schroeder, Susanne. "Die Wahrheit des 'Den-Anderen-Suchens': Imagologische untersuchunger zu Camara Laye: *Le Regard du Roi*," *Ngam* 6 (1981), pp. 73–85.

Sellin, Eric. "Trial by Exile: Camara Laye and Sundiata Keita," *World Literature Today* 54 (1980), pp. 392–395.

Sissoko, F. D. "Glossaire des mots français passés en Malinké," *Bull.. I.F.A.N.* 1 (1939), pp. 325–366.

Songolo, Aliko. "Surrealism and Black Literature in French (with emphasis on Césaire and Camara Laye's *Les yeux de la statue*)," *Fr.R.* 55 (1982), pp. 724–732.

Sow, A. I. "Notes sur les procédés poétiques dans la littérature des Peuls du Fouta-Djalon," *C.E.A.* 5 (1965), pp. 370–385; *P.A.* n.s. 54 (1965), pp. 181–197.

Tcheho, I. C. "Etat Présent de la recherche sur l'ouevre de Camara Laye," *Ngam* 6 (1981), pp. 119–122.

"Three Soussou Tales ['Sweetness,' 'The Moon,' 'The Well']," *Black Orpheus* 15 (1964), p. 5.

Umeh, Ambrose O. "Etude socio-politique et économique des thèmes de la violence et de la protestation dans le 'Cercle des tropiques' d'Alioum Fantouré," *Le Mois en Afrique* 18 (August–September, 1983), pp. 133–143.

LINGUISTICS

Books

Delafosse, Maurice. *La Langue mandingue et ses dialectes.* Paris: Geuthner, 1929.

Greenberg, Joseph H. *The Languages of Africa,* 3rd ed. Bloomington, IN: Indiana University Press, 1970.

Heine, Bernard. *Status and Use of African Lingua Franca.* Munich: Weltforum Verlag, 1970.

Articles

Conil-Lacoste, Michel, and Tracoré, Kamori. "No More Secret Languages," *New Africa* 9, no. 3–4 (1967), p. 14.

Diakité, Drissa. "Le Manden: Une Langue d'Intercommunication éthnique en Afrique de l'Ouest," *Binndi e jande* 7 (1982), pp. 21–26.

Hair, P.E.H. "Ethnolinguistic Continuity on the Guinea Coast," *J.A.H.* 8, no. 2 (1967), pp. 247–268.

Kastenholz, Raimund. "Note sur les marques prédicatives en koranko," *Mandekan: Bulletin semestriel d'études linguistiques mande* (1983), pp. 55–73.

Santos, R. "Quelques aspects de la classification nominale en wèy," *Annales de la Faculté des lettres et sciences humaines de Dakar* 12 (1982), pp. 281–301.

Winters, Clyde-Ahmad. "The Ancient Manding Script," *Journal of African Civilization* 5 (April-November, 1983), pp. 207–214.

ART AND MUSIC

Books

Bravmann, René A. *Islam and Tribal Art in West Africa.* London: Cambridge University Press, 1974.

Hennebelle, Guy *et al.,* eds. *Les Cinémas Africaines en 1972.* Paris: Société Africaine d'Edition, 1972.

Laude, Jean. *The Arts of Black Africa.* Berkeley, CA: University of California Press, 1971.

Leuzinger, Elsy. *Africa: The Art of the Negro Peoples,* Ann E. Keep, trans, 2nd ed. New York: Crown, 1967.

Teel, William. *An Outline of African Art.* Cambridge, MA: University Prints, 1970.

Articles

Diaré, Ibrahim Khalil. "Musique guinéenne: audience et prestige," *Horoya* 2098 (March 24, 1974), p. 7.

———. "Les Orchestres modernes aux compétitions régionales," *Horoya* 1935 (September 28, 1972), p. 2.

"Les Films guinéens remportent la médaille d'or," *Horoya* 1979 (March 11, 1973), p. 2.

"French Guinea," *Encyclopedia of World Art* (1959), pp. 56–58.

Germain, J. "Extrait d'une monographie des habitants du cercle de N'Zérékoré (Guerzé, Kono, Manon). Les Artisans, les techniques et les arts," *E.G.* 13 (1955), pp. 3–54.

Kaba, Lansiné. "The Cultural Revolution, Artistic Creativity and Freedom of Expression in Guinea," *Journal of Modern African Studies* 15 (June, 1976), pp. 201–218.

Knight, Roderic. "Record Reviews (Musique malinké: Guinée; and Musique d'Afrique occidentale: Musique malinké, musique baoulé)," *Ethnomusicology* 18, no. 2 (May, 1974), pp. 337–339.

Okpaku, Joseph. "Les Ballets Africains Sont Belles: Guinea's National Ensemble in San Francisco," *Journal of the New African Literature and the Arts* no. Fall 1967 (June, 1968), pp. 65–67.

Rouget, G. "Les Ballets africains de Keita Fodeba," *P.A.* n.s. 7 (1956), pp. 138–140.

Sano, M. "De la mélodie populaire *Alpha Yaya,* à l'hymne national Liberté," *R.A.* 2–3 (1963), pp. 28–32.

Suret-Canale, Jean. "Chronique de Guinée," *Cultures et Développement* 10 (1978), pp. 297–314.

Government Documents

Guinea. Le Haut Commissariat à l'Information au Tourisme et à L'I.N.R.D.G. *Chefs d'Oeuvre de l'Art Guinéen et Africain: Catalogue.* Conakry: Institut National de Recherches et de Documentation, 1967.

TOURISM

Books

Greene, Graham. *Journey Without Maps,* 2nd ed. New York: Viking, 1961 (1936).

Miller, Stefan. *Guinea.* Berlin: Verlag Volk u. Welt, 1979.

Renaudeau, Michel. *La République de Guinée.* Paris: Delroisse, 1978.

Articles

Balachowsky, A. S. "Le Fouta-Djalon," *La Nature* no. 3227 (March, 1954), pp. 83–88.

———. "La Guinée forestière et les monts Nimba," *La Nature* no. 3229 (May, 1954), pp. 161–167.

———. "Le Pays mandéni en Basse-Guinée," *La Nature* no. 3215 (March, 1953), pp. 65–68.

Barry, S. "Le Chasse en Guinée," *R.A.* 1 (1960), pp. 51–57.

Diop, A. "Impressions de voyage," *P.A.* n.s. 29 (1959–1960), pp. 3–7.

Government Documents

Guinea. Ministère de l'information et du tourisme. "Quatre Années d'indépendence et de liberté." Conakry: I.N.R.D.G, 1962.

———. Office of the Secretary of State for Information and Tourism. "Guinea and Its People." Conakry: Office of the Secretary of State for Information and Tourism, 1965.

REFERENCE AND BIBLIOGRAPHY

Books

Africa South of the Sahara, 22nd ed. London: Europa Publications, 1993.

Almeida, Damien d'. *Premier Répertoire des archives nationales de Guinée.* Conakry: I.N.R.D.G., 1962.

Annuaire des mission catholiques en Afrique française. Paris: Editions Paul Balsey-oep, 1955.

Asamani, J. O. *Index Africances.* Stanford, CA: Hoover Institution Press, 1975.

Bederman, Sanford H. *Africa; A Bibliography of Geography and Related Disciplines.* Atlanta, GA: Georgia State University Press, 1974.

Bogaert, Jozef. *Sciences humaines en Afrique noire: guide bibliographique (1945–1965).* Brussels: Centre Documentation Economique et Sociale Africaine, 1966.

Booth, Richard. *The Armed Forces of African States* (Adelphi Papers no. 67). London: International Institute for Strategic Studies, 1970.

Brasseur, P., and Maurel, J. F. *Les Sources bibliographiques de l'Afrique de l'ouest et de l'Afrique équatoriale d'expression française.* Dakar: Bibliothèque de l'Université, 1970.

Busch, Lawrence. *Guinea, Ivory Coast and Senegal; A Bibliography on Development.* Monticello, IL: Council of Planning Librarians, 1973.

Carson, P. *Materials for West African History in French Archives.* London: Athlone Press, 1968.

Conover, H. F. *Official Publications of French West Africa, 1946–58.* Washington, DC: Library of Congress, 1960.

Désiré-Vuillemin, G. *Les Capitales de l'ouest-africain.* 2 vols. Paris: Service d'Etudes et de Recherches Pédagogiques pour les Pays en Voie de Développement, 1963.

Dictionary of African Biography, 2nd ed. London: Melrose Press, 1971.

Duignan, Peter, ed. *Guide to Research and Reference Works on Sub-Saharan Africa.* Stanford, CA: Hoover Institution Press, 1971.

Dupuy, Trevor N., ed. *The Almanac of World Military Power.* Dunn Loring, VA: T.N. Dupuy Associates, 1970.

European Economic Communities. Statistical Office. *Annuaire Statistique des E.A.M.A.* Luxembourg, annual, 1969–.

———. ———. *Foreign Trade Statistics. Associates Overseas Areas.* Brussels: 1959–65.

Imperato, Pascal James. *Historical Dictionary of Mali.* Metuchen, NJ: Scarecrow Press, 1986.

Kobele-Keita, Aboubakar. *Les sources coloniales de l'histoire de la Guinée jusqu'en 1939.* Conakry: I.P.C., 1970.

Organisation de Coopération et de Développement Economique, Centre de Développement. *Bibliographie de la Guinée.* Paris: O.E.C.D., Centre de Développement, 1965.

Panofsky, Hans E. *A Bibliography of Africana.* Westport, CT: Greenwood Press, 1975.

Ryder, A. F. C. *Materials for West African History in Portuguese Archives.* London: Athlone Press, 1965.

Rydings, H. A. *The Bibliographies of West Africa.* Ibadan: Ibadan University Press, 1961.

Standing Conference on Library Materials on Africa. *United Kingdom Publications and Theses on Africa.* Cambridge, England: Heffer, 1963–.

Ternaux-Compans, Henri. *Bibliothèque asiatique et africaine ou catalogue des ouvrages relatifs à l'Asie et à l'Afrique, qui ont paru depuis la découverte de l'imprimerie jusqu'en 1700.* Paris: 1841 (repr.: Amsterdam: B.H. Gruner, 1968).

Wieschnoff, Heinrich A. *Anthropological Bibliography of Africa.* New Haven, CT: American Oriental Society, 1948.

Witherell, Julian W. *French Speaking West Africa: A Guide to Official Publications.* Washington, DC: Library of Congress, 1967.

Articles

Africa. London (quarterly).

Africa News. Durham, NC.

Afrique. Casablanca (six times a year).

Afrique Contemporaine. 1962–.

Afrique Nouvelle. Dakar (weekly).

Année Africaine. Paris (yearly).

Année Politique Africaine. Dakar (yearly).

Autra, Ray (Mamadou Traoré). "L'Institut national de recherches et de documentation de la République de Guinée," *R.A.* (1964), pp. 5–35.

Chronologie Politique Africaine. Paris (bimonthly).

The Economist Intelligence Unit—Country Report. London (quarterly).

Etudes Guinéennes. Conakry (irregular).

Europe-France-Outre-Mer. Paris (monthly, including the annual June survey of all African states).

Horoya. Conakry (daily).

Horoya-Hebdo. Conakry (weekly).

Jeune Afrique. Paris (weekly).

Johnson, G. Wesley. "The Archival System of Former French West Africa," *African Studies Bulletin* 8, no. 1 (April, 1965), pp. 48–58.

Klein, Martin A. "Report on Archives of the Popular and Revolutionary Republic of Guinea at Conakry," *Hist. Africa* 8 (1981), pp. 333–334.

Le Monde. Paris (daily).

Marchés Tropicaux et Méditerranéens. Paris (weekly).

Mauny, Raymond. "Contribution à la bibliographie de l'histoire de l'Afrique noire des origines à 1850," *Bull. I.F.A.N.* 27, no. 3–4 (July–October, 1966), pp. 927–965.

Overseas Associates: Statistical Bulletin. Brussels (5 issues annually).

West Africa. London (weekly).

Wright, Donald R. "The Western Manding: A Bibliographical Essay," *Africa Journal* 6 (1975), pp. 291–302.

Government Documents

France. Institut National de la Statistique et des Etudes Economiques. *Compendium des Statistiques du Commerce Extérieur des pays de la Zone Franc.* Paris (annual, 1938–1946).

Dissertations

Kaké, Ibrahima Baba. *Bibliographie critique des sources imprimées d'histoire de la Guinée.* Dissertation, Dakar, 1962.

Maps

Mercier, Paul. *Carte Ethno-Démographique de l'Afrique Occidentale,* no. 5. Dakar: I.F.A.N., 1954, p. 4.

Richard-Molard, Jacques. *Cartes ethno-démographiques de l'Afrique occidentale.* Dakar: I.F.A.N., 1952.

ABOUT THE AUTHORS

THOMAS E. O'TOOLE (B.A. cum laude, St. Mary's College-Minnesota; M.A., University of Minnesota; Doctor of Arts, Carnegie-Mellon University) is Professor in the Department of Interdisciplinary Studies and a member of the African Studies faculty at St. Cloud State University. Dr. O'Toole is active in the African Studies Association nationally and participates regularly in the YMCA African Forum locally. A returned Peace Corps volunteer, former Senior Fulbright lecturer, and first Director of Minnesota Studies in International Development, he maintains an active interest in African affairs. He has published several articles in professional journals, written many book reviews, translated the *History Dictionary of the Central African Republic* (by Pierre Kalck, Scarecrow Press, 1992), and authored *The Central African Republic: The Continent's Hidden Heart.*

IBRAHIMA BAH-LALYA is a graduate (Licence ès lettres) of the Conakry Polytechnique Institute and also holds an advanced professional diploma (D.E.S.) in African History and Sociology from that institution. He earned his M.S. and Ph.D. from Florida State University. Dr. Bah-Lalya has worked with the Learning Systems Institute of Florida State University and currently is Education Project manager of the Critical Languages Institute at Florida Agricultural and Mechanical University. Dr. Bah-Lalya taught high school, was a university professor and assistant dean of social science at the Julius Nyéréré Institute, and served as deputy director of education in the Ministry of Higher Education as well as interim general director of education at the National Ministry of Education before leaving Guinea. He has written widely on Guinea and Francophone Africa.